JERUSALEM PRAYER TEAM

"Pray for the Peace of Jerusalem..."

www.jerusalemprayerteam.org

DR. MICHAEL D. EVANS

#1 *NEW YORK TIMES* BESTSELLER

MIKE EVANS

A NOVEL

GAMECHANGER

TIMEWORTHY
·BOOKS·

P.O. Box 30000, Phoenix, AZ 85046

Published by TimeWorthy Books
P. O. Box 30000
Phoenix, AZ 85046

Design: Lookout Design, Inc.

ISBN: 978-0-935199-04-7

NOTE FROM AUTHOR

THE NEO-GOTHIC BOUTIQUE HOTEL in the Tudor neighborhood one block from the United Nations skillfully merged Old World architecture and contemporary furnishings. In the lobby silhouettes of men and women depicting different time periods were surrounded by sculptured moss and hanging mirrors. The impression was of a vibrant and hip place to be.

As I sat in one of the six cream-colored contemporary chairs, my attention was drawn to a charming man with a full head of white hair. I happened to know he lived a stone's throw from Washington, D.C. Everyone seemed to know him, and I watched as both mullahs and diplomats warmly embraced him. Eventually he walked over to greet me.

By the way he addressed me one would have thought we were former college roommates. He said with a huge grin, "I am Mohammad, an American like you."

Everyone seemed to know Mohammad; mullahs and diplomats embraced him warmly. He smiled and asked, "You're having a hard time with names, aren't you?"

I nodded. "Yes. It seems like all Iranian diplomats are named Mohammad."

He laughed loudly. "We are; we're all Mohammad."

I was curious. "But who is the boss? I'm having a hard time understanding the chain of command."

He chuckled and waved his hands. "They are all the boss, or at least they think so." He spoke more softly and pointed to a man across the room, "But *that* Mohammad is the one you want to talk to."

I took note of the direction in which he pointed and sighed. "Getting into the hotel was a nightmare. There must be at least four hundred police officers forcing the public away. That did not include the SWAT team, CIA, and Secret Service. This hotel is guarded more tightly than Fort Knox."

Mohammad gave a slight nod. "Nobody gets in unless they have been pre-approved by Iran and cleared by the Secret Service."

The cast of strange characters in the hotel was surreal—mullahs, Iranian spies, representatives of terrorist-harboring (or supporting) regimes, such as Sudan, Syria, and even some Europeans. A few Holocaust-denying rabbis with their hands out were in attendance. They were trying to cash in on Iran's notoriety. The most infamous guest, of course, was Mahmoud Ahmadinejad. The U.S. government had provided almost as much security for him as for the president of the United States. Ahmadinejad had just delivered another ire-raising speech at the U.N., accusing the United States of blowing up the World Trade Towers to support Zionism.

I was keenly aware that by this time next year, if the world slept, Iran would have the atomic bomb. A quote by President Barack Obama reverberated through my mind: *"We can absorb a terrorist attack. We'll do everything we can to prevent it, but even a 9/11, even the biggest attack ever . . . we absorbed it and we are stronger . . . A potential game changer would be a nuclear weapon in the hands of terrorists, blowing up a major American city."*

Later on I met with twenty-one diplomats from Ahmadinejad's inner circle. I was told that in less than two hours I would meet with the Iranian president in a private room. He had agreed to a half-hour exclusive interview with the Fox Network. Little did I know that this tiny man with the obsessive smile would bring three mullahs to the meeting to pray for him. When he sat down for the interview, his eyes lit up in response to one of the questions I had written for the host.

"Is the Mahdi coming soon?" asked Eric Shawn. "According to your theology, an apocalypse will usher him in."

Ahmadinejad nodded. "Yes, the Mahdi is coming very, very soon."

During the next twenty minutes, past hateful, anti-Semitic words of Ahmadinejad kept spinning through my mind like bright lasers:

- *The Jews are "filthy germs and savage beasts . . . A stinking corpse and rotten, dried tree . . . A cancerous bacterium stuck in a cesspool created by itself and its supporters."*

- *"Zionists are the true manifestation of Satan . . . They kill women and children, young and old . . . Behind closed doors they make plans to advance their evil goals . . . They want to dominate the world."*

- *There is only one solution to the Middle East problems, namely the annihilation and destruction of the Jewish State."*

- *Israel should be "wiped off the map."*

Iran will soon be a Persian, Shia, nuclear state, and the center of gravity for world terrorism. It could put nuclear arms into the hands of rogue regimes such as Hezbollah, Hamas, and al-Qaeda. This would precipitate a trillion-dollar nuclear arms race among the Sunni countries that reside along the two-hundred-mile stretch of the Persian Gulf.

I knew in my heart that the obsession of the mullahs to confront the Great Satan, America, and the Little Satan, Israel, was stranger and deadlier than fiction. Indeed, it would be a *GameChanger*.

1

NORTHERN IRAN

SUNRISE BROKE OVER THE MOUNTAINS as the dune buggy worked its way up the next hill. Known officially as a Light Strike Vehicle, the buggy was little more than a tubular frame with seats bolted to a steel floor pan. A modified, air-cooled Volkswagen engine hanging off the back provided enough power to send the buggy scooting across the desert and over the roughest terrain. Painted the color of sand, it blended with its surroundings and, in spite of the engine's noise, all but disappeared against the muted colors of the desert.

Seated behind the steering wheel was Adam Kirkland. Twenty-three, Kirkland had enlisted in the Army the day after graduating from high school in Eustis, Florida. Following a year of training, he had been deployed to Iraq as part of a peacekeeping mission, patrolling the hills along the border with Turkey. While on patrol in a remote region of Iraq north of Dahuk, Kirkland and a three-man team had come under fire from radical forces. Pinned down and cut off, they held out for three days before maneuvering into a position from which they could be removed. Kirkland's leadership during those tense days had proved decisive in avoiding a major international incident. As a result, he had been sent to Ranger school and assigned to a special missions unit tasked with the Army's most sensitive covert operations.

Six weeks ago Kirkland and his partner, Chris Martin, were inserted into an isolated area of northern Iran. Satellite imagery and intercepted transmissions suggested the region was the site of an underground nuclear testing facility, but flyovers from unmanned drones had been unable to detect anything more than background radiation. Someone at the Pentagon's Nuclear Support Center wanted a conclusive answer. Kirkland and Martin were sent to get it.

Kirkland jerked the steering wheel to the left and maneuvered the dune buggy around a ravine, then pressed the throttle and continued their climb up the hill to the right. At the crest he brought the buggy to a stop and took out his binoculars. The hill they had just topped was a steep rise halfway across the floor of a broad valley. To the left and right, ominous craggy peaks of the Zagros Mountains towered above them. Kirkland raised the binoculars to his eyes and scanned the valley to the left.

"You see anything?"

"No," Martin replied. "Nothing but—" He stopped in midsentence. "I got a truck over here."

"Where?" Kirkland lowered the binoculars and turned to see. "You sure it's a truck? We're a long way from anywhere."

"A hundred yards," Martin pointed. "Behind that clump of bushes."

Kirkland turned in that direction. He squinted against the morning glare and looked past the bushes. "I think I see it." He raised the binoculars to his eyes again. "Yep. It's a truck all right."

Painted the same tan color as the terrain, the truck was all but invisible in the early morning light. Only the square corners of its van body gave it away. Kirkland adjusted the focus on the binoculars and searched along the side of the truck for markings that might give a hint of its identity or purpose. "Don't see any markings on it," he mumbled. "Do you?"

"Looks like one of those seismic trucks they use to search for oil."

"A thumper truck?"

"Say what?" Martin grinned.

"Thumper truck," Kirkland repeated. "That's what we call them down in Florida."

"We call them boomer trucks in Louisiana. That thing's so square and clunky. Not sure how they got it out here."

Something in the tone of Martin's voice ignited a memory in Kirkland's mind. Clear and crisp, it struck him so hard his eyes blinked and his head jerked spontaneously to the side. For one brief moment he was back home—riding to Leesburg with his grandfather, standing in the family orange grove at Yalaha, spending one more night parked with Lisa at the tennis courts on Bates Avenue. Most days he kept those memories well out of reach, but sometimes, at the sound of a word or when the light hit the bushes just right, he could smell the orange blossoms and see the look in Lisa's eyes. As quickly as it surfaced, the memory vanished. He turned back to Martin.

"I don't know," Kirkland continued. "I'm not sure it's a… thumper." He studied the truck through the lens of the binoculars. "Doesn't look like it to me." He turned his head farther to the right. "I don't see any blast holes. If they were looking for oil, they should have blast holes. We'd see little red flags to mark the charges." He twisted from side to side, searching through the binoculars. "I don't see anything. Do you?"

"No," Martin replied. "Nothing but sand and rocks. We got a lot of rocks," he chuckled. "And scraggly bushes."

Kirkland lowered the binoculars and rested them on his lap. With his left hand he reached across his body to his right shoulder and keyed the microphone on his radio. "This is Delta Six."

A voice crackled in reply, "Delta Six, this is Olympus. Go ahead."

"Olympus, we've got a truck out here. Looks like a geological team. Any way you can confirm that?"

From high above someone in a JSTARS airplane answered. "Negative, Delta Six. That's not an oil field crew. We're picking up their telemetry. They're sampling the air."

Kirkland glanced over at Martin and frowned. Martin shrugged in response. Kirkland pressed the microphone once more. "Roger that. What do we do?"

"Hold your position. NADAK thinks you're right on top of them. You see anything?"

"Any what? Nothing out here but—"

Suddenly Martin's shoulder exploded. Blood spewed across the front of the buggy. Bone fragments peppered Kirkland's cheek. Traveling faster than the speed of sound, the bullet had arrived without warning. As the sound of that first shot echoed from the mountains to the right, a second round struck Martin's skull. His head flew forward then snapped backward against the seat. Seconds later, he slumped to the right and hung precariously from the opposite side of the buggy.

Kirkland rolled to his left out of his seat and spread himself flat on the ground. His heart pounded against his chest and veins in his neck throbbed as he grappled with the microphone. "Be advised! Be advised!" His voice was excited and tense. "We are under fire. One man down." The sound of the second shot rumbled through the valley. He scanned the mountains to the right and shouted into the microphone. "Sniper! Sniper! On the ridge to our south!"

"Roger, Delta Six," the JSTARS answered. "We're checking his position now."

Slithering across the ground on his knees and elbows, Kirkland crawled to the rear of the vehicle and peered over the engine. His hands shook as he raised the binoculars to his eyes and scanned the mountains to the south. At first he saw nothing, and then he caught sight of a man lying prone on a smooth flat outcropping two thirds of the way to the top. Kirkland raised the microphone near his lips and pressed the key to talk.

"This is Delta Six. I see—"

Searing hot pain sliced through Kirkland's forehead. He jerked forward, slamming his cheek against the surface of the engine's muffler. His flesh sizzled against the white-hot metal, filling his nostrils with the smell of burning meat. Then his arms went numb. The binoculars and radio slipped from his hands and clattered against the frame of the buggy. His legs buckled as his body slumped backward, striking the ground with his buttocks first, followed by his shoulders.

Overhead, he caught a glimpse of the cloudless blue sky as his head flopped to one side and bounced against the sand. Then the world fell silent.

2

ACROSS THE VALLEY

HIGH UP IN THE ROCKS YITZHAK HAREL tugged at the rope as he led a mule up the winding, steep, mountain trail. At the next switchback he paused and scanned the opposite ridge. A white puff of smoke caught his eye. He reached inside the folds of his robe and took out a pair of binoculars to study the rocks and crags on the face of the mountain that lined the far side of the valley. Fifty feet below the top ridge, he caught sight of a man lying flat beside a boulder. While Yitzhak watched, the man stood, slung a rifle over his shoulder, and scrambled over the crest.

With the man gone, Yitzhak turned his attention to the valley floor. There he saw the tubular frame of an all-terrain buggy. Lying near the back wheels was the body of an American soldier. From the gaping wound to his head, Yitzhak was certain the man was dead. The body of a second soldier dangled from the frame rail on the opposite side. Yitzhak had been following the two-man team since they first appeared in the valley three days before. As he shadowed their trail, he wondered how long it would take before Iranian snipers located them. He had given them two days. That it took the Iranians three to find them told him Iran's snipers were not as good as their reputation.

As he scanned the valley floor beyond the buggy, he caught sight of the angular outline of a truck with a van body in back. Parked beside a clump of bushes, it was all but invisible. "That is why the Americans stopped," he mumbled to himself. *If they had kept going, they would be alive. The sniper might be better than I thought… watching them all this time and waiting to move until absolutely necessary … waiting to take them out until he had no choice.* He stared through the binoculars at the truck a moment longer. *Ruthless and cunning might be a better description.*

Moments later the ground beneath his feet trembled. Rocks tumbled around him and cascaded down the mountain. The mule brayed and kicked, then bolted up the trail toward the top. A boulder bounced in front of it, and then a second one landed on its back. With a loud cry the mule lost its footing, stumbled to the left and plummeted eight hundred feet to a ledge below. Packs, pots, and tent stakes littered the mountainside.

Yitzhak backed away from the edge. He covered his head, pressed his body flat against the mountain, and waited for the shaking to stop. Ten minutes later he felt safe enough to move. As he leaned over the edge, he saw the mule lying on the stone outcropping far below.

I need my backpack, he thought. *But how can I get it?*

Moving cautiously, he stepped across the trail, laid on the ground, and eased himself over the edge. Working from foothold to handhold, he lowered himself down the face of the mountain to the ledge and made his way to the animal. Blood trickled from its nose and ears. A gash tore its side. Yitzhak felt along the animal's side, searching for a heartbeat. Suddenly the animal kicked its feet and struggled to its knees. As it jerked and hopped, Yitzhak caught sight of his backpack dangling from a pack brace still strapped to the mule's back. He grabbed hold of the backpack with one hand

and snatched it hard. The mule stood to its feet and bolted forward, away from Yitzhak. The backpack came free in his hand. Yitzhak stumbled back against the mountain as the animal lunged forward, braying loudly. Its hooves clattered against the rocks as it stumbled over the ledge. Yitzhak closed his eyes and listened as the animal fell to its death two thousand feet below.

Shaking and unnerved, he opened the backpack and took out a small satellite telephone. He turned on the power switch, pointed the solar collector toward the sun, and popped up the antenna. Moments later he was talking to a controller at the Mossad operations center in Ashdod, Israel, a small town north of Nazareth.

3

KARACHI, PAKISTAN

NASSER HAMID SAT IN THE REAR SEAT of a Mercedes sedan as it made its way through the streets of Karachi, Pakistan. Dressed in a dark gray suit with a white shirt and red tie, he looked more like a Western businessman than an Iranian on a lethal mission. On his right hand he wore a gold ring. Plain along the sides, it had a six-point star engraved on top. Around the star was a stylized crescent moon. With the ends tapered to sharp narrow points, the crescent was positioned so that it all but surrounded the star. As he stared out the window, Hamid twisted the ring round and round on his finger.

Hamid had visited Pakistan on many occasions over the past three years, and on each trip he was amazed that the country remained intact. Suicide bombers had become commonplace, assassinations and kidnappings a way of life. Yet it seemed the country not only survived but thrived on the political chaos that appeared always on the verge of destroying it.

A smile crept across Hamid's face. *Chaos. That has been the key.* No one really wanted to topple the government. Just create an environment conducive to their purposes. That had been Iran's method in dealing with its neighbors. A military invasion of Iraq and Afghanistan would have brought the Americans scurrying back with their bombs and machines. Conventional military confrontation with Pakistan troops would have brought swift action from India and China. The world would have lined up to destroy the belligerent and evil Iran. Hamid chuckled to himself at the thought of it, especially in light of all he knew about Iran's capabilities. They had chosen a more... unique tack. Rather than calling it chaos or confrontation, they had dubbed it "creative instability," choosing tribal factions over organized armies and improvised weaponry over sophisticated technology. The approach had worked well in destabilizing Iraq, and now it was doing the same in Pakistan.

The car slowed and made a sharp right turn into yet another narrow alley. In the space of a few feet, Hamid was in a Karachi much like it had been centuries earlier. On either side of the alley were low, one-story buildings. Made of mud bricks, they were crowded together in a continuous stream of open doorways and paneless windows. The smell of cooking fires and the foul stench of raw sewage seeped into the car. Hamid frowned at the sight and wrinkled his nose at the smell. Instinctively, his fingers slipped around the handle of the briefcase and pulled it close.

Although he was an Iranian citizen, Hamid was born in Saudi Arabia. His parents worked as economic advisers on the staff of the Iranian embassy, posts to which they were appointed by Mohammad Reza Pahlavi, the last Shah of Iran. Though they feigned loyalty to the Shah, Hamid's parents were followers of the Ayatollah Ruhollah Khomeini, a radical Moslem cleric who, at the time of their appointment, lived in exile in Paris. From his position at the Iranian embassy, Hamid's father secretly funneled money from sympathetic Saudi families to the Ayatollah and resistance groups working inside Iran to topple the Shah. When the Shah was ousted from power in 1979, Hamid's family was recalled to Iran, where his father became an adviser to the Ayatollah's son, Mustafa. At the time they returned, Hamid was four years old.

After studying at a madrasah in Qom, Hamid attended the University of Tehran, where he graduated with a degree in philosophy. The following year he moved to Boston and obtained a master's degree in American history from Harvard. When he returned to Iran he had hoped to follow in his parents' footsteps with a position in Iran's Foreign Service, but his father advised against it. Instead, he suggested Hamid establish his own freight forwarding company, arranging shipments of essential material for vital government projects and operations. With his father's help, Hamid landed his first job, delivering a shipment of drilling parts from Russia to an oil field near Esfahan.

A few weeks after that first job, Hamid met his father for lunch at a café near the Tehran airport. Accompanying his father that day was Adnan Karroubi, a powerful member of the Assembly of Experts and an authority on ancient Islamic history and traditions. Hamid knew Karroubi only by reputation and was surprised to learn he and his father were old friends.

Over lunch that day, Karroubi explained the predicament of a friend, who needed to move a large quantity of drilling mud from Texas to an oil field in western Iran. The mud, a specially blended compound used in the drilling process, was packaged in five-gallon containers. With the West tightening sanctions against Iran, no one seemed able to obtain the permits necessary to pry it loose from a warehouse in Houston. Perhaps Hamid would like to try?

With little trouble Hamid secured an airplane to fly the shipment to Yemen, where it was transferred to a second plane bound for Iran. One week after his lunch with Karroubi, the shipment arrived safely in Tehran. Eager to please his newest client, Hamid accompanied the shipment to its final destination. There he learned the five-gallon containers actually held C-4 explosives, and the destination was anything but an oil field.

Hamid's quick delivery impressed Karroubi, and his willingness to participate without asking questions gave him a reputation as one devoted to the Shi'a cause. When news of it reached the Ayatollah, Hamid became the government's preferred source for covert logistical support. Many assignments followed, each more complex than the one before and all accomplished without fail or delay. Now, at last, Hamid was in Karachi on the most important project of all.

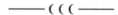

The Mercedes jostled Hamid from side to side as the car emerged from the alley and turned left onto a broad avenue lined with modern commercial buildings. Two blocks later, the car came to a stop at the curb outside a fifteen-story steel and glass building in Karachi's central business district. A small brass sign on a column near the lobby entrance identified it as Perwaiz Tower.

Briefcase in hand, Hamid opened the door and climbed from the car. As he stepped to the curb, he glanced back at the driver. "Pick me up in one hour." The driver nodded in response. Hamid closed the door and started toward the building.

Halfway across the sidewalk, an old man brushed past. Dressed in dirty khaki pants and a ragged white shirt, his face was lined with wrinkles and creases that made him seem even older and dirtier than he first appeared. Yet behind the weathered complexion, his eyes sparkled. As he glanced at Hamid his face lit up with a smile that stretched from ear to ear. He called out to him in a gravelly voice, but Hamid could not understand the words.

Distracted for the briefest of moments, Hamid collided with a woman carrying a basket of flowers. The basket tipped to one side and flowers spilled on the sidewalk. Irritated by the interruption,

Hamid scowled at the woman and continued across the sidewalk to the building entrance.

From the doorway Hamid crossed the lobby and made his way past the security desk to the elevator. He stepped inside and pressed a button for the tenth floor. As he rode the elevator, he thought again of the look on the old man's face and the woman on the street with the basket of flowers. It seemed a curious encounter, made more so by the Islamic prohibition against...

The elevator doors opened, and Hamid stepped out to a broad hallway with walls painted a dusty taupe color. Carpet woven in brown and gold colors covered the floor. Directly opposite the elevator was a reception desk. Track lights on the ceiling illuminated the words, "Pakistan Shipping," written in raised gold letters on the wall behind the desk. A young man standing near the end of the desk glanced up.

"May I help you?"

"I am here to see Nabhi Osmani."

The young man gave Hamid a polite but inquisitive look. "And you are?"

"Olek Kamati." Hamid never used his real name in public. "I am sure he is expecting me."

The young man ran his finger down a list on the desk then quickly looked up with a smile. "Very well. Follow me."

Hamid trailed behind as they walked down the hall to the far side of the building. They came to a set of large double doors. Made of mahogany, the doors were smooth as silk and fitted with brass knobs and hinges. Hamid waited while the young man rapped lightly on the door. There was a muffled response from inside.

The doors swung open, revealing a large and expansive corner office. Windows that reached from floor to ceiling stretched along two sides of the room. Light streamed through them, flooding the room with a brilliance that made everything seem to shine and sparkle. In the corner was a large, wooden desk, polished and gleaming in the sunlight. Nabhi Osmani sat in a leather chair behind the desk. He glanced up as Hamid entered.

"Nasser," he called. "So good to see you." He rose from the desk, came briskly around the corner, and embraced Hamid with a hand on one shoulder and a kiss on the cheek. "I trust all is well with you."

"Yes," Hamid replied, returning the gesture. "I am fine."

Osmani pointed to a chair. "Please. Have a seat." By then the young man was gone, the doors were closed, and the two were alone. Hamid took a seat in a chair to the right, in front of the desk, and set the briefcase on the floor. Osmani sat in a chair to the left, a few feet away. "You had a good trip?"

Hamid nodded. "It was without event."

"That is the best kind. Are you hungry? Perhaps some tea?"

"Tea would be nice."

Osmani leaned forward in his chair and reached over the front of the desk. He pressed a button on the telephone then eased back to his seat. "When I was younger, I enjoyed trips that were more… adventurous. Now that I am older, I prefer the ones with the least surprises."

"You're not that old," Hamid smiled.

"Perhaps." Osmani patted his stomach. "But there is more of me to move around now."

The doors opened and a young woman carrying a silver tray entered. On it were two glasses of tea with a plate of cheese and sliced tomato. Hamid studied her as she set the tray on the desk. Little more than five feet tall, she was slender but not skinny, with dark eyes and an olive complexion. She reminded him of his cousin Ameena.

When Hamid had reached school age, his parents sent him to live with Ameena's family in Qom while he attended school. At first he and Ameena were only cousins. Then, slowly, they became friends, playing together in the afternoons, laughing and giggling over a childhood game in the street or in the alley behind the house. As they grew older the attraction between them grew stronger, and they became more than friends, a taboo strictly forbidden by Sharia law and a secret no one could ever know.

The young woman slid the tray onto the desk and glanced in Hamid's direction. He smiled at her as she bowed, then she retreated toward the door and disappeared down the hall. All the while, Hamid worked the ring on his right hand round and round.

Osmani chuckled, "You like her?"

"There is no time for such distractions," Hamid said quietly.

"Distractions?" Osmani cackled. "There was a time when all you wanted was a 'distraction.'"

"Not now." Hamid's face turned serious. "Your ships are ready?"

"Yes." Osmani lifted a glass from the tray and set it on the desk near Hamid. "Have some tea." Osmani took a slice of cheese from the tray and leaned back, gesturing with it in his hand. "You should try this. It is very good. I know you must be hungry."

Hamid slid forward in his chair and lifted the glass from the desk. He took a sip of tea and settled back. "Everything must go as planned. There can be no mistakes. This operation must work perfectly."

"The ships are in position." Osmani's face had turned sullen, the laughter gone from his eyes. "We have done just as you said."

"They have called on the ports as we instructed?"

"Each of them called on all the ports at least twice." Osmani's smile returned. "These are magnificent ships, built only for the containerized cargo trade. Highest quality. Latest technology. And self-loading, as you suggested." He took another bite of cheese. "They have called on their regular routes and on the ports as you instructed. No one could possibly suspect them of anything but carrying cargo containers."

"You are certain?"

"Positive. Anyone researching the records of our ships would find them to be nothing but container ships, carrying goods that could not possibly raise suspicion or question."

"And they have called on ports in the United States?"

"Yes."

"And there were no problems?"

"No," Osmani frowned. "There were no problems. How could there be? They are registered in Panama. They fly the Panamanian flag. They have names like *Panama Clipper*, *Amazon Cloud*, and *Santiago*." Osmani chuckled. "They look like any other container cargo ship."

Hamid took a slice of cheese from the tray and slipped it into his mouth. He nodded his head as he swallowed. "This is good."

"We did our best to follow your instructions."

Hamid smiled. "I meant the cheese."

Osmani grinned. "We chose it especially for you."

4

NEAR THE PERWAIZ TOWER

AROUND THE CORNER FROM THE PERWAIZ TOWER, Zvi Amit took a wallet from the pocket of his khaki trousers and handed it to Shabtai Admoni. With the wallet in his hand, Admoni stepped to the curb and ducked inside a Chevrolet Suburban. As he closed the door, he leaned over the seat and handed it to Joseph Yegel, seated in back. "Here," Admoni said.

Yegel took the wallet and opened it. Inside he found three hundred dollars in U.S. currency and a driver's license issued from the State of Florida in the name of Nigel Hamatti. Sitting on the rear seat was a black case that contained a portable scanner. Yegel opened the case, took the license from the wallet, and laid it on the scanner screen. The machine hummed as a laser scanned the card.

"You are certain this belongs to Hamid?"

"Yes," Admoni replied. "But I am curious why he would carry a Florida driver's license."

"Probably travels on a U.S. passport. Did we get photos of him?"

"Yes. You think he could move in and out of the United States without being noticed?"

Yegel gave Admoni a wry smile. "You think such a thing is not possible?"

"Even after September 11?"

"Especially after September 11." Yegel took the card from the scanner. "You are certain our men have photographs of Hamid?"

"Yes. They are on the building across the street."

"I assure you," Yegel began as he returned the driver's license to the wallet. "This man intends to leave no trail. Our job is to make certain that he does." He handed the wallet back to Admoni. "Tell them to put it back in his pocket."

"Very well," Admoni nodded.

"Make certain it is not noticed."

"Of course."

Yegel looked Admoni in the eye. "Hamid must suspect nothing. If necessary, make him think it was the Americans."

"Right." Admoni opened the door and stepped from the Suburban.

5

AL-AKBAR TESTING FACILITY, NORTHWESTERN IRAN

FROM THE AIR, THE AL-AKBAR TESTING FACILITY looked like a barren valley in the Zagros Mountains of western Iran. As far as the eye could see there was only a treeless, mountain plain, punctuated by an occasional herd of goats. Beneath the stark landscape, however, lay a complex system of modern tunnels connecting an array of testing facilities that housed Iran's most extensive nuclear weapons program. Only the control room, located in a gas processing plant twenty miles east of Bakhtaran, was above ground.

Under the code name Raj'a al-Mahdi—Return of the Mahdi—development of Iran's first nuclear device had been entrusted to the control and direction of two men, Josef Yazid and Elian Razan. Virtually unknown beyond the borders of Iran, both men had worked in absolute secrecy to prepare their first nuclear device, using only material obtained from inside Iran.

Now, on the morning of November 4, the Al-Akbar control room prepared to monitor a critical test that would determine whether Iran could successfully place a nuclear warhead on its most important existing missile, the Shahab-3. If the test proved successful, production of strategic warheads could proceed immediately and the world would know beyond all doubt that Iran had entered the nuclear age.

Present in the control room was Karim Atef, the lead physicist in Iran's weapon program. It was his responsibility to take the technology developed by Yazid and Razan and turn it into strategic weapons. He had been chosen for that task not by the Assembly of Experts but by Nasser Hamid himself. The choice had been an excellent one.

The oldest man in Iran's nuclear program, Karim had attended Tehran University and then pursued graduate degrees in Paris. Well educated and a scholar in his own right, he had eschewed academic life in the 1970s to devote his talent to creating a completely Iranian missile, one designed entirely by Iranian engineers, using parts manufactured in Iran from raw materials mined there. It had been a task as arduous as that of Yazid's and Razan's, but Karim had found success. One final step remained—arming the missile with a nuclear warhead. Whether that could be easily accomplished would be determined in a few short hours.

Near the center of the room, Elian Razan sat facing the central control board. Mounted atop a large metal desk, the panel before him contained digital displays that provided electronic data transmitted directly from a warhead buried in the ground twenty-five miles away. Two small monitors tracked radioactive rays emitted by the device. Green lines rolled in waves across the monitor screens. All night the lines had followed a uniformly undulating pattern. If everything went according to plan that morning, the green waves on the screens would show the results immediately—one forming an angular spike to the top of the screen followed by an equally dramatic drop, the other forming a perfect arc.

For the men in that room, ten years of long days and sleepless nights had come down to this single moment. They had spent years wondering if the Israelis would find them, if the Russians would tip the Americans, and if the next moment would be their last.

Somehow, their program had escaped the watchful eyes of American satellites and the ever-inquisitive probing of Israeli agents. Now the day finally had arrived when Iran would detonate a nuclear bomb worthy of the minds that had created it, ushering in a new age of Islamic rule. Iran would be the undisputed regional power. Not Saudi Arabia. Not Syria. Not Iraq with its lingering American occupation. Only Iran. Everything was in place. No one could stop it.

Razan glanced away from the instrument panel and rubbed his eyes. From across the room, Yazid called to him. "Do not go to sleep on me."

"I am awake," Razan smiled. "I am wide awake." He glanced at the clock on the wall and noted the time. *Six in the morning.* His mind wandered back to his wife and daughter in Tehran. They were warm and safe in their beds. Before long they would awaken to start their day, but at that moment they were still fast asleep. He imagined his wife lying there peacefully, the smell of the room, the cool morning air, the way the floor creaked when she rolled from bed...

Just then a light flickered on the control panel to the left. Razan pressed a tiny black button beneath the red light and sat up straight. "We have the first phase in place." He glanced at Karim. "Soon we will know."

Karim nodded. "Soon we will see."

"Soon," Yazid grinned, "the world will know and see. They will talk for weeks, even months, about what we are going to do here today."

Fifteen minutes later a light glowed on the panel to Razan's right. He pressed a button beneath it and leaned back in his chair, his hands rested in his lap. After all their work, cajoling others to go along with their plans, begging for money to keep the program active when nothing seemed to work, then crafting parts from bits and pieces of outdated equipment for the first tests... Razan sighed.

Yazid was right. Karim was right. They all were correct. In a few short minutes they would prove once and for all that they knew what they were doing. All would know it was possible for Iran, on its own, to do what others thought could never be done.

Yazid called out. "How are we coming over there?"

Razan slowly turned his head in Yazid's direction. Tears formed in his eyes. "We are ready," he whispered.

Technicians who had been shuffling between instrument panels suddenly stopped and turned toward Yazid. The room fell silent. Yazid stepped to a desk in the corner and picked up a phone. Razan heard him talking but could not make out what was said.

Suddenly the door to the room swung open. Startled by the intrusion, Razan jumped to his feet and shouted, "What are you—" He stopped short when he saw an army officer stride through the doorway. Adnan Karroubi followed close behind. Dressed in a long gray robe, Karroubi wore a gray turban bound tightly around his head. The robe hung loosely from his shoulders, covering his arms to the wrist and his legs to the tops of his ankles. Taking quiet, measured steps, he seemed to float effortlessly across the floor.

Razan folded his hands and bowed his head, "Assalum alaikum."

"Wa alaikum assalam," Karroubi nodded, "wa rahmatu Allah."

A technician stepped quickly to the doorway, glanced outside to check the hallway, then pushed the door closed.

Karroubi gestured toward the instrument panels along the walls. "You are ready for the test?"

"Yes," Razan nodded. "We are ready."

"I should like to observe the event."

Yazid crossed the room. "It would be our pleasure."

Karroubi glanced around once more, a pleasant smile on his face. He cut his eyes at Yazid. "This is impressive technology."

"Let us hope it works," Yazid grinned nervously.

The smile disappeared from Karroubi's face. "Let us hope so."

Karroubi turned away, nodding to the technicians as his eyes scanned the instruments once more. Yazid stepped to the instrument panel along the wall to the right. In quick succession he flipped three switches, then he paused. He glanced down at his wrist watch. "I have 6:29 a.m. in ten seconds."

"Ten seconds," Razan replied.

A few feet away, Karroubi stood waiting, motionless, as if frozen in place. The army officer who had accompanied him stood to his left, hands folded behind his back. As the seconds ticked slowly by, the officer rocked gently on the balls of his feet.

Razan studied the instrument panel, watching for the slightest change in the lines on the screens before him. Then he heard the click as Yazid flipped the last switch. A row of lights across the top of the panel turned green. Razan felt his heart leap against his chest.

Ten seconds went by. The room was quiet and still. Twenty seconds. Razan felt his palms grow sweaty. He wiped his hands on his pants and rested his finger tips against the edge of the desk. Still nothing happened. Karroubi glanced over his shoulder.

"Is that all there is to such a—"

Suddenly the room shook violently. Panels along the walls rattled and the floor trembled. Ceiling tile fell from overhead. A piece struck Karroubi on the shoulder. Instinctively, he covered his head with his hands and ducked to one side. On the desk in the corner, where the telephone sat, coffee sloshed from a ceramic cup. A brown stream of liquid dribbled onto the floor.

Razan gripped the edge of the desk and steadied himself, more for psychological comfort than for physical protection. If the explosion went out of control, nothing in the room could protect them from its fury. All the while he kept his eyes focused on the readouts coming across the monitor screens on the panel. A grin spread across his face as the wave form on the screen to the left spiked to the top of the scale. An instant later the lines on the screen to the right popped up to form a perfectly symmetrical arc.

"Gamma rays are off the chart!"

Yazid called to him, "What about the promethium?"

"Seventy-eight," Razan shouted.

Karroubi turned in Yazid's direction. "What does that mean?"

"It means we have a bomb," Razan shouted. "We have a bomb!"

The room erupted with cheers. When Razan looked around for Karim, he was nowhere to be found.

6

KARACHI, PAKISTAN

FROM THE MEETING WITH OSMANI, Nasser Hamid walked back to the hallway and pressed the button for the elevator. A slender young man dressed in a light brown business suit approached. Hamid glanced in his direction then quickly looked away. He shifted the briefcase to his left hand and slipped his right hand in his pocket. The elevator doors opened.

Hamid turned to step inside the elevator and collided with a tall, athletic man dressed in a tan suit. "Pardon me," the man said with a smile. He had broad shoulders and fair skin. From the color of his hair and his hazel eyes, Hamid was certain he was an American. The man patted Hamid on the back as he brushed past. "Didn't mean to get in your way." Then, without waiting for a reply, he turned to the right and moved toward the reception desk.

Hamid stared after him a moment, then stepped into the elevator. The man in the brown suit looked over at him. "Lobby?"

"Yes," Hamid nodded.

They rode in silence to the lobby. When the elevator doors opened, Hamid turned to the right and started toward the exit to the street. The man who had been with him on the elevator followed a short distance behind. When Hamid reached the street, the man caught up with him and stood at his side.

"You have seen Zaheden?"

"Yes," Hamid replied. "He sailed last week. And the others?"

"Sirjan boarded *Amazon Cloud* today. Tabas departed yesterday aboard the *Santiago*."

"You are certain about this Tabas?"

"As certain as you are of Zaheden."

"You have their passports?"

The man handed Hamid a passport. "This is for Tabas."

The cover was green with the official seal of Pakistan emblazoned in gold. Hamid held it in his hand and used his thumb to push it open. Inside, he saw a picture of Tabas and a stamp indicating he had used the document when leaving South Korea. Hamid nodded and slipped the passport into his pocket.

"This is for Sirjan," the man said. He handed Hamid another passport.

The cover was brown with the great seal of Iran stamped on the front. Hamid opened it and glanced at Sirjan's picture. He had known Sirjan for many years and had spoken with him two days before.

Hamid slipped the second passport in his pocket and set the briefcase on the sidewalk near his feet. "I trust you will have a good trip."

The man beside him reached down and took hold of the case. "Perhaps we shall work together again one day."

"Perhaps we shall," Hamid smiled.

The man took the briefcase and started up the sidewalk to the right. Near the corner a silver Mercedes was parked at the curb. He walked to the rear door of the car, opened it, and slipped inside. As the door closed the car moved from the curb, blended with the midmorning traffic, and continued across the intersection.

Hamid watched the Mercedes move away. As it crossed the intersection at the corner, he took a cell phone from his pocket. He held it in his left hand and pressed the buttons with the index finger of his right hand. Carefully, deliberately, he pushed one number at a time, then pressed a button to send the call. The phone rested in the palm of his left hand as he listened for the sound of a ringtone.

At the first ring an explosion erupted in the middle of the next block down the street to Hamid's right. Smoke billowed in the air as people ran yelling and screaming in every direction. Cars and trucks veered erratically to the left and right onto the sidewalks. In the center of the street was the burning wreckage of a Mercedes sedan, its silver trunk lid the only recognizable part still intact.

A smile broke over Hamid's face as he closed the phone.

7

POTOMAC, MARYLAND

DENNIS KINLAW SAT ON THE BACK PEW at Potomac Community Church in Potomac, Maryland. Outside, the first light of dawn broke through the eastern sky, but in the sanctuary the only light came from candles burning on the altar table near the front of the church. Scattered across the sanctuary were thirty-five or forty other congregants. Like Kinlaw, most were dressed for work.

Born the son of a North Carolina attorney, Kinlaw had worked his way through Yale, earning a degree in Near Eastern history. With it, he obtained a proficiency in Arabic and ancient Hebrew. He had contemplated pursuing a PhD, perhaps teaching at a college or seminary. Then, at the last minute, he bowed to family pressure and followed his friend, David Hoag, to Harvard Law School.

He and Hoag had shared a long-time interest in the Near East, but Hoag was more focused on the archeological side, spending summers in digs and enjoying the hands-on experience. While at Harvard they roomed together and, until two years ago, shared an apartment in Bethesda. Since his marriage, however, Kinlaw lived in Rockville with his wife, and Hoag had a townhouse in Georgetown.

During their last year at Harvard, Kinlaw and Hoag were recruited by the CIA, Kinlaw for his language proficiency and both of them for their unusual ability in deductive reasoning, as well as their knowledge and understanding of the Middle East. Six months after graduation, they were sent overseas as field officers. Working together from the embassy in Istanbul, they learned the craft of espionage from two of the Company's last great operatives in the art of gathering human intelligence. But that was all in the past. Now, in spite of lessons learned from the war against Al-Qa'ida, the CIA had no Americans abroad listening, infiltrating, or building relationships. Instead, intelligence officers reviewed analyst reports derived from electronic eavesdropping, satellite imagery, and information gleaned from published news accounts. When interviews were necessary, they were outsourced to local police.

In the years following their work in the Middle East, Kinlaw and Hoag tried to apply what they had learned about field operations, but they were soon pushed aside. They served a stint together in London and worked for a year in Paris. Then, at the ripe old age of thirty-five, they were placed on loan to Georgetown University. Kinlaw taught courses in ancient Semitic languages. Hoag conducted research in Near Eastern archaeology. They worked for the CIA on a part-time basis, providing speculative analysis of terrorist capabilities derived from actual terrorist incidents.

Ten minutes into the early morning service, Kinlaw felt his phone vibrate inside the pocket of his jacket. He took it out and glanced at the number. The call was from Winston Smith, his supervisor at the CIA. Kinlaw pressed a button to send the call to voicemail. Before he could return the phone to his pocket, it vibrated again. He slipped quietly from the pew and made his way through the rear doors.

In the vestibule the phone vibrated again. Kinlaw pressed a button to answer it. Winston's voice was clear and sharp.

"You asleep?"

"No," Kinlaw replied quietly. "I'm in church."

"Church? It's seven o'clock in the morning."

"Yeah. What's up?"

"We have a problem."

"What kind of problem?"

"Technical Services says their seismographs detected geological activity inside Iran."

"An earthquake?"

"They haven't finished analyzing their data, but they're pretty certain Iran detonated a nuclear device."

"When?"

"Last night."

"Where?"

"Western Iran. Somewhere up in the mountains. They don't have an exact location yet. Looks like it was an underground test."

"Did we know this was coming?"

"We'll talk about it when you get here. Find Hoag and bring him with you."

Kinlaw switched off the phone and walked outside.

8

WASHINGTON, D.C.

AS THE STREETS OF WASHINGTON, D.C., filled with morning traffic, David Hoag sat at a table in the Starbucks café in the Georgetown section of the city, a mile west of the White House. Slouched in his chair, he read the morning edition of *The Washington Post* and did his best to think of nothing else. His eyes darted from article to article between sips of hazelnut latté. As he reached up to turn the page, his cell phone rang. He took it from his pocket and checked the screen. A text message appeared. "Let's go."

Instinctively, he looked out to the street through the front window of the store. Parked at the curb was a black Chevrolet Suburban. Seated behind the steering wheel was Dennis Kinlaw.

Something's up, Hoag thought. He and Kinlaw hadn't planned to meet until after lunch. That Kinlaw was there now could mean only one thing. *Trouble*, he sighed. Through the windshield he watched as Kinlaw waved his hand to hurry him. Hoag tossed the newspaper on the table, picked up his coffee cup, and started toward the door.

A car horn blared as Hoag made his way across the sidewalk. An angry commuter scowled at him from a car stopped behind the Suburban. Hoag gave an apologetic wave, opened the passenger door, and climbed inside. "What's up?" He set the coffee cup in a holder and pulled the door closed.

"Got a call from Winston Smith." Kinlaw pressed the gas. The Suburban lurched ahead. "NORAD thinks the Iranians have detonated a nuclear bomb."

"Where?"

"Western Iran."

"A test?"

"Yeah."

"That changes things," Hoag said sarcastically. He pulled the seatbelt over his shoulder and clicked it in place. "When did they do it?"

"Last night."

"Last night?" Hoag frowned. "They did a nuclear test at night?"

"No." Kinlaw shook his head. "It was daytime there. Last night here, for us." Kinlaw picked up Hoag's coffee cup and took a sip. "About ten o'clock. I'm sure you were sleeping."

"They called you last night, and you're just now telling me?"

"No. Winston called me an hour ago."

Hoag glanced at his watch. "Got you out of the shower?"

"Got me out of church."

"Have time to get your daily dose of religion?"

Kinlaw frowned. "Get as far away from me as possible."

"Why?"

"So when lightning strikes you, it won't hit me."

Hoag cut his eyes at Kinlaw as he took the coffee cup from his hand. "What did Winston say?"

"They want us out at Langley this morning."

"I can't," Hoag protested. "I have a meeting at ten."

"Not any more."

Kinlaw steered the Suburban into the left lane and drove toward the entrance to Rock Creek Parkway.

9

BERLIN, GERMANY

GERMAN CHANCELLOR JOSEF MUELLER stood at a large plate glass window and stared at the reflecting pool that surrounded the official residence. As he stood there, hands behind his back, a satisfied sense of confidence swept over him, bringing a smile to his face and a certainty that destiny was unfolding before him. His assurance of pending success was not without foundation.

Born in Bavaria, Mueller burst onto the political scene ten years earlier as an advocate of a more prominent leadership role for Germany in world affairs. He was swept to power as governor of Bavaria in a landslide election that marked a resurgence of German nationalism. After two terms as governor, his overwhelming popularity made him an obvious choice for chancellor. A week after the German parliament elected him to that office, Mueller was shot by a disgruntled Czech extremist. For three days he lay in a coma on the verge of death. Then Gregor von Bettinger paid Mueller a visit.

A mysterious figure, Bettinger masqueraded as an Orthodox archbishop. In reality, he practiced a heretical blend of Christianity and ancient Germanic religion that eventually had led the Orthodox prelate to defrock him. When he visited Mueller in the hospital, Bettinger prayed for him. Almost immediately Mueller regained consciousness and his condition improved rapidly. His physicians declared his recovery nothing short of a miracle.

Bettinger became a regular visitor at the Chancery, instructing Mueller on the ancient Germanic arts, a practice that fed on Mueller's sense of German pride. On one of those visits Bettinger gave Mueller a small sun wheel medallion as a gift. About the size of a two Euro coin, it had an open circle in the center with ten spokes that extended in jagged lines to an outer rim. Mueller carried the medallion in his pocket as a reminder of the destiny Bettinger assured him was his.

While Mueller stared out the window of the chancellor's residence, he thought of all that had transpired to bring him to a position of power. His rise to high office, two successful terms as Bavarian governor, and the attempted assassination—he could not have orchestrated it better. Now, his vision of a global market centered on a German economy rather than the American markets seemed at last a real possibility. Germany and the German people could once again take their rightful place at the center of world events. Unlimited prosperity would be theirs, and with it the world domination they had longed to obtain. Today he would initiate the final phase of his efforts to bring that vision to pass.

An aide appeared at Mueller's side. "Chen Wu has arrived."

"Very well," Mueller turned and nodded. "Show him in." He turned back to the window for one last gaze. As he did, he slipped his left hand into his pants pocket. His fingers curled around the sun wheel and traced lightly over the spokes.

Chen Wu, the Chinese foreign minister, had spent the past two weeks traveling throughout Europe conducting talks with his counterparts in European Union member-nations. Made to appear routine, the trip was a carefully planned cover for his stop in Berlin and his meeting with Mueller. As China's largest European trading partner, Germany played a vital role in the life of China's economy. Conversations with other heads of state in Europe would be informative. Wu's conversation with Mueller would be strategic.

Footsteps from the hall behind him drew Mueller's attention away from the window. He glanced to the left as Wu entered the room. The two men approached each other and shook hands. Wu bowed respectfully.

"Chancellor Mueller. I am honored to meet with you."

"I assure you," Mueller replied, "the pleasure is all mine."

Mueller laid his hand on Wu's shoulder and guided him toward a small table and chairs on the opposite side of the room. "Would you care for coffee?"

"Yes," Wu nodded. "Coffee would be nice."

The two sat at the table and chatted amicably about Wu's trip, the things he had seen and the experiences he had had as he traveled about the continent. Then, carefully, Mueller turned the conversation to the topic of Iran.

"I suppose you have heard the news from Iran."

"A most unfortunate event."

"Have you seen the markets today?"

"Yes."

"They have not reacted too severely, but incidents like this indicate once again how fragile the world's economy really is."

"Disruptions of this nature are very expensive, indeed."

Mueller took a sip of coffee. "We have all been lulled into relying on the United States to ensure our economic success. Dependant on their military to provide global stability and their consumers to purchase our goods."

"They have an ability to project power none of us has yet been able to match."

"That was true in the past, but that is only one component. The other element is America's consumption of the world's production."

"They are the largest economy in the world. No producing country can ignore their markets, regardless of how much one might wish."

"Again, that was true in the past, but as you know, American economic dominance peaked a decade ago. Their sovereign debt now equals their gross domestic product. Debt service is now second only to defense spending." Mueller pointed to Wu. "China has replaced the U.S. as the world's leading economic power."

Wu took a sip of coffee. "So it would seem."

"You enjoyed ten percent growth last year?"

Wu nodded. "We had a good year."

"Your own internal demand accounted for eight of those percentage points."

"Our people are growing accustomed to a life of consumption themselves. They have seen how Americans live and have sought to emulate that style." Wu looked away. "It was inevitable, I suppose, though we have tried in the past to limit their exposure."

"China no longer needs the U.S."

Wu looked back at Mueller. "We need them to repay their debts."

"But going forward, you have better use for the money you earn than spending it on their bonds."

Wu smiled at Mueller. "What would you suggest we do with it: purchase European Union bonds, perhaps?"

Mueller shook his head. "Invest the money in China's infrastructure."

"We have been doing that and are continuing to do so." Wu set his coffee cup on the saucer. "But I am curious. Why would Germany have any interest in whether China purchases United States debt obligations?"

Mueller rested his hands together on the tabletop and leaned forward. "The United States can no longer provide the world stability both of our countries require. The U.S. response to Iran's nuclear test will show their inability to address Middle East issues in a way that accounts for either of our interests in the region."

"And what is our interest in the region?"

"China's interest is oil, and of course Iran is China's major source of foreign oil. China needs Iran just as Iran needs China. Your economy cannot operate without their oil."

"And Germany?"

"Iran running loose in the region with nuclear arms is not a problem for most Germans. Our people care little whether they and their neighbors blow each other up. But the disruption that would follow is something we cannot allow. German companies sell to Iraq and the growing industrial base in Afghanistan. We would like to sell to Iran. And, we have a large presence in Pakistan."

Wu's face brightened. "China is grateful for your work in Pakistan. Unlike the Americans, Germany understands the strategic significance of the Chinese-Pakistan alliance. It is the only thing that keeps India's regional hegemony in check."

"Germany is glad to assist in obtaining regional stability along the Indian Ocean. And you have made my point quite eloquently. The United States has neither the vision nor the will to impose stability on the region."

"And how do you suppose they see the region?"

"At their core, Americans view the Middle East as part of a global struggle with Islam. For all its talk of tolerance and justice, the United States is captivated by the historic conflict between Christianity, Judaism, and Islam. They see the Middle East region as part of a religious war. That religious conflict, not economic considerations and certainly not China's interests, drives U.S. policy for the region."

Wu agreed. "Religions have spawned wars throughout human history. Ridding humanity of its religious obsession would take us far toward global peace and unity."

"Precisely. And we have reached a critical point once again. Iran with nuclear weapons places us at a time when the nations of the world will have to choose between survival and religious expression. You have already seen some of this in your struggle with Tibet."

Wu nodded thoughtfully. "And with the Uyghur, too."

"One day soon we will face the very real possibility of making all religious expression illegal." Mueller leaned away. "Or face a religiously motivated nuclear holocaust."

"The United States would oppose any decision that limits religion."

"Perhaps, but not necessarily."

Wu took a sip of coffee and smiled at Mueller. "And how do you propose their cooperation for such a measure could be obtained?"

"Quite simply." Mueller leaned forward once again and lowered his voice. "Stop purchasing their bonds."

Wu could not suppress the startled look on his face. "Such a move would be catastrophic for them and for us." He gestured with his left hand. "You cannot be serious. Germany would suffer, too."

Mueller gestured with a tap of his finger against the tabletop. "For you, U.S. debt is an investment. The bonds you hold are excess profit from trade, most of it foreign trade. Whether the value of that investment goes up or down has little bearing on the Chinese economy. For the United States, your purchase of those bonds has been their livelihood, and your continued purchase is their only hope. Your support for their debt is the only thing keeping them afloat."

"And if we suspended our debt purchases?"

"The dollar would collapse. America would be forced to shrink its global reach." Mueller paused. "The United States, with all its military machinery, would be neutralized."

"And what would China gain from such a thing?"

"Control of the world's economy."

Wu's eyes opened wide. A smile spread across his face. He gestured with his empty coffee cup. "Perhaps you should pour more coffee."

10

DOWNTOWN LOS ANGELES

JABBAH ILMIR CROSSED THE LOBBY of the U.S. Bank Tower and made his way past the newsstand. Located on Fifth Street, the building loomed over downtown Los Angeles. Barely six thirty on the West Coast, the sun was just rising, its long, sharp rays piercing the haze of dawn and casting brilliant streaks of light through the lobby windows.

Dressed for work, Ilmir wore a navy blue suit, white shirt, and red tie. He had arrived early that morning, hoping to catch up on assignments he had missed the day before. No one seemed to like it that he had left early to attend his son's soccer game. He hoped that by making up the time, he could prove to them that he really was serious about his job.

Around the corner from the security desk, he passed the coffee shop. A television mounted above the counter showed the morning newscast. Ilmir slowed his pace as he came within sight of the screen then stopped to watch. The broadcast showed images of the Zagros Mountains in Iran. He recognized them immediately. Ilmir moved closer to the counter to listen to the report.

"According to newswire reports, Stanford seismologists suspect Iran has detonated a nuclear bomb," the reporter said. "Seismographic data indicates the event occurred near Bakhtaran, on the western slopes of the Zagros Mountains. The blast is believed to have been a five-kiloton explosion."

A grin spread across Ilmir's face. He put his hand to his mouth to conceal his joy.

The reporter continued, "White House spokesman Ron Nielsen and Iranian news agency officials have yet to either confirm or deny the blast. However, when asked about the report earlier today, Iranian Foreign Minister Abadeh Ardakan had this to say…"

The newscast cut to videotape of Ardakan entering the foreign ministry building in Tehran. Ilmir's eyes grew wide with anticipation as he watched. His heart raced. Veins in his neck throbbed. Ardakan climbed the steps and turned to look squarely into the news camera, "Allah has been moving the events of human history toward a time when all peoples of the world will learn to deal with us in fairness and justice. Now is that time."

Ilmir gasped. *The Mahdi. A time when all will learn to deal with us in fairness and justice. The day of the Mahdi has arrived.* There had been cryptic messages before, Ahmadinejad in his speech to the United Nations, an open letter in *The New York Times*, but those were only to alert the millions of Shi'a that the time was drawing near. These words today from the foreign minister—this was the call to action.

A man behind the counter glanced up. "You ready to order?"

Ilmir ignored him and turned away without responding. He started back across the lobby, retracing his steps toward the front entrance. He took a cell phone from his pocket and scrolled down the contacts list to the name of Shamil Minab. Then he pressed a button to place the call. When Minab answered Ilmir could hardly contain himself. "The day of the Mahdi has arrived."

For a moment the phone was silent. Then Minab spoke in a halting, skeptical tone, as if what he had heard was too good to be true. "Do not joke with me. This is no joking matter."

"I am not joking."

"You are certain?"

"Yes," Ilmir replied, confident and certain. "You know what to do?"

"Of course. You are sure this is correct?"

"I heard it with my own ears. You know where to go? You remember the location?"

"Yes," Minab answered. "I remember."

"Good. Get busy. Meet me there in half an hour."

Ilmir pressed a button to end the call. By then he had reached the main entrance. With one hand still holding the phone, he pushed through the doorway and stepped outside to the sidewalk. He stopped and switched the cell phone to a text screen. Using his index finger, he punched in the message, "The day of the Mahdi has arrived."

When he had finished inserting the proper letters, he searched through his contacts list for a number, found it, and pressed the button to send the message. He smiled as he waited for confirmation that the message had been sent, then he slipped the phone into his pocket.

Ilmir walked to the corner and crossed at the traffic light. As he stepped to the curb on the far side of the street he met Steve Roth, walking in the opposite direction. Roth worked in Ilmir's office, two cubicles down. He called to Ilmir in jest, "Hey, Jabbah." He pointed toward the building. "The office is this direction."

"Ahh, I forgot something." Ilmir feigned embarrassment and waved him off, slapping his palm to his forehead. "Talking on the phone. I have to go to my car. It won't take long."

"Johnson will be there in an hour." Roth held up his wrist and pointed to his watch. He had left early the day before, too. "You want to be there before she gets in."

"Take care of it for me," Ilmir grinned. "Punch me in."

Roth stopped and turned to face him. "Really? You want me to log you into the system?"

"Yeah. Punch me in. I'll be right behind you anyway."

"Okay," Roth laughed. "Just make sure you show." He turned away and crossed the street. Ilmir continued in the opposite direction.

When Ilmir reached his car, he took the cell phone from his pocket, tossed it on the seat beside him, and started the engine. From the parking garage downtown, he drove east to Park Mesa Heights. At Fourth Avenue he slowed the car to an idle and looked for the house number. Halfway down the block he found the location—a one-story house with stucco and stone exterior. He turned into the driveway and let the car roll slowly toward the fence at the back corner of the house.

As he switched off the engine, a blue Honda Civic turned into the drive behind him. He watched in the mirror as Minab stepped from the car. Together they opened the gate and made their way around the back of the house to the rear door. Minab tried the door knob.

"It's locked. Do you have the key?"

"No," Ilmir replied. "It's supposed to be here. Check around. They said it was here for us."

Minab lifted the doormat but found nothing. A flowerpot sat nearby. Ilmir moved it aside but the key wasn't there. Minab glanced over at him. "You sure this is the day? What if you were wrong? What do we do if it's just a setup?"

"It's not a setup," Ilmir frowned. "I heard him say it on the news this morning. A time when all will learn to deal with us in fairness and justice." Ilmir's face brightened. "I remember."

A small concrete slab covered the area at the foot of the steps near the back door. No more than four feet wide, it was protected from the weather by a stoop that jutted out from the roof. Wooden braces on either side ran at an angle from the edge of the stoop to the rear wall of the house. Ilmir reached overhead and ran his fingers along the top edge of the brace. He found the key and held it up for Minab to see.

"They told me where to find it," he grinned, "but it took Allah to remind me where to look." Minab nodded and smiled as he waited nervously for Ilmir to open the door.

The rear door opened to a small kitchen. Near the wall to the left was a counter with a sink. To the right was a table with four chairs. Beyond the table, an archway opened to the living room. A sofa and one overstuffed chair sat near a window on the front wall.

A hallway led from the living room to the right through the center of the house. Two bedrooms opened on the front side, one opened to the back. A bathroom was located at the far end of the hallway.

Ilmir crossed the kitchen. Minab followed close behind.

"I don't see the bag."

"It's here," Ilmir replied. "They said it would be in the bedroom closet."

"Which one?"

"Front." Ilmir started toward the hallway. "On the end."

They walked up the hallway to the bedroom near the end of the hall. An empty bed frame sat in the center of the room. Ilmir made his way around it to the closet and pulled open the door. "Here it is," he sighed.

A green canvas duffle bag lay on the closet floor. Ilmir tugged on the handle then glanced at Minab. "Give me a hand, will you? This thing is heavy." Minab hesitated. Ilmir looked over at him. "What is the matter?" He turned toward the front window. "Is someone here?"

"No." Minab shook his head. "It's not that. It's just… I knew I would carry the backpack. I just didn't think I had to prepare it."

"I will prepare it, but I can't carry this by myself. Come on." Ilmir gestured toward the duffle bag. "Give me a hand."

Reluctantly, Minab took hold of the bag at one end. Together they lifted it from the floor and carried it to the kitchen. As they came around the corner of the living room, Minab glanced over his shoulder, "Where do we put it?"

"On the table," Ilmir said, out of breath.

"Can it take the weight?"

"Yeah," Ilmir groaned as he lifted the bag higher. "It will be just fine."

They set the duffle on the table and took a deep breath. Minab looked warily at the bag. "There's a lot in that bag."

"More than enough to do the job." Ilmir unzipped it. "They should be here soon with the backpacks."

The bag was filled with packages of plastic explosives and an envelope with maps and drawings of Los Angeles. Ilmir took out a map of the city and spread it over the duffle.

Just then the rear door opened. Ilmir looked up to see four men. He caught the eye of the first one, Kundi Mastung, and gave him a puzzled look. "Where are the backpacks?"

"In the car."

"We need them in here."

"I'll get them. Just wanted to make certain everything was ready."

Ilmir pointed to the duffle bag protruding from beneath the map. "We are waiting on you. Do you have the truck?"

"Yes," Kundi nodded. "It's in the warehouse. You know where that is?"

"Show me." Ilmir pointed to the map on the table. "I want to make certain I go to the correct location."

Kundi came from the door and leaned over the table. "Here," he pointed. "Along this street, off of Crenshaw. It's not far away."

"You have it loaded?"

"Yes," Kundi nodded. "Eshabon is loading it now."

Ilmir looked confused. "Right now?"

"He began last night. As soon as we received the notice." Kundi dismissed Ilmir's look of concern with a wave of the hand. "Don't worry. It will be ready when you arrive."

Ilmir propped his hand against the back of a chair. "You received notice last night?"

"Yes."

"How? How did you receive notice?"

"A text message." Kundi scowled. "Just like you." He frowned. "They are not stupid, you know. No one would risk revealing our mission now. Not after all the many details we have worked to address. They would not call and talk to us by phone."

"Then it is true? Iran has exploded a nuclear bomb?"

"Yes," Kundi grinned. "We have exploded a bomb. A nuclear bomb."

"This is good," Ilmir said, nodding. They stood there a moment, then Ilmir stood up straight. He pointed again to the duffle bag. "We need to prepare the backpacks."

Kundi nodded, "I will bring them from the car." He turned toward the door and stepped outside.

When he was gone, Ilmir glanced at Minab. "I don't like this. Coming inside, looking around, then going out."

"Neither do I," Minab replied.

Ilmir stepped away from the table and followed Kundi outside.

11

CIA HEADQUARTERS, LANGLEY, VA

HOAG AND KINLAW ARRIVED AT CIA HEADQUARTERS and were cleared through building security, then made their way downstairs to the bottom level of the basement. At the far end of the hall, they entered the Operations Control Center. Four large screens covered the wall to the left of the door. To the right, the room was filled with desks arranged in arcs that stretched the width of the room, forming a semicircle around a central workstation. Atop each desk were computer screens, keyboards, and phone sets. Bright young analysts were busy pecking away at the keyboards. Headsets on, everyone talked and chattered at the same time, filling the room with an endless stream of conversation.

Near the workstation in the center of the room stood Winston Smith, dressed in a blue blazer, khaki pants, and white shirt. The collar of the shirt was open. His tie hung loosely against his chest. With his hands resting on his hips, he looked more like a basketball coach than an operations control officer.

For a man of his rank and stature, Winston Smith was an oddity. Unlike most senior operations officers, he was not a graduate of an Ivy League school or a prestigious prep school, and his parents were not wealthy. Instead, he came to Langley from the University of Kentucky, where his proficiency in languages caught the attention of a professor with connections. Fluent in Spanish at the age of twelve, he taught himself French and German while enrolled in public high school. At the university he picked up Arabic, Chinese, and Hebrew. Language skills, timing, and dogged determination propelled his career forward at a rapid pace. Now, twenty years later, he was a senior control officer supervising a team that worked the agency's most intractable issues. He looked up as Hoag and Kinlaw entered the room.

"Good of you all to join us," Winston quipped.

Kinlaw lingered near the front of the room, watching the screens on the wall. Hoag moved past the rows of desks toward Winston.

"Are we sure it was a nuclear device?"

"It was nuclear," Winston replied. An ironic smile turned up the corners of his mouth. "No doubt about it."

"Anybody on the ground confirm it?"

"Not yet." The look on Winston's face turned serious. "We had a team on site but they got 'em."

"Got 'em?"

"Snipers."

"What kind of team?"

"Rangers. I don't know their names. Two Green Berets."

"So, how did we confirm it was nuclear?"

"Seismic data. And, the army team found a truck just before they were hit. A JSTARS plane tracking the team picked up telemetry from the truck. They were taking air samples and sending the results back to a station near Bakhtaran. We traced their signal to a control room in a gas processing facility." Winston cut his eyes at Hoag. "They were checking for gamma rays. Promethium. Alpha particles."

"What's the army say about the two guys?"

There was a twinkle in Winston's eyes. "Oh, they're pretty angry." The ironic smile returned.

Hoag looked disgusted. "But they're not mad at the Iranians."

"No, not the Iranians." Winston shook his head. "They're mad at me for requesting the team. Said their guys should have never been there in the first place."

Hoag shook his head in disbelief. Winston turned back to the others and raised his voice. "Okay. What do we have?"

Someone spoke up. "NORAD confirms a blast occurred."

"Instruments at Incirlik back that up," someone else offered.

"Aviano Air Base says the same."

"Call from Doha to the Defense Ministry in Riyadh last night noted the blast."

"We had a—"

"Okay." Winston cut them off. "There was a blast. We're certain it was a nuclear explosion. We were certain of that twelve hours ago. What else? Anybody got anything new on this? Satellite imagery? Communications intercepts?" Winston paused. When no one responded he raised his voice a little louder. "Am I talking to myself? I got a room full of people here, and I'm not getting much."

Billy Jones spoke up. "I think we ought to move on to the implications."

Others chimed in. "Implications? Iran has the bomb. Now they'll rule the Persian Gulf. End of story."

"No, they won't rule the region," another answered. "I mean, they might, but that isn't our biggest concern."

"Oh? And what is that?"

"Saudi Arabia."

"Oil prices are spiking through the roof," someone else offered.

"Not that." Jones snapped, frustrated. "Look, if Iran has nuclear weapons, the Saudis will want them. Then the Iraqis.

Syria will be next. They all have the money. They can buy them or develop their own. This thing will go all the way around the Gulf."

"A Middle Eastern nuclear arms race," someone snickered.

"Yes," Jones replied. "That's exactly what it'll be. An arms race." His tone grew ominous. "An arms race among countries with enough money to spend us under the table."

"Why?" A guy near the front of the room turned to face the others. "Why does it have to come to that?"

"Why?" Jones retorted. "Because the Iranians have them. Haven't you been paying attention the last ten years? If we're the ene-my, they're all against us. But if we aren't the enemy, they'll fight each other. After us, they hate each other the most. We're out of Iraq—"

"Sort of," a voice interrupted.

Jones ignored the intrusion and continued, "We forced the Israelis to make concessions. We aren't the bad guys anymore. Now they're back to their regional conflicts. I assure you, Saudi Arabia will want its own nuclear force. They don't trust the Shi'a, no matter what they say in public."

Hoag spoke up, "Billy's correct, but that's not our problem right now, either."

Jones glanced in that direction. "Then what's our problem?"

"New York. Los Angeles. Washington, D.C. And they don't have to obliterate them to destroy us."

Someone across the room dismissed Hoag with a wave of the hand. "They don't have a missile that can reach us."

"But they have missiles."

"Not any that can reach us from inside Iran. Or from Iraq. Or from Syria, for that matter. They'd have to put a missile in... Bermuda to reach us."

Laughter tittered across the room. Hoag continued. "They won't launch them from inside Iran or Iraq or Syria. All they have to do is put one…"

A voice interrupted him. "The real problem is what if Osama bin Laden gets one of those bombs. He's our real enemy."

The conversation started again, this time in a different direction.

"I don't think so," a voice replied.

"Why not?"

"Iran has worked hard to get to this point. They stand on the verge of dominating the region."

"They already dominate the region."

"More a regional pest than anything dominant."

"Whatever they are, if they sell bin Laden a nuclear bomb, they'll hand him the power that goes with it. He'll dominate the region. Iran isn't giving it up that easily. Not now."

The discussion moved on. Winston glanced over at Hoag. "Welcome to my world." Hoag shook his head. Winston chuckled. "It's like this all the time."

"They think they're invulnerable," Hoag scoffed. "They don't realize just how fragile all that electronic gear they're using really is."

"Yes, it is," Winston agreed, his voice suddenly serious. "One high-altitude, nuclear detonation and they'd be in the dark instantly, along with everything on the East Coast."

Hoag nodded in agreement. "Do one over Kansas and you could just about blanket the entire country."

"Technology works great when it works, but when it doesn't you're in deep trouble." Winston had a nervous smile this time. "No one remembers how to function without it." He gestured to the room around them. "In a nuclear attack this building could be useless two seconds after an explosion that hits anywhere on the East Coast."

"You really think so? Aren't all our buildings shielded now?"

"Supposed to be, but who knows if it'll actually work."

"I'm sure they tested it."

"Oh, it's been tested. Just not with an actual explosion."

Hoag found Winston's skepticism amusing. "Let's hope we never have to find out. Every system in here relies on a microchip to make it work."

"That's right." Winston stuck his hands in his pockets. "Lights. Air conditioning. All the security measures. Every car in the parking lot. It all runs on microprocessors. A nuclear explosion over any target within three states of here would give off a high-voltage electromagnetic pulse strong enough to compromise the entire system."

Hoag looked back over the room. "They seem smart enough."

"They're plenty smart," Winston nodded. "And they aren't a bad bunch." He let his eyes slowly scan the room. "I didn't always think so. I used to argue with them and try to change their minds." He chuckled again. "Spent a lot of time shouting at them. Now I just let them talk." He patted Hoag on the shoulder. "And I remind myself that Western civilization has survived worse than these."

"I think the stakes are a little higher now."

"Which is why I need you and him." Winston nodded toward Kinlaw. "I need you two to get to the bottom of this."

Hoag glanced over his shoulder toward the others in the room. "I thought that's what they were doing."

"Yeah," Winston chuckled. "That's what they think, too." He pulled Hoag away and leaned close. "These guys can cover the technology end of it. Whatever's out there in an electronic file or a databank, they'll find it and mine it for all it's worth. I need you and Kinlaw to work the human side."

"The human side? We don't really have any sources in the field. We aren't case officers."

"No one's a case officer anymore." Winston pulled Hoag closer. "Look, you heard their analysis just now. They have none. I need you and Kinlaw to 'what if' this situation, like you did with that guy in Turkey and the thing in Houston. Just do whatever it is you do and find out what the Iranians are really up to."

"Okay," Hoag nodded. "We'll get to work."

Winston let go of Hoag's shoulder and turned away. Hoag started across the room toward the door. As he made his way past the rows of desks, Winston called after him. "David." Hoag turned to look back at him. Winston looked grim. "Work fast. The game has changed. We don't have a lot of time on this one."

12

DENVER, COLORADO

AT JAKE'S DELI, BANK EXECUTIVES in town for a conference crowded the line. Behind the counter, Mustafa Bandar took a bagel from the toaster, placed it on a plate, and handed it across the counter. A woman reached up and took the plate. Mustafa smiled at her, "Would you like cream cheese with that?"

"No," she replied, shaking her head. "This will be fine. I like it plain."

As she moved away, Mustafa turned to the next person. "What could I get for you?"

A man scowled from behind a newspaper. "Sausage biscuit," he groaned.

"One sausage biscuit coming up." Mustafa reached inside the deli case, took a biscuit from the hot tray, and placed it on a plate. "Anything else?" The man shook his head. Mustafa handed him the plate.

The cell phone on Mustafa's hip vibrated. He slipped his hand beneath his apron, unclipped the phone, and brought it around to see the screen. His heart leaped at the sight. "Rj'l Mhd." He stared at it a moment, suddenly transported back in time to a dusty madrasah in Bojnurd, a small village in northern Iran. He was fourteen and listened with rapt attention as a teacher told about the Mahdi, one great and final prophet who would come at the end of time to lead all peoples everywhere to faith in Allah. Arrival of the Mahdi would be preceded by a great war against the infidels, a time of tribulation for all mankind, and then he would come. And then all of the infidels—Jews and Christians alike—would bow before him or lose their heads.

Mustafa glanced down at the phone once more. The message—Rj'l Mhd—though formed with English letters, was actually written in Arabic, the vowels omitted to make it less obvious. He recognized it immediately. "Raj'a al-Mahdi. Return of the Mahdi."

Just then, a voice called from the far end of the counter, "Mustafa! We got a line waiting."

Mustafa jerked around to see Sam smiling at him from the cash register. Sam gestured toward the phone, "Trouble?"

"No," Mustafa shook his head. "It's all right," he smiled.

Mustafa closed the phone and returned it to the clip on his belt. As he turned back to face the line of waiting customers, someone nudged his shoulder. He glanced to the left to see Sam now standing next to him.

"Wash your hands." Sam nodded toward the sink. Mustafa started toward the sink near the grill behind the counter. Sam moved around him and stepped to the counter for the next customer.

—— (((——

Later that morning Mustafa finished his shift and left the deli. From downtown, he drove to a white frame house on Utica Street in the Edgewater section of Denver. A car was parked in the driveway, another down the street. Mustafa brought his car to a stop at the curb, climbed from the driver's seat, and walked to the front door.

As he came through the doorway into the living room, he saw Munir Esfandak seated on a sofa to the right. Next to him was a thin, wiry man. Mustafa had seen him before but did not know his name. Across the room someone was seated in a chair. Through a doorway to the kitchen he saw Robat Sedeh standing at the stove, slowly stirring a pot. Sedeh turned to look over his shoulder. "Mustafa!" he called. "You are late."

"I had to finish my shift."

"We sent you a text message two hours ago. This is the most important day of our lives. Your job at the deli is of no consequence now."

"If I had left early, everyone would have noticed. I thought it best to complete the shift. Leave at my regular time."

Sedeh gestured with a nod for Mustafa to come near. Mustafa walked to the kitchen. Sedeh lowered his voice. "Zanjan will not be joining us."

The news startled Mustafa. A frown wrinkled his forehead. "Why not?"

"His interest in the project has… waned."

"But he will give us all away," Mustafa protested. "We must not proceed now. The whole thing is of no use. He will tell someone."

"No." Sedeh smiled. "He will not be a problem."

"You mean—"

Sedeh looked grim. "Esfandak gave him a ride."

Mustafa glanced over his shoulder toward Esfandak, who turned his head to face Mustafa. The look in his eyes sent a chill through Mustafa's body.

Sedeh continued. "You will take his place."

Mustafa was startled by the suggestion. "Me?" He snapped his head around toward Sedeh. "But," he protested, "I have not driven the route. I don't know the way. I've never done anything like—"

"Shhhh," Sedeh cut him off with a wave of his hand and a gentle pat on the shoulder. "It will be okay. You will drive the route this afternoon. After school is closed. And you can drive it again later. We have time." He rubbed his hand lightly across Mustafa's shoulder. "It will be okay. Use your own car to make certain of the route. No one will notice. It will be all right."

He moved his hand from Mustafa's shoulder, took him by the elbow, and ushered him into the front room. "Look at the map." He squatted near the sofa and unfolded the map on the floor. "The school is here." He pointed. "You will pick up the Suburban here, at the house." He pointed with his thumb over his shoulder. "It will be parked in the garage out back." He looked back at the map and traced the route with his index finger. "All you have to do is drive right along here, turn here, and pull in this drive, at the front entrance to the school. It's the morning drop-off." He smiled at Mustafa. "You were present when we went over this before. You've seen the map a thousand times."

"Yes," Mustafa nodded. "A thousand times. But always it was Zanjan who would not be coming back."

Sedeh looked up. His gaze was sharp and piercing. "What are you saying?" He stood. "Are you saying you will not give your life for the cause of Allah?"

"No," Mustafa shook his head. "I am not saying that. It just…" He sighed. "It takes some getting used to. Some preparation. Zanjan had time to prepare."

"I understand." Sedeh patted Mustafa on the shoulder again. "You will be ready. Esfandak will help you with the route. I will help you with the Koran. Allah will help you find peace." He looked Mustafa in the eye. "You will be ready."

13

WASHINGTON, D.C.

AFTER MEETING WITH WINSTON SMITH, Hoag and Kinlaw walked up the hallway to the elevator. As they stood there waiting, a woman appeared from around the corner. Her sudden appearance startled Hoag.

"David," she smiled.

Hoag responded with a tense smile. "Jenny. Good to see you." His eyes darted away. A knot formed in the pit of his stomach. His hands were damp and clammy.

She turned to Kinlaw, "Dennis." Her tone was polite but disinterested. "How is Debby?"

"She's fine." Kinlaw smiled and nodded. "You're looking well."

"Thanks." She turned back to Hoag. "Thought you might be out here today."

"Ahh, yeah. You know," Hoag shrugged. "Always something going on."

"Right." She looked him in the eye. "That was our problem, wasn't it?"

"Yeah," Hoag nodded. "Among other things."

"Well…" Her countenance dropped, but she quickly recovered and put on a good smile. "You guys want to get lunch? I was on my way to the cafeteria."

"Can't today," Hoag replied. "We're in the middle of something and… it just…" A bell rang. The elevator doors opened. Kinlaw brushed past him and stepped inside. Hoag smiled at Jenny as he stepped backward into the elevator. "I'll call you."

"Okay."

The doors closed. The elevator started up. "Don't say a word," Hoag growled.

Kinlaw stared up at the floor numbers above the door. "She's a nice girl," he chuckled.

"I said, don't say a word."

Kinlaw ignored him. "You know, of all the things that happened in college, I never quite understood what happened with her. Why'd the two of you break up, anyway?"

"Gregg what's-his-name," Hoag sighed.

"Gregg?" A frown wrinkled Kinlaw's forehead. He glanced over at Hoag. "The football player?"

"Yeah."

Kinlaw looked up at the lights above the door once more. "She never seemed that superficial."

"You didn't know her that well."

"People change."

"She was interested in who she thought could do something for her. His father was some big-time Wall Street guy. That's what she thought she wanted."

"And?"

"His daddy's firm went belly up. Gregg turned out to be interested in other things besides her. By then college was over. Everyone else had moved on."

The elevator doors opened to the lobby on the first floor. Kinlaw and Hoag stepped out.

"You know," Kinlaw continued, "people have a way of changing."

"Not that much."

"I don't know. She seems okay to me." Kinlaw gestured toward their surroundings. "She got a job here." Sarcasm dripped from his voice. "Must be something right about her."

"I don't know."

"You should call her," Kinlaw urged.

"Maybe." Hoag was ready to change the subject. "By the way, thanks for taking my back in that meeting," he smirked.

"You're welcome."

"Everyone in the room ignored what I was saying." They reached the exit. Hoag pushed open the door. "I'm only thirty-five, and I felt like the oldest guy in the room."

"You probably were." Kinlaw followed him outside. "But it does us no good for them to know what we're both thinking. One of us has to remain detached."

"Does us no good if they don't think," Hoag retorted.

"Winston knows what's going on. Jones is pretty sharp."

"They should have put Jones in Clandestine Operations. He knows the region, and he's great with people. They could have made a great field agent out of him, if they still made field agents. But as an analyst, he never pushes his conclusions."

They reached the Suburban and Kinlaw pressed a button on the remote to unlock the doors. Hoag got in on the passenger side. Kinlaw slid in behind the steering wheel. "They were right about the Saudis. They'll want the bomb."

"Yes," Hoag replied. "I'm sure they will. They always have. But that's a few years away. It isn't what we face right now."

Kinlaw put the key in the ignition and started the engine. "I noticed nobody in that meeting got to 'why.'"

"Why?"

"Why today?" Kinlaw glanced over his shoulder as he backed the Suburban from the parking space. "No one asked whether it was a coincidence that the Iranians exploded their first nuclear device today."

"And you have an answer?"

"November 4."

"So," Hoag shrugged. "What's special about November 4?"

"It's the day they took our embassy staff hostage in Tehran. November 4, 1979."

Hoag was silent for a moment. Then he looked over at Kinlaw. "You sure about that?"

"Positive."

"We better get back to the office."

14

CHICAGO, ILLINOIS

SHAIR KASHAN OPENED THE DOOR and stepped from the sidewalk into Pizano's Pizza. A favorite spot among office workers in Chicago's downtown loop, the restaurant was crowded and noisy. Already a line of young professionals waited at the front for a table. Kashan worked his way between them and scanned the dining room.

Seated at a table along the opposite wall was Tabuk Sabzevar. Short and slender, he was born in Yemen to Saudi parents. His father worked as a welder at a shipyard. His mother took in laundry. The family had been poor for generations, but they were devout Muslims and made certain all their children received an Islamic education. When he reached the age of eighteen, Tabuk, their oldest, got a job working on an oil tanker. With the money he earned, he came to the United States and attended college. He had been recruited by one of Hamid's connections at a mosque on Chicago's south side.

Sitting there, dressed in a dark gray business suit, Sabzevar looked like any other office employee. Men at tables on either side of him paid him no attention. Had they known him better, they would have been concerned.

Kashan crossed the dining room and slid quietly into a chair across from Sabzevar. "Why did you pick this place?" Kashan spoke

in Arabic. He kept his voice low and calm. "We should not be meeting like this. These places have security cameras."

"Relax," Sabzevar smiled. He tapped the newspaper folded
beside his plate. "Read the paper." He scooted his chair back from
the table and stood. "Enjoy lunch."

When he was gone, Kashan slipped around the table to take
his seat. He unfolded the paper and scanned the front page. Near
the bottom was an article with a circle drawn around it. The title of
the article read, "Stanford Scientists Suspect Iranian Nuclear Detonation." He was engrossed in the article when a waitress appeared.

"You need anything else?"

Kashan was caught off guard by her sudden appearance. He
glanced up from behind the paper, "Excuse me?"

"We're crowded today," she frowned. "You need anything
else?"

"Oh," he smiled. "A glass of tea."

"Tired of water?"

Kashan looked down at the table. A glass sat to the right, half
full of water. In the center of the table was a small, metal pan. On it
were two uneaten slices of pizza. There were two crusts sitting on
the plate in front of him. Kashan grinned. Sabzevar had not paid for
his meal. He chuckled as he looked back at the waitress. "Make that
tea hot."

"Hot tea?"

"Please." Kashan took a slice of pizza from the pan. "With
plenty of sugar."

An hour later Kashan entered a warehouse on Lowe Avenue. A
truck was parked nearby. Sabzevar and others were gathered around
the truck. A map was spread across the hood. They stood around

it talking. Kashan called out as he entered the room, "You owe me fourteen dollars."

"I only owe you for half," Sabzevar laughed. "I left you half the pizza. And I only had water to drink."

Kashan cuffed him on the back of the head as he joined them around the hood of the truck. "We are ready?"

Sibi Kalat glanced up from his place on the opposite side. "There is one problem."

"What is that?"

"How do we know for certain the truck will detonate?"

"It's a forty-foot tanker truck," Kashan replied. "Loaded with gasoline."

Someone else spoke up. "But unless the tank ruptures, it won't explode."

"That is the problem," Kalat nodded. "If the tank ruptures and gasoline leaks out, it will explode. But there is no guarantee it will rupture. And everything would be for nothing."

Farah Shinad spoke up. "I can take care of that."

Kalat glanced at the others then back to Shinad. "And how is that?"

"An explosive with a timer. Explosive detonates, the truck goes up."

"And you can get this explosive? And the timer?"

"Yes." Shinad said quietly. "I will take care of it."

Kalat took a deep breath. "You are certain of this?"

Shinad looked him in the eye. "I am certain of it. If I do not, I will personally open the valve and strike the match."

The mood was suddenly tense. This wasn't the first time Kalat and Shinad had stood face-to-face.

"Well," Kashan grinned, breaking the mood. "That problem is solved." He slapped Shinad on the back. "Anything else?"

15

GEORGETOWN UNIVERSITY

HOAG AND KINLAW ARRIVED at the campus of Georgetown University, Kinlaw parked the Suburban in its assigned space, and the two made their way to Ryan Hall. Home to Woodstock Theological Center on the floors above, the basement in the building went unused until Hoag and Kinlaw took it over. They located their official campus offices near the elevator, where they were easily accessible to students, two offices with a shared secretary in between. Most of their time, however, was spent across the hall. Access to that area was guarded by two doors. The first with a coded lock opened to an alcove, where entry through a second door required retina, voice, and palm print verification.

Beyond the second door were three offices which had been constructed as a building within a building. Made of steel and reinforced concrete, the self-contained structure was sturdy enough to support the weight of the entire building. Hoag's office was on one side, Kinlaw's on the other. In between was space for an assistant, a bathroom with shower, sleeping cots, and a fully-stocked galley kitchen.

Hoag entered his office and logged into the CIA's computer system through a terminal on his desk. Kinlaw took a seat on a chair nearby. Hoag glanced up from the monitor screen. "What time was the detonation?"

"Our time or theirs?"

"Theirs." Hoag continued to work at the keyboard while he talked. "What time was it in Iran when the bomb went off?"

"NORAD says…"

"Never mind." Hoag pressed a key on the computer keyboard. "I've got it right here." He pointed to the monitor screen. "Almost exactly 6:30 a.m." He looked up at Kinlaw. "You were right."

"About what?"

"About November 4." Hoag leaned back in the chair and folded his hands behind his head. "Our embassy was taken at 6:30 on the morning of November 4, 1979. And last night, while we were sleeping and they conducted their test, it was 6:30 in the morning on November 4 in Iran. "

Kinlaw rocked his chair on its back legs and propped his feet on the edge of the desk. "You know, Iran is an interesting country with an intriguing history."

"Here we go," Hoag moaned.

"What?"

"I wondered how long it would take for you to start in about all that prophecy and the end-of-time stuff." Hoag waved his hand in a dismissive gesture. "Gog and Magog, wasn't it?"

"Some of what has been written about prophecy is a little contrived, but it doesn't take a biblical scholar to see that Islam and Judaism are on a collision course."

"Maybe so, but parsing all the imagery in those writings is like trying to decipher a single line in a Faulkner novel. There's just too much for the minute details to be of any use."

"I'm not talking about trying to decipher all the details."

"Look, I'm sure this is all very interesting and that church you visit every morning will have a conference on the subject any day now…" Hoag paused and cut his eyes in Kinlaw's direction. "Does Winston know you go there in the mornings?"

"Why would Winston care?"

"I don't know," Hoag shrugged. "I just think some of the people we work for and with might think it was a little strange."

"Strange? Who would think it strange that I stop at a church in the morning to pray?"

"The people in that room today, for one. They would be shocked to think that you might actually interpret intelligence information in light of some ages-old religious text."

"The people in that room would be shocked if they ever saw any real intelligence." Kinlaw rested his hands in his lap. "Have you ever read any of the prophets?"

"Not really." Hoag looked away. "And I'm not interested in doing it now."

"You ought to at least read some of what you hold with such disdain."

"Why should I? I have you." Hoag leaned back in his chair. "Look, we've talked about this stuff before. Yes, Scripture indicates a final battle is coming, and there seems to be a consensus about what the so-called Rapture might be, but no one can agree on when it might happen, if at all. And I realize Iran isn't Arabic but Indo-European, with a long history that predates Islam by thousands of years. But I—"

Kinlaw cut him off. "You just don't want to think it's possible that those ancient prophecies are true."

Hoag leaned forward. "I want to deal in facts, Dennis. Not speculation."

"Excuse me?" Kinlaw tossed back his head at an imperious angle. "You don't want to deal in speculation?"

"Does that offend you?"

"David, speculative analysis is what we do. It's why we have this office. It's why the federal government pays us a monthly salary. It's been our work since we graduated from law school."

"We speculate about historic events, real-time events that happen in the here and now. And we analyze them in terms of actual information."

Kinlaw folded his arms across his chest. "Do you listen to yourself when you talk, or do you just spout out words and wait to see what sticks?"

"What do you mean by that?"

"I mean, we're already analyzing an event that happened yesterday in terms of the 1979 seizure of our embassy, an event that happened almost four decades ago. We're already looking to the past to find clues about the future for an event that is just now hitting the news."

"These were historic events, Dennis," Hoag leaned back once more, "not ancient prophecies."

"And you don't think that the ancient writings of Islam are driving current events in the Middle East?"

"Yes. I agree that people of the Middle East are influenced by their past, but we're not dealing with what they... Well, I guess we are dealing with what they believe, but it's not the same."

Kinlaw took a deep breath. "I think the real problem is that when I bring up the possibility that ancient Jewish and Christian prophecies might be true and accurate, you feel confronted by the implication that you ought to believe it, and you've always had a problem with Christians."

"No, I haven't."

"Yes, you have. You've always thought of them as weak and mindless. You don't think that of Muslims because you deal with them in a context of terrorism—people running around with assault rifles and explosives blowing things up and killing people, which you see as strength."

Hoag reacted with a smile. "I don't think of you as weak and mindless."

"But that's because I've pinned you to the wall a few times."

The smile on Hoag's face turned into a grin. He ran his hands over his face. "I don't know," he sighed. "It just doesn't seem like what we're supposed to do."

"I'm just saying, we should be open to the possibility that we're dealing with something bigger than simply Iran and its neighbors, and that events unfolding today have been foretold in the past."

"So, where do we begin?"

"Let's begin with today."

Hoag threw up his hands. "After all that, you want to begin with today?"

"You were the one who took us down the prophecy path. I was merely remarking about how unique Iran is when compared to its neighbors."

Hoag shook his head. "This is going to be one of those days."

Kinlaw leaned forward and rested his elbows on the desk. "Come on. Let's work this out. We'll start with today and work our way out in every direction." Kinlaw took a deep breath. "Bomb goes off in northern Iran at 6:30 in the morning on November 4."

"The precise date and time when they seized our embassy," Hoag replied. "Back it up, chronologically. What else happened in 1979?"

Kinlaw drummed his fingers on the desk. "They took our embassy."

"Yes," Hoag pointed. "But push it. They removed the Shah from power. They took Iran. Islamic students."

"University radicals."

"Islamic radicals. A ragtag band of university students."

"Revolutionaries."

Hoag leaned forward. "Islamic revolutionaries." His eyes were wide. "Islamic revolutionaries, seizing our embassy, kicked off a revolution. An Islamic revolution."

"A revolution focused on what?"

"Not what, but whom?"

"On taking back their country."

"And on driving infidels from the region."

"So that's what this is." Kinlaw slapped the desktop with his hand. "A second Islamic revolution, but does it mean there is more to follow? Or is this all there is—just a general, broad shift to nuclear power? The dawning of the Iranian age, the rise of Iran as a regional superpower—or the beginning of a specific military action?"

"Not just any military action, but a military action against us."

"And Israel."

Hoag frowned. "I agree that Iran is opposed to the existence of Israel, but adding that to our analysis now adds a variable we don't have, at least not yet. The attack on our embassy in 1979 wasn't an attack on Israel. It was an attack on us. So, what would that involve?" He drummed a pen on the desk. "A specific action against the United States. What would it involve?"

"I have no idea," Kinlaw shrugged. "Logistically, there could be a hundred things."

"Well, let's push this a little further." Hoag suggested. "Since this second revolution is based on a new, nuclear Iran… and the US is the target… Iran can't reach us with a warhead on a missile from anywhere inside Iran. They don't have a missile with that kind of range."

"Why would we be the target?"

"We were the target then. Do you think they chose the date by accident?"

"The date? To attack the embassy?"

"No. That they detonated their first nuclear device on precisely the same date and at precisely the same time. Six-thirty a.m. on November 4. The exact date and time they took the U.S. embassy in 1979."

Kinlaw shook his head. "No. I don't think it was an accident. That's why I brought it up."

"Okay. We were the target then, in 1979. I think we should assume we're the target now. So, back to my question: If they don't have a missile that can deliver a warhead this far, how else could they attack us?"

"Suicide bombers."

"That might work to inflict terror, disrupt things, maybe drive the stock market down a few hundred points; but if their nuclear test was the opening shot in a nuclear attack on us, I don't think they can miniaturize a nuclear device quickly enough to make it that portable."

"Well," Kinlaw stroked his chin, "then it's either an airplane or a ship."

"How would that work?"

"It's a nuclear bomb. You don't have to get very close to create a lot of damage. Load one on a ship. Sail it in as close as you could get to a major port. Detonate it."

"Can't get within the farewell buoy at most places without attracting attention."

"You could if you stopped to pick up the harbor pilot and let him guide you in, same as usual. They don't inspect cargo until it's offloaded."

"Most of the time."

"Yeah, but even then you'd already be at the dock. Set off a nuclear bomb at Red Hook and you'd level New York City." Kinlaw leaned back. "Otherwise, they need an airplane."

"Okay," Hoag said, gesturing with his hand. "Anything else?"

Kinlaw was silent a moment then shook his head. "Ship or plane. Those are your only options." He folded his hands behind his head. "I mean, the warhead would be in Iran. And you'd have to get it from there to here. If you don't have a missile that can make it, then you have only two ways to do it. Either on a plane or a ship." He paused a moment before continuing. "I suppose they could launch a warhead into space and drop it down on us from a couple hundred miles up."

"They can't reach space."

"Maybe."

Hoag shoved the pen he had been drumming into the corner of his mouth and chewed on it nervously. "They could fly a plane from Iran, or a neighboring country, to the U.S. and detonate a bomb onboard while over a U.S. city."

"That would work, but it's a little obvious." Kinlaw rocked the chair on its back legs. "Too many places for someone to detect the radiation. A bomb of any strategic size would leak off obvious radiation. It would be heavy, too. Unless they've been working on this longer than we think, it would be big and bulky. A ship would be better."

"They sail a ship over here from Iran and we'd know it, too."

"Don't use a ship registered in Iran," Kinlaw countered. "Use… North Korea. They have ships that call on Iran all the time."

"But North Korean ships don't call on us."

"They don't have to dock in port. They just have to get close."

"Who else could they use?"

"I don't know. Who else trades on those routes? Let's make a list." Kinlaw pointed to the monitor on Hoag's desk. "Ask Langley. Check their system. We need lists of all ships that have called on ports in Iran and on ports in the U.S. in the last two years."

"Why that? Why just Iran? Couldn't they transport it somewhere else first, then load it on a ship from there?"

"Yeah, they could. But they would want to use the least risky delivery method, the one with the least risk of detection. Let's assume they put as much planning into this as they did the 9-11 attacks. They would want to use a ship that had been here before so we wouldn't pay much attention to it."

"All right. Ships that have called on… ports in Iran, Oman, Saudi Arabia." He looked over at Kinlaw. "Pakistan?"

"Yeah," Kinlaw shrugged. "I guess. Include all the countries in the region and see what we get. We'll work backward from the ships to the companies that own them."

Hoag keyed in the request then pressed a button to execute the search. He leaned back in the chair while he waited for the results. "This could be a long list."

16

ATLANTA, GEORGIA

HARAD AL-MUBARRAZ SAT ON A SOFA in the student center on the campus of Georgia Tech. Born in Espaken, a small town in the southeastern corner of Iran, Mubarraz's parents had sent him to live with relatives in Dubai. There he attended a secular school and was exposed to a broad, Western education. His mind flourished and he excelled in mathematics. During his senior year he became interested in physics and received a scholarship from an unnamed Middle Eastern source to study in the United States. Someone at his school pointed him toward Georgia Tech. He had lived in Atlanta for two years.

As he sat in the student center, Mubarraz held a textbook from a second-year physics course. He needed to study but found it difficult to concentrate. Words on the page ran together as his mind wandered from thought to thought. Every few moments he glanced up from behind the book and scanned the room, watching, waiting, hoping. Early that morning he had heard the newscasts about a suspected nuclear test in Iran. He had heard the statement from Foreign Minister Abadeh Ardakan. "Allah has been moving human history toward a time when all peoples of the world will learn to deal with us in fairness and justice. Now is that time."

All morning Mubarraz had repeated in his head and privately whispered on his lips, "Raj'a al-Mahdi." The return of the Mahdi. The day when the true and final prophet of Islam would come, bringing with him fairness and justice for all. The day when all people throughout the world would worship Allah. He whispered the words again, "Raj'a al-Mahdi." Surely this was that day. Someone would call. Someone would come to find him.

Thirty minutes later a text message arrived on his iPhone. "Study group meeting this afternoon." Mubarraz felt his heart leap when he read those words. "Yes," he said in a coarse whisper, barely able to contain himself. He had been right. This was the day. He read the message again, then slipped the phone into his pocket.

A little before three that afternoon Mubarraz arrived at a house on Melrose Avenue in Decatur, five miles east of downtown Atlanta. The older wood frame home had been constructed during World War II. It had white siding with stone columns on the front porch. Inside was a living room that opened into a dining area with a kitchen to the right. A hallway opened to the left and led to three bedrooms and a bath.

When Mubarraz arrived, six people were seated in the living room. Two occupied chairs to the left of the door. Three sat on a sofa against the wall to the right. One person sat on the floor. Mubarraz had seen none of them before. Feeling more than a little nervous, he found a spot near the door and leaned against the wall. A few minutes later a man appeared from the hallway.

"Good afternoon." The group murmured a response. "I am Yazan Emrani," he continued. "You are all here today because you were chosen by someone, either in your mosque or in your group at school."

While Emrani spoke, Mubarraz remembered the day he had been approached. Ali Makbani, one of the older graduate students, invited him to lunch. Afterward, as they drank coffee, Makbani had suggested Mubarraz work with him in the physics lab. A few months later Mubarraz was introduced to Emrani. The next three months were spent scouting locations, plotting routes, evaluating and analyzing every alternative, every contingency, every possible problem that might emerge. Then there was the waiting. Now, all that effort brought them to this day.

"Someone chose you as one worthy of the cause of Allah." Emrani smiled as he spoke to them. "And you know by now what that cause is and the service to which you have been given." He glanced around the room once more. "So, let us begin."

A fourth man entered from the hallway. Tucked beneath his arm were three maps and two large, loose-leaf binders. As he moved toward the center of the room, two more men came from the hallway behind him. Mubarraz wondered how they had all arrived at the house with so few cars parked outside. While he was still mulling this over, the first man set the maps and books on the table in the living room and glanced around at the group.

"I know you've been over this many times in your groups, but we need to go over it once more together. This is perhaps the only time we will all meet in the same location. If you have any questions, speak now." He unrolled one of the maps and pointed, "This is the airport in Albany." He held the place with his finger and glanced around the room. His eyes met Mubarraz. "You will drive the car." Mubarraz nodded. The man continued. "You drive up to the building and let them out." Mubarraz nodded once more. "And what do you do then?"

"I drive to New Orleans," Mubarraz answered. "Someone will contact me."

The man unrolled another map. He looked across to someone seated on the sofa. "This is the airport in Montgomery, Alabama. You know how to find it?"

"Yes," the man responded. "I have been there twice."

For the next hour they went over the details for each location: arrival time, where to park, how to act. Remember to obey the speed limits. Allow plenty of time for traffic. Avoid accidents at all costs. And above all, do not get in an argument with the police.

Finally, Emrani spoke up. "Okay. That is it, I think." He looked around the room. "Anyone have any more questions?" When no one responded, he stood. "All right. We'll leave as inconspicuously as we arrived." He looked over at Mubarraz. "You came in last. You get to leave first."

Mubarraz nodded and turned to the door. As he reached to open it, Emrani called after him. "Not a word of this to anyone." He looked Mubarraz in the eye. "You understand me?"

"Yes," Mubarraz replied.

Emrani glanced around the room, his eyes focusing for a moment on each one present. "That goes for all of you. Lives are at risk. Therefore, your life will be at risk, too. Do you understand?" Heads nodded around the room. Emrani stared at them a moment longer and then turned to Mubarraz. "You may go now."

Mubarraz opened the door and stepped outside.

17

PRESS BRIEFING ROOM
THE WHITE HOUSE

U.S. PRESIDENT JACK HEDGES entered the press room at the White House. The room was packed. Every assigned seat was filled. Additional reporters and staff stood along both walls and filled the area at the back of the room. They all stood as Hedges loped through the door and stepped onto the dais.

Hedges had come to the presidency from Vermont, where he had been a two-term governor. A moderate Democrat, he unseated Frank Gordon, the Republican incumbent president, with promises to revamp domestic policy and turn the nation's attention once again toward business with China. To do that he pledged to sell the government's stake in banking and insurance companies and withdraw America from involvement in the Middle East. Peace in the region, he argued, had been achieved by Bob Nelson, the previous Democratic president, who had tethered Israel with a short leash and appeased Iran by providing fuel for two of its reactors. Hedge's goal was to build on that peace and reap its benefits, which included freeing the country from unwarranted fear of Islamic political groups and downsizing American troop commitments abroad.

On election night, voters responded by handing Hedges a landslide victory. As he took office, the world appeared to have entered a new age of peace and harmonious economic expansion.

With the threat of war no longer at the forefront, the price of oil plummeted, sending securities markets around the world soaring to new heights. Hedges seemed to have the touch. The world appeared his for the taking. Now, as he stepped to the podium in the press briefing room, he appeared tired and haggard.

Tall and lanky, Hedges usually stood erect with his shoulders squared and his chin up. When he addressed an audience, he stepped back from the podium, hands at his side, in a relaxed and confident manner. Today, as he faced a press corps that was anxious for news about the latest developments in Iran, he gripped the podium with both hands and hunched forward in a way that made him seem to glower at reporters assembled in the room.

"I have a statement to make, and then I will take your questions." Silence fell over the room, broken only by the sound of cameras snapping his photograph. Hedges cleared his throat, looked down at a single sheet of paper lying on the podium, and began to read. "Last evening at 9 p.m. Mountain Standard Time, instruments at NORAD facilities in Colorado detected a seismic event with an epicenter located in northwestern Iran. Additional instruments located at other sites in the region and in Europe, along with data obtained through other sources, have since confirmed that the event was the successful detonation of a nuclear device. While we regret this, there is no indication Iran poses any immediate military threat to the United States or its allies." He paused and then looked out at the crowd. "I'll take your questions." Hands shot up. Hedges pointed to a woman seated on the second row. "Mrs. Allen."

"How large was this device?"

"Analysts believe it was a five-kiloton explosion."

"Most people won't have a clue what that means. How does that compare to other bombs?"

Hedges cleared his throat again. "The bomb dropped on Hiroshima produced a thirteen-kiloton blast."

"So this was obviously smaller."

"Yes." Hedges looked to the man seated at Mrs. Allen's left. "David—"

"Excuse me, Mr. President." Mrs. Allen cut him off. "Iran is now a member of the nuclear community?"

"Yes. I think we can say that with certainty."

Hedges raised his hand to point, but Mrs. Allen kept going. "What will be the U.S. response?"

"Obviously, sanctions have not worked." Hedges stood up a little straighter. "Perhaps talking might offer the hope of stable relations."

A murmur rippled across the room. Mrs. Allen leaned forward. "You're ready to talk to Iran in face-to-face negotiations?"

"Yes."

"Wouldn't it have been better to do that before they exploded a nuclear bomb?"

"Yes. I suppose it would." He gestured to a man seated beside Mrs. Allen. "David, you have a question?"

"You're prepared to meet with Iranian President Kermani?"

"Yes."

"Any idea when or where that meeting might take place?"

"I'll meet him at a mutually agreeable site as soon as he is ready."

"Is that meeting in the works? Do you have someone making overtures to the Iranian government?"

"I am making one right now." Hedges looked into the television camera. "We are prepared to talk if they are."

A reporter to the left spoke up. "You sound grim, yet you said just now we are in no danger."

"No immediate danger," Hedges reiterated. "I didn't say we were in no danger. Anytime a country acquires a nuclear weapon, the world becomes a more dangerous place in which to live."

A hand went up. Hedges nodded in that direction.

"Mr. President, have you spoken at all with President Kermani?"

"No, I have not." Hedges glanced down at the podium. His eyes darted to the right. "We don't have a secure connection to them. This isn't like Moscow during the Cold War, where we had a direct line with a red phone on the desk."

Another hand went up to the left. "Have you delivered a formal response of any kind to the Iranian government?"

"The statement I read to you just now was delivered to them earlier today."

"Who delivered it?"

"Our attaché." Hedges ran his fingertips along the edge of the podium. "Working through the Swiss embassy in Tehran. They took care of it."

A hand went up. Hedges pointed. A reporter stood. "Was this nuclear device created with fuel from the reactors we supplied under the previous Democratic administration?"

"As of right now, we have no way of knowing."

Another reporter spoke up. "So, just to be clear, Mr. President. How serious is this situation?"

Hedges took a deep breath. Linda Reynolds, the press secretary, stepped forward as if to end the conference. Hedges glanced at her and shook his head. Reynolds backed away. Hedges squared his shoulders and looked up from the podium. "A nuclear Iran, solely and simply, would not appear to be of strategic or tactical concern. However, I'm sure you're aware of the region's history of chronic instability. During President Nelson's administration, a permanent peace agreement was reached that brought us to the brink of finally ending the cycles of violence and unrest. However, President Gordon failed to follow through on many of the basic commitments in that peace accord. As a consequence, we have inherited a situation that now increases the likelihood a radical group might acquire a nuclear bomb. Based on that, I'd say the situation in the Middle East is gravely serious."

Once again, murmurs rippled through the room. Hedges concluded, "This permanently changes the game. And I can't think of any way this makes the region or the world more peaceful or stable."

18

BERLIN, GERMANY

JOSEF MUELLER STROLLED SLOWLY down a garden path outside his residence. Paved with large, flat stones, it wound its way past the reflecting pools and down to the river. As he came around a clump of wax leaf bushes, he found Franz Heinrich seated on an iron bench.

Born in Munich, Heinrich was Mueller's closest friend. As children they had grown up on the same street. They attended the same schools, went to university together, and began their professional careers in the same investment banking firm. When Mueller first entertained the notion of standing for election as governor, many had advised against it, suggesting that he stick to banking. Heinrich had been his lone supporter and soon became his closest adviser.

When Mueller was elected governor of Bavaria, he appointed Heinrich his special assistant, eventually entrusting to him the most delicate political issues. Later, when Mueller was elected chancellor, he arranged to have Heinrich placed in charge of national security policy, ignoring the accepted practice of promoting from within the permanent staff. Some thought it an affront that one as valuable as Heinrich was placed in less than a cabinet-level role, but Mueller had other ideas. With Heinrich in charge of the Chancery's national security apparatus, he was able to create a foreign affairs channel separate and apart from the official Foreign Office. Of all the people in the German government, Heinrich was the lone official Mueller trusted as unwaveringly loyal, a loyalty and trust that were vital to the success of Mueller's plans.

Heinrich stood as Mueller approached. "Chancellor, I came as quickly as I could without creating a scene."

"Good," Mueller nodded. "Did anyone follow you?"

"No, of course not."

"Does anyone at your office know you are here?"

"I told them we were meeting to discuss the Iranian situation."

"Hmm." Mueller frowned. "I suppose that will hold."

"I had to tell them something."

"Yes, certainly." Mueller took Heinrich by the shoulder. "Walk with me."

They moved down the path, walking side by side. Mueller paused at a fountain and turned to face the gurgling water. He spoke without looking up. "I should like for you to arrange a private meeting with Vladimir Vostok."

"Shouldn't this be a task for the foreign minister? The Foreign Office has an efficient staff. They do these things regularly."

"No." Mueller shook his head. "I want you to arrange it." He looked at Heinrich. Their eyes met. "I want you to arrange it yourself. Personally."

"What shall I tell them?"

"You must deal with Vostok directly. You are attending the conference in Luxembourg?"

"Yes."

"Good. You will see Vostok there."

"I did not know he would attend."

"He'll be there," Mueller grinned. "When you see him, take him aside on a pretext. Anything. It doesn't have to be much. When you have him alone, tell him I wish to see him about the Radinsky matter."

"Radinsky?"

"Yes. The Radinsky matter. Vostok will know what to do."

"But what of the Foreign Office? Surely they will want to know the details of such a trip. What shall I tell them?"

"Tell them nothing," Mueller replied.

"Nothing?"

"This meeting must be absolutely secret. No one must know about it. You and I shall fly there together and return together. We will be gone only one day, two at most. No one else will know."

"And where will this meeting take place?"

"In Russia."

Heinrich leaned away, an astonished look on his face. "You wish to travel to Russia and meet with the Russian president, and you want me to mention nothing of it to the foreign minister or anyone at the Foreign Office? And keep the entire trip secret from them?"

"Precisely," Mueller nodded.

"But why?"

Mueller pulled Heinrich close. "The Americans have spies in the Foreign Office." He wagged his finger. "I want no one to know of this meeting. Not in Washington. And not in Berlin."

Heinrich stood erect and squared his shoulders. "Very well, Chancellor. It shall be as you request."

19

PAKISTAN'S NORTHWEST FRONTIER

NASSER HAMID LAY ASLEEP in a dusty hotel room in Mingora, the largest city in Pakistan's Northwest Province. Located along the River Swat, near the base of the Hindu Kush mountain range, Mingora once was a popular tourist destination for Europeans. With the mountains as a backdrop, it looked more like a village in Switzerland than a city in the Himalayan foothills. After American troops drove Islamic radicals from Afghanistan into Pakistan, the city fell under Taliban control. Strict imposition of Sharia law transformed it from bustling and crowded to bloody and deserted. Attempts by the Pakistan army to retake it by force only made conditions worse and left the entire region decimated. Now, ten years later, the Taliban held the city firmly in its grip and used it as a major export point for its lucrative opium trade.

Hamid had arrived there three days earlier, traveling by bus from Peshawar. He appeared for prayers at a Mahabat Khan mosque, sipped tea at a shop across the street, and spent an afternoon seated on a bench near the square at the center of town. Avoiding the traditional robe and lungee headdress, he made no attempt to blend into the crowd or hide his presence. Instead, he wore the Western garb to which he had grown accustomed—a dark gray business suit with a white shirt and black wingtip shoes.

Hamid came to Mingora for a critical meeting with the most powerful man in all Islam, a man whose cooperation was essential to the success of their plans. Deep in hiding for the past twenty years, he kept no office, no appointments, and no schedule. Those who sought him made their interests known in the ancient, traditional way. They appeared at the center of town and waited. At the end of each day, Hamid returned to his room in the hotel and lay on the bed, staring at the ceiling, hoping the meeting would come soon.

Today was no different from the others. He saw no one who appeared even remotely curious about his presence. People passed by him as if he weren't there. When he nodded or smiled at a passer-by, they seemed to look right through him. As the afternoon waned, he went across the street to a shop for tea. He sipped it while he ate a light supper of bread and cheese. With darkness approaching he sauntered back to the hotel, walked quietly up the steps to his room, and lay across the bed. Sometime later he drifted off to a dreamless sleep.

Hamid was jerked awake by a hand against his shoulder. He gasped for breath and tried to speak, but a second hand clamped his mouth shut. A man leaned over him. "You must be quiet," he whispered in Arabic.

Hamid took a deep breath through his nose and forced himself to relax. *Surely*, he thought, *if they meant to kill me they would have done so already.*

In the dark shadows of the room, Hamid saw a man standing near the door. The man whispered something, his voice little more than a grumble. At the sound of it, others in the room lifted Hamid to a sitting position and swung his feet to the floor. Calmer now, he could see the man to his left was middle-aged, perhaps forty. Hamid held his right hand out to him. The man pushed him away.

Without warning a hood was slipped over his head, plunging him into total darkness. His heart raced, and his breath came hot against the cloth. Once again, fear welled up inside him. He pushed it aside and forced his mind to work. He had been through this before. For the past three days he had reminded himself it would happen this way. These men were not there to harm him. They had come to escort him to the meeting. This was the purpose for which he had traveled to Mingora.

The first voice spoke again, "Get dressed." Hamid felt something drop onto his lap. He groped with his hands and discovered it was his pants. He found the waistband, slid his feet inside, stood, and pulled his pants to his waist. When he had buckled the belt, a hand took him by the arm, "Let's go." Someone tugged him forward. Hamid felt the soles of his feet against the floor. With halting, uneasy steps, he started from the bed, his shoulders bumping into men on either side as they made their way across the room.

A few steps later he felt the air change. It was warmer and the smell was different. He was certain they had entered the hall. From the sound of their voices and the scuffle of their steps, two men accompanied him. Perhaps there was a third.

Down the hall a little way he heard a door open. Footsteps echoed as they moved into a stairwell. He felt a cool concrete floor beneath his feet. Gingerly, he placed one foot in front of the other. He stumbled. Someone caught him and guided him to the handrail. Carefully, they worked their way down the first few steps. Then one of them said something. Hands reached under Hamid's armpits and hoisted him up. His feet dangled beneath him, barely touching the tops of the steps. In quick order they carried him down the stairs.

When they reached the bottom, they lowered him to the ground. The hands that had been beneath his armpits moved away. Fingers squeezed tightly against his biceps as they hustled him forward into the crisp night air. His feet scraped across rough, stony ground.

A hand shoved his head down. Another pushed him forward. He banged his shin against something hard and pitched forward. His forearm slammed against the seat. A dirty, stuffy smell filled his nostrils with the aroma of sweat and cigarette smoke all blended into one. Someone pushed him from behind, whispering, "Hurry. Hurry." He slid to the right and fell headlong against the cushion of a seat. As his cheek pressed against the coarse fabric he realized he was inside a car, lying across the rear seat. Another voice growled, "Sit up." Hamid tucked his legs beneath him and rolled to a sitting position. Someone nudged him. Doors banged closed. An engine started. The car moved forward.

Jerking and twisting, they wound through the city streets. A few minutes later they made a sharp turn to the right and then sped along at a rapid pace. Wind blowing through the open windows filled the car with a rumbling sound. Once or twice Hamid heard the sound of passing traffic.

Twenty minutes later, the car came to a stop. Doors opened. The car rocked from side to side as people stepped out. A hand grabbed his arm and tugged him to the left. A voice commanded, "Come."

Hamid squirmed across the seat and groped for the door. A hand took his ankles and guided his feet to the ground. He scooted forward, ducked low, and stepped outside. As he stood, someone took him by the elbow and ushered him forward. Less hurried than before, they guided him a few paces, then a hand moved to the top of his head.

"Careful," someone said. "You are entering a car." The voice was different than before; kinder, softer, and gentler. "Don't bump your head."

Hamid bowed low and eased forward. He reached out with his hands and touched the side of the car, then slid inside and took a seat. Doors closed as men took a seat on either side of him, then the car started forward.

Not too long afterward Hamid heard the brakes squeak as the car came to a stop. Doors opened. A hand took him by the arm and guided him to the right. Moving slowly across the seat, he made his way out of the car. As he stood, a hand grasped his elbow. Someone was standing next to him. Hamid could feel their arms touch as they stepped forward.

"Carefully now," the man beside him said. "We are entering a building."

Hamid slid his foot forward, found the threshold, and took a step. His bare foot landed on a smooth, wooden floor. They moved to the left, then turned right and started up a flight of stairs. Hamid groped with his hand, found the handrail, and steadied himself against it.

At the top they turned left. Then the hand at his elbow nudged him to stop. He heard a chair slide across the floor. A voice spoke, "You may sit now." Hamid felt behind him for the chair then slowly lowered himself onto it.

A chair scooted across the floor. Footsteps. Whispers. And then the room was silent. Hamid took a deep breath and forced his body to relax. His hands were not bound. His feet were not tied. With one motion of his hand, he could remove the hood. But he knew better. This was a land of custom, tradition, and respect. Better to sit and wait.

A few minutes later he felt a hand against his shoulder. The hood was snatched from his head, and the darkness he had known just seconds before was suddenly replaced by a bright light that shone in his face. He blinked and squinted at the glare. Behind him a door slammed closed. From beyond the light a voice spoke. "Would you care for some tea?"

Hamid smiled at the sound of that voice. "Tea would be good."

A hand extended through the glare. In its grasp was a glass filled with tea. Steam rose from it as the hand passed the glass forward. Hamid grasped it between his thumb and forefinger. As he drew the glass toward his lap, he noticed a small table to the right. The voice spoke to him again.

"Perhaps you would like something to eat?" The hand appeared again, this time with a plate of bread and cheese. Hamid took the plate and set it on the table. He raised the glass to his lips and took a sip of tea then set the glass on the table.

With his head tipped slightly to the right, Hamid could see the leg and shoulder of a man seated opposite him. He could not see the man's face, but he knew from past experience the man was waiting for him to speak. Hamid cleared his throat and began.

"Everyone is ready?"

"Yes," the voice replied.

"Chicago? Atlanta? All the places we discussed?"

"Yes. Just as you requested. You have taken care of the other details?"

"Yes," Hamid nodded. "They are all in place."

"Your people are on the ships?"

"Yes."

"And the devices? The devices are with them?"

"Yes."

"I would not want my people to be the only ones who showed up for the fight this time."

"You won't be alone."

"I have your word on that?"

Hamid took a breath. This was not a question of trust or assurance in the Western sense. This was a request for an oath. Not a request for a written guarantee but for something much deeper and far more serious. This was a request for the ancient oath of Islam. If all did not go as Hamid said, he would pay with his life; and if that seemed insufficient, his family would pay with theirs.

"Yes," Hamid nodded. "You have my oath."

"Very well." The man behind the glaring light sighed. "You may proceed."

There was the sound of feet shuffling against the floor, then a click as the light was turned off. For a moment, Hamid found himself in total darkness. He blinked as his eyes adjusted once again. Slowly, the room came into focus.

The walls were painted turquoise, the ceiling white. Directly opposite Hamid, a framed picture of Ayatollah Khomeini hung on the wall. From the left, gray predawn light drifted into the room through a tall window with a wooden frame. A fan turned lazily overhead. A few feet in front of Hamid was a floor lamp. Its shade missing, there was only a bare bulb at the top of the stand. Beyond the lamp was an empty wingback chair.

Just then a door to the left opened and a young man appeared. He gestured with a wave of his hand. "You are ready to go now?"

Hamid stood and made his way toward the door. As he reached the hallway, a hood slipped over his head. Someone grasped his elbow. A voice spoke in a kind and assuring tone. "We are moving to the right. Can you feel the wall with your hand?" Hamid extended his arm. His fingers brushed against the smooth plaster finish.

20

POTOMAC, MARYLAND

KINLAW SAT IN HIS USUAL SPOT on the back row at Potomac Community Church. He did his best to listen as the pastor led the congregation through morning prayers, but his mind was distracted and he found it difficult to concentrate. When the service ended, he rose from the pew and turned to leave. As he did, he bumped into Jenny Freed.

"Oh," he said, surprised. "Didn't expect to see you here."

"Didn't expect to see you, either," she replied. "Bring David with you?"

"No," Kinlaw smirked. "Not hardly." They walked toward the rear doors. "I don't think I've seen you here before."

"I don't come here too often." She glanced at him. "Most of the time I stop at St. Stanislaus, down in Bethesda." Her voice sounded nervous. "But if I'm running late, I stop by here. This is right on the way." She took a deep breath. "I'm sure that strikes you as odd."

"Well yes, actually," Kinlaw chuckled. "I always thought you were more the David Hoag cynical type."

By then they were in the vestibule. "I never was the David Hoag type, and that was something he never understood."

"Really?" Kinlaw frowned.

"Really. That's why things never worked out for us."

"Hmm," Kinlaw mused. "That's interesting." A broad grin spread across his face. "David always prides himself on his keen insight."

"What keen insight did he share about me? I'm sure he had plenty to say after I saw you guys the other day."

"Well, for one thing, he thinks you dumped him when we were in college for that football player. The center or guard or whatever he was. His father worked on Wall Street."

Jenny shook her head. "That is so like David." She gave a heavy sigh. "I didn't dump him for that guy."

"You started going out with him."

"Yeah, but he wasn't the reason." She moved aside, out of the way of the front doors. "I was a Christian before I went to college, but it sort of got lost during those first few years. That's when I met David, and we started seeing each other. But in my junior year I got back to my relationship with God. By then, David and I were pretty serious. I thought I could see David and still be faithful to the Lord, but I just couldn't take his skepticism. He is so... secular. It just wasn't working. I had a choice. Either I could love the Lord, or I could love David."

"And now?"

Jenny blushed. "What do you mean?"

"Come on, Jenny. You know what I mean."

"It shows that much?"

"Yeah," Kinlaw nodded. "On both of you."

Jenny shrugged. "I thought I was over him. Until I saw you two the other day."

"You've seen us out there before."

"Yeah, but all the other times I knew in advance. That one caught me by surprise."

21

MINGORA, PAKISTAN

SHABTAI YATOM LEANED AGAINST the corner of the building. Dressed in cotton twill pants and a heavy wool sweater, a three-day beard covered his face. Atop his head was a leather cap, and on his feet were dirty work boots. With a cigarette hanging from his lip, he looked like all the other men who worked the poppy fields around Mingora.

Yatom took a long draw on the cigarette, then poked his head around the corner and glanced to the right. Fifty meters away, a black BMW sat idling near the entrance to the mosque, three buildings over. The car had a dent in the trunk lid and black smoke came from the tailpipe. He studied it a moment longer then pulled back out of sight around the corner and leaned against the wall.

In a few minutes he heard the car's engine rev. Moments later the BMW appeared. Through the rear window he could see Hamid seated in back. The car turned left, passed in front of Yatom, and disappeared out of sight down the road.

As the sound of the car faded in the distance, Yatom took a cell phone from his pocket and entered a text message. "Sbjct mving." He pressed a button to send the message and put the phone back in his pocket.

A few minutes later a truck rounded a curve to the right. The engine rumbled as the truck gradually slowed to a stop near the building. Yatom took the cigarette from his mouth, dropped it on the ground, and crushed it out with the toe of his boot. He straightened his cap and started toward the truck.

When he was just a few feet away, the driver of the truck stuck an assault rifle out the window. In a quick burst of gunfire, bullets ripped through Yatom's body and ricocheted off the wall behind him. For an instant his body stood on its own, as if the muscles of his legs somehow did not recognize what had happened to the rest of his body. Then, as the driver pulled the rifle from the window and put the truck in gear, Yatom's body crumpled to the ground.

Yatom gasped for breath and felt it gurgle in his chest. Thick red blood oozed out of the corner of his mouth and dribbled down his neck. Lying there on the ground, time seemed to slow. He remembered sitting in a synagogue on Long Island with his grandfather. The Yom Kippur War was on and everyone was talking about it. He had wanted to leave for Israel that day, to join the fight, but his father reminded him he was only fifteen.

Sad and dejected, Yatom had wandered out to the garage. Late that afternoon his grandfather found him there and took him to temple. As they sat listening to the reading of the Torah, his grandfather leaned close and whispered in Yatom's ear, "You must submit to your father," he had said. "But you must never let them steal the fire from your belly."

Sitting there with his grandfather, Yatom resolved that one day he would return to Israel and join the fight. If not in the war being fought that day then in another, for he was certain the enemies of God would never rest until Israel was pushed into the sea. And he would never rest so long as the fight was his to take.

A chill ran over his body. Yatom's shoulders and arms shuddered. His sweater felt damp and heavy against his chest. Someone rolled him onto his back. A hand went into his pocket and took out the cell phone. Another hand checked the other pocket and pulled out a fold of bills.

"Dollars!" a voice shouted. "A rich Jew."

A foot kicked him in the ribs. "Jewish swine." He heard the sound of someone spitting. Then another kick to the ribs, and Yatom heard his favorite chant from the temple. "El na refa na la…"

22

WASHINGTON, D.C.

HOAG SAT AT HIS DESK, reviewing the list of ships generated from their search through the database at Langley. Kinlaw sat in a chair across from him, reviewing a copy of the same list.

Hoag spoke up. "*Texas Star* called on Bandar-e 'Abbas last month." He pointed to the list. "Then went to Karachi. Two months before that it was at Inch'on."

"There must be a better way to sort this out," Kinlaw groused. "I had no idea it would take this long for them to produce this information."

"I suppose they had other things to do with their computers." Hoag rubbed his eyes. "We could do it with paper and pencil."

"The computer ought to be able to give us better information without having to search each ship individually." Kinlaw leaned over the desk and peered around the monitor. "Tell it to search the results by fields." He pointed to a box on the screen. "Right there. Check that box."

Hoag moved the cursor over the box and placed a check mark there. Moments later, a new screen appeared. "Here we go," he said, triumphantly. A printer on a table across the room came to life. Soon he and Kinlaw were looking at a new list.

"Okay," Kinlaw began. "This is more like what we need." He shuffled through the papers in his lap. "During the past two years, fifteen ships from the region called on ports in Iran and ports in the U.S."

"That's good," Hoag replied. "But now we need to find out who owns those ships."

They spent the remainder of the morning tracking down information about each ship. Early that afternoon Kinlaw looked up from his notes. "Did we work all the way through the list?"

"I think so." Hoag rubbed his eyes. "The *Santiago*, *Central Gold*, *Costa del Sol*, *Panama Clipper*, *Ocho Del Rio*, and *Amazon Cloud* are all registered in Panama, fly a Panamanian flag, but they're owned by Pakistan Shipping in Karachi. That takes care of the first six."

"*Isildor*, *London Kite*, *Alba*, and *Africa Coast* are out of service."

"That's ten. Five left."

Kinlaw turned a page on his legal pad. "*March Wind* sank off the Australian coast last winter."

"Four more," Hoag sighed.

"Hmmm."

Hoag looked up. "What?"

"Those ships are all new."

"Which ones?"

"Three from Pakistan Shipping," Kinlaw glanced at the legal pad again. "*Panama Clipper, Amazon Cloud*, and the *Santiago*."

"That strikes you as odd?"

"Well, these ships aren't cheap." Kinlaw adjusted his position in the chair. "But what's curious is the kind of ship. All three are self-loading container ships."

"Container ships are odd?"

"No. The self-loading type. Ships like that have their own cranes, which means they can't haul as much as other container ships. Most of the new ones are sleek and designed to carry the maximum amount of freight."

"Maybe they call on ports that don't have cranes."

"Maybe so."

Hoag pointed. "Keep going down the list. What's left?"

Kinlaw checked his notes. "The *Burgundia* and *Cabo San Lucas* are owned by Del Mar Shipping in Spain."

"And…" Hoag scribbled a note, then checked the computer screen. "The *Maid of New Orleans* is owned by Rio Tonto, which is actually a legitimate Panamanian company. I think."

"*Savannah Breeze* is owned by Goodman Watts Ltd. of London."

"Okay. Pakistan Shipping, Del Mar Shipping, Rio Tonto, and Goodman Watts. Those are the companies from this list that had ships that called on ports in the Arabian basin and Indian Ocean and also called on ports in the United States."

"Right," Kinlaw nodded.

Hoag tossed his notes on the desk and leaned back. He looked at Kinlaw. Their eyes met. Kinlaw smiled. "Seems a little thin, doesn't it."

"Yeah. A little thin." Hoag stretched. "We've made several suppositions, any of which could be wrong. The whole exercise could be absolutely meaningless."

"Then again," Kinlaw sighed, "we could be right." He leaned forward and placed his hands on the armrest of the chair. "Let's keep going."

"You don't want to widen the list?"

"If we widen our search, we'll make it meaningless for certain."

"I guess so." Hoag scooted his chair up to the desk. "All right. The next thing we need to do is to find out about these companies."

"That could take weeks," Kinlaw replied. "I mean, we don't even know what we're looking for."

"Then we better get started. I don't think any of those kids working for Winston will tackle this project."

"Not glamorous enough, that's for sure."

"Didn't come from a satellite."

Kinlaw tossed his pen and notepad on the desk. "Won't come from me today, either."

"Why not?"

"I have a class to teach." He stood and stretched. "Although I suppose I could cancel it."

"Better not," Hoag warned. "Someone will come down here looking for you, and then they'll want to know what you were doing besides teaching your class."

"Good point." Kinlaw started toward the door. "I'll be back in an hour."

———— (((————

When Kinlaw returned, Hoag was still seated at his desk. On the floor around him were stacks of books. He glanced up as Kinlaw entered. "How was class?"

"Not bad." Kinlaw pointed to the stacks on the floor. "What's all this?"

"Annual reports and government filings on all those shipping companies we were talking about."

Kinlaw took a seat and picked up a report. "Must be ancient history if it's in a book or annual report."

"That's what we need," Hoag quipped. "History."

Kinlaw shot a knowing look in Hoag's direction. "Turning to the past to find out the future?"

"Don't start on me again."

"What do you know about the Mahdi?"

Hoag looked up. "You've been reading non-canonical books." He had a wry smile. "Do the folks at that church you've been attending know about your reading habits?"

"I try to stay informed," Kinlaw quipped. "What do you know about the Mahdi?"

"Last known legitimate heir of Muhammad. Thrown down a well in Jamkaran when he was four years old. Came to be thought of as the Twelfth Caliph. Gradually deified into a messiah figure—the returning caliph who will unite the world in a single Muslim caliph-ate. One world. One religion. We'll all be Muslim or die."

"You've been reading, too."

"I do try to keep up."

"If you spent half as much time on Christian prophecy, you'd be a lot less belligerent toward Christians."

"I don't believe any of it, Christian or Muslim. I just know a little something about it. Why do you ask about the Mahdi?"

"The Mahdi is more than just a deified notion of who might be the proper successor to Muhammad. Belief in his return is the thing that drives radical Shi'a Islam. Most of Iran's leadership believes the Mahdi will not return until the world is on the brink of destruction. They see it as their duty to create an environment in which he will return."

"I thought the point was to force everyone to convert to Islam."

"Sunnis want you to convert. Shi'a want you to die. Sunnis are content to dominate the world and obtain grudging obedience from us. Shi'as want to annihilate everyone."

"And that's different from the Christian version?"

"Very different."

"How so?"

"Hebrew prophets and the prophecies aren't a call to destroy the world or force anyone to convert to any religion. Those prophecies reveal what will happen not what should happen or ought to happen. They are based on fact."

"Come on," Hoag scoffed. "There's no 'fact' in it. It's all about faith."

"Read the book of Daniel. He foretold the end of the Babylonian Empire and then the rise of the Syrians, Greeks, and Romans. And he foretold the end of the Roman Empire a thousand years before it happened. They weren't even in existence when he received that prophecy."

"But that's not what we're dealing with here. We're talking about the end of time, imagery no one can decipher, and a timeline on which no one can agree."

"I don't know how to explain this to you, point for point, but there are people who can show you how it fits with things that have happened in recent history. Want me to find someone to explain it?"

"Maybe," Hoag sighed. "But I don't see how that's going to help us with this."

"With what?"

"Ships and nuclear bombs and Iran."

"I think it would help us see both sides of this. You can't deny this is a religious war. I know it's not politically correct to call it that, but this is Islam against Christianity, and when that's done it'll be Islam against the rest of the world."

"Well, right now it's you and me and these." Hoag pointed to the stack of books that surrounded his desk. "Pick a stack and get started."

They spent the remainder of the afternoon and into the evening working through company reports. Late that night Kinlaw leaned back in his chair. "This is useless."

"Not completely."

"Pretty close," Kinlaw insisted.

"We have a list of the players in all these companies."

"But we don't even know if this means anything." Kinlaw raised his hands in a gesture of frustration. "What are we looking for? Why are we doing this?"

"I said Iran could hit us with a nuclear device dropped from an airplane," Hoag grinned. "You said a ship would be better. That's how we got to the list of ships. And that got us to these four companies."

"But this doesn't really mean anything. It's just an exercise."

"It's an idea," Hoag replied. "That's what we do. We develop ideas. We get paid for this sort of thing."

"They pay us a lot for not very much in return," Kinlaw groaned.

"At least it's not digging ditches."

"You have a point." Kinlaw looked over at Hoag. "Ever dig ditches for a job?"

"Once. On a construction job when I was in high school. You?"

"No." Kinlaw shook his head. "Cleaned out horse stalls all summer but never dug ditches." He smiled at Hoag. "So, what do we have so far?"

"A list of names." Hoag handed him a legal pad.

Kinlaw pointed to the list. "We need to see Winston with this."

"Maybe," Hoag shrugged. "I don't think we're ready to write a report."

"Me either. Which is why we need his help."

Hoag moved a book from his lap. "But what do we tell him?"

"Tell him what we have and see if we can get some help." Kinlaw leaned forward and dropped the legal pad on the desk. "Maybe get the FBI or somebody to help us. It's a long shot, but we can't do this alone. I mean, we're just two people, and this is like searching for the proverbial needle in a haystack. We could flip through reports and charts and still be right here, surrounded by the same stack of books two months from now."

"That's not a bad idea." Hoag brightened. "The FBI has been collecting all kinds of information on people since the World Trade Center attacks. If they had a file on one or two of these people, we could see where they intersect. This could take us a long way."

"But will it be a long way toward anything we're interested in?"

"I don't know. But the FBI might be intrigued. Give them an opportunity to follow someone new."

"Okay," Kinlaw stood. "We can see Winston tomorrow." He checked his watch. "I gotta get home. It's late."

"Wait for me." Hoag switched off the computer terminal and stood. "I'll walk out with you."

23

CIA HEADQUARTERS LANGLEY, VIRGINIA

HOAG AND KINLAW ARRIVED at Winston Smith's office. Located down the hall from the Operations Center, it was a windowless room with dark wood paneling and a mahogany desk. Built-in cabinets lined the wall behind him, with a shelf at waist level that held a computer terminal and telephone. Winston was seated at the desk when they walked in.

"You two better have something good," he growled.

"What's the matter, Winston?" Hoag took a seat near the desk. "Kids in the think tank letting you down?"

"Think tank," Winston chuckled. "They're too busy playing with their computers to notice what's really going on." He leaned back in his chair and folded his hands behind his head. "We've been getting a lot of pressure on the president's suggestion he would meet with the Iranians."

"Suggestion," Kinlaw chortled. "More like he called them out in front of the world." He pulled a chair from across the room.

Hoag raised an eyebrow. "They want to actually do something about Iranian capabilities?"

"Nah," Winston shook his head. "The White House is just getting cold feet on the meeting with Iran."

"Cold feet?" Kinlaw leaned back in his chair. "Do they really think they can back out now? The entire world was watching when he suggested they meet."

"It's not the president," Winston sighed.

"Then who?"

"Braxton Kittrell."

"Kittrell." Hoag groaned. "Mr. Chief of Staff."

"I see you've met him," Winston grinned.

"A few times."

"I thought meeting with Iran was a good idea," Kinlaw offered. "One of his better moves so far."

"So did I," Winston replied. "But apparently Kittrell was livid."

"Was he mad about the idea, or was he mad that Hedges didn't tell him about it ahead of time?"

Winston pointed at Kinlaw, "That's a man in tune with the times."

Hoag shifted positions in the chair. "Are they going to meet?"

"That's just it." Winston leaned forward and propped his elbows on the desk. "They have no meeting. Not even one in the works. At least not yet."

"Would have been better if we did this last year."

"Yeah," Winston sighed. "Well, now they're feeling boxed in. Kittrell's calling me every five minutes wanting to know what the options are."

"Options?" Kinlaw ran his fingers through his hair. "There aren't any options. And certainly none Jack Hedges would consider. What's Kittrell think they can do besides sit down with them?"

"He keeps talking about a way to contain Iran without getting our hands dirty." Hoag and Kinlaw shook their heads. Winston turned his chair to one side, opened a desk drawer, and propped his feet on it. "So, what's on your minds? I can tell you didn't come here prepared to talk about this."

Kinlaw and Hoag exchanged glances again. Hoag straightened himself in the chair. "This might not be the best day for it."

"Can't be that bad," Winston shrugged. "And if it is, maybe it'll be a good diversion." He folded his hands in his lap. "What've you got?"

Hoag leaned forward. "We'd like you to request some information for us from FBI and NSA."

"What kind of information?"

"Information about these people." Kinlaw leaned forward and handed him a list of names.

Winston scanned the list and tossed it on his desk. "You've got eight names here. None of them jump out at me as anybody we're interested in. What's so important about them?"

"They're all major players in key international shipping companies," Hoag explained. "Their ships have called on ports in the Arabian basin and the United States within the last two years."

"Interesting information." Winston propped his head back. "Something special about that?" His eyes looked alert. "You two aren't really pursuing that missile idea you floated the other day, are you? Missiles on a cargo ship, wasn't it?"

Kinlaw ignored the question. "If Iran has a nuclear weapon, we think it's targeted at us."

Winston smiled. "I'm sure they'd like to hit us, but they don't have a missile that can reach us." He cocked his head to one side and peeked in Kinlaw's direction. "You know that."

"That's why we thought of ships."

Winston closed his eyes. "You two realize they exploded that thing on November 4?"

"Yeah," Hoag nodded. "At 6:30 in the morning."

"I knew a couple of people who were in that embassy. News reports never gave the full story. It wasn't pretty."

"Beginning of the revolution," Hoag replied.

"Beginning of a lot of things," Kinlaw suggested.

Winston opened his eyes. "Most people don't realize Ahmadinejad was there." He looked over at Hoag. "Why Nelson agreed to deal with him is beyond me. First time I saw Ahmadinejad I wanted to shoot him." Winston sighed. "I still want to shoot him, but that day I actually had a pistol."

Hoag chuckled. "Good thing you didn't."

"Why's that?"

Hoag pointed to the desk. "Because we need you to check the names on that list."

A frown wrinkled Winston's forehead. "You sure you want me to ask the FBI for help?"

"They still have people on the ground," Hoag argued. "Actual human sources."

"Yes, but asking them tells them what we're looking for."

Kinlaw shook his head. "Aren't we ever going to get past this kind of agency rivalry?"

"Maybe. Homeland Security was supposed to solve it, but as you know, that hasn't worked." Winston sighed. "If we tell them what we know, there's a good chance they'll take over and cut us out of the whole thing. Better to go to them at the end. After we know what we're up against. Then all they can do is confirm our information."

Kinlaw propped his elbows on the arms of the chair. "If I'm right, we might not have that much time."

Winston looked at Hoag then back to Kinlaw. "You're sure about this? Both of you?"

"Yes," Kinlaw said.

Hoag nodded. "As sure as any theory I've had before."

Winston cut his eyes at Hoag. "That's not very reassuring." He swung his feet to the floor, sat up straight, and glanced at the list once more. "I don't know." He tossed the list aside, slid open a desk drawer and took out a photograph. "Either of you know this guy?" He handed Hoag the photograph.

Kinlaw looked over Hoag's shoulder. "Who is he?"

"Nasser Hamid."

"What about him?"

"FBI's been asking about him." Winston ran his fingers over his eyes. "They think he works for the Iranians. That photo was taken a few weeks ago outside the offices of Pakistan Shipping, in Karachi." He pointed toward the list that lay on his desk. "I see a guy from Pakistan Shipping is on your list. You might want to look into the connection."

"Where'd you get the photo?"

"I have sources," Winston replied.

Kinlaw looked at him. "So, we spy on the FBI. They spy on us. That's what it's come to now?"

"Something like that," Winston smiled.

The telephone rang, and Winston turned to answer it. "Leave me the list. I'll see what I can do."

24

WHITE HOUSE, WASHINGTON, D.C.

SECRETARY OF STATE Lauren Lehman looked out the window of her black limousine and watched as the White House came into view. She had seen the building many times, and even now, after all these years, the sight of it still made something inside her leap with anticipation.

Lehman had spent her entire life in politics, first as a student organizer at Wellesley College, leading campus opposition to the war in Vietnam, then as a law school student working to defend radicals from the 1960s. Elected to the U.S. Senate from Florida, her home state, she served two terms. Most of that time was spent carefully cultivating relationships, gaining committee assignments, and shepherding strategically placed bills through the legislative process. Hard work and attention to detail paid off as she steadily rose in prominence among Democratic Party faithful.

During the previous election cycle, she stepped out of her role as senator and entered the race for president. Campaigning hard, it came down to a contest between her and Jack Hedges. In the end, voters in Texas and California chose Hedges. It was a bitter loss, but Lehman soldiered on, campaigning vigorously for the party ticket in the fall.

Now, as she looked out the window at the lawn with the towering oaks and the portico facing Pennsylvania Avenue, she still felt a twinge of jealousy. This should be her house. Everything had been set. She had done everything right. She had raised more money, had higher favorables in every poll, recruited more volunteers, and swept all the early primaries. Victory was within sight. But then the rumors started again. Her husband. A waitress in Oregon and something about a… She pushed the thought from her mind and focused on the matters at hand. Braxton Kittrell waited for her inside. *Why Hedges named Kittrell chief of staff is a mystery to me*, she mused.

Born and reared in Virginia, Kittrell was the son of Maddie Wainwright Kittrell. She was a Wainwright from South Carolina, and if you happened to forget, she would quickly remind you. Not like those Wainwrights from Tennessee or even North Carolina. Maddie and her brother, Robert, were heirs to a fortune made in the textile business. With the help of the family fortune, Braxton had grown up to be arrogant, bombastic, and overbearing, forever certain he was the smartest person in the room. Lehman cringed at the thought of him occupying an office so close to the president.

The car rolled to a stop under the portico at the entrance to the West Wing of the White House. The driver opened the rear door and waited as Lehman stepped out. A U.S. Marine Corps guard stationed at the building snapped to attention as she approached. When she was a few paces away, the guard opened the door and held it as she moved past.

Inside, Lehman crossed the reception lobby and turned right. She wound her way down the hall to a small office in the back corner of the first floor. Mrs. Wilson, a petite woman of sixty who served as Kittrell's secretary, smiled politely as Lehman appeared at the doorway. "Madam Secretary."

"Mrs. Wilson," Lehman nodded. "Good to see you again."

"He's ready for you."

"Thank you."

Mrs. Wilson opened the door to reveal Kittrell seated at his desk. As Lehman stepped inside, Mrs. Wilson closed the door behind her.

Kittrell stood. "Madam Secretary."

"Braxton," she nodded politely.

Kittrell came from behind the desk and gestured to a chair a few feet away. "Please. Have a seat. Let's sit over here near the window."

Lehman took a seat in the chair to the right. Kittrell sat to the left.

"Would you like some coffee?"

"No, thank you," Lehman replied. "I'm fine."

"Have you—"

"Look, Braxton," Lehman began, cutting him off. "I know you were caught off guard by the president's remarks at the press conference, but I think he was right. He has to meet with Kermani. It was a good idea."

"We're not kowtowing to some Arab sultan," Kittrell scoffed.

"That's why you've been calling the CIA every five minutes?"

"What do you mean?"

"You know exactly what I mean."

"I'll call whoever I want, I'm the—"

"I know very well who you are." Lehman raised an eyebrow. "And I'm sure you think you can find some way out of this. But you can't. It won't work. Diplomacy is the only way to keep this from escalating into a major incident."

"Escalating?" Kittrell raised his voice. "You don't think it's already a major incident?"

"Listen, Braxton." Lehman placed her hands on the armrests of the chair. "Iran has been after us for three years to meet with them. Ever since—"

"And that's exactly why we shouldn't go," he snapped.

"Germany tried to get us to talk to them. France. Even England wants us to sit down with them. We should have done this in our first year. Instead, we sat around playing it safe."

"Arabs think they can—"

"Kermani isn't a sultan, and he isn't an Arab," Lehman scowled.

"He's a thug."

"He's an Iranian."

"That's Arab to me."

"Well it's not to the rest of the world."

"What is it then?"

"Kermani is Persian," Lehman explained.

"Well, we're Americans—"

"We're the only superpower left. And we need to act like it."

"We're not meeting with some third-world dictator at the point of a gun."

"Iran isn't a third-world country." Lehman gave a frustrated sigh. "They're the world's third largest supplier of oil."

"They think they can dictate their terms to us."

"They aren't dictating anything to us. They're a sovereign nation, pursuing their own strategy. We need to engage them. It worked with the Soviets. It worked with China. It'll work with Iran."

Kittrell shot her a wary glance. "Why are you so interested in a meeting?"

"Look, Braxton. The president's remarks were instinctive. He has a good head for what's right, and meeting with Kermani is the right thing to do. Besides which, it makes great political sense. The American people like to see this sort of thing. They like to see their president taking the initiative, cutting through the red tape, meeting face-to-face with the other side to solve our problems. It'll do wonders for his approval rating."

"Short-term."

"We don't have any other option. He's made his position public. The whole world heard his press conference. If he doesn't meet with Kermani, there may not be any long term, strategically or politically."

Kittrell shook his head. "There's no way this is going to happen."

"Yes, there is," Lehman responded. "I already have people working on a site."

Kittrell's eyes flashed. "Where?"

"I'll tell you when we get it all worked out."

"You're talking to Iranian officials about this?"

"I'm talking to whomever it takes."

"Who authorized you to do this?"

"Congress."

"Congress? When?"

"When they created the post of secretary of state."

"Need I remind you, the president sets foreign policy?"

"And need I remind you? The president announced our foreign policy at his press conference just a few feet down the hall."

25

BREMERHAVEN, GERMANY

MANFRED ROSLER WALKED AMONG the stacks of cargo containers. After years as a foreman on the docks, he had become suspicious of everything—regulations handed down from Berlin, inspectors sent from the port authority, agents from the Federal Police filled with a sense of self-importance about their latest innovations for security. He had seen all of them come and go, and he knew that security, real security, meant getting close to the cargo. Others who worked the wharfs were content to simply follow the rules and procedures outlined in the memos stapled to the bulletin board, to let the automated scanners and the air samplers handle it, but Rosler insisted on following a different routine.

Each day, after handing out the shift assignments and sending the crews out to work, Rosler took a handheld dosimeter from his locker, checked to make sure it was functioning properly, and then went for a walk among the stacks of cargo. He couldn't reach all the containers, as many of them were stacked five and six boxes high, but he could reach the first two levels. And that allowed him to return home knowing he had done his best.

As Rosler turned the corner at the end of a blue container stack, he came to a row of oversized containers. Painted a light cream color, they were stacked three boxes high. He held the dosimeter at arms length and walked slowly down the line. Near the center of the row, the dosimeter began to whine. Rosler stopped and glanced down at the digital reading on the instrument. What he saw sent a rush of adrenaline through his body. Numbers on the dosimeter's screen indicated radiation levels five times the allowable level. He pressed the reset button and restarted the device. Still, the reading came back the same.

Carefully, he moved back and forth along the stack, first lifting the dosimeter high over his head and then low to the ground. In a few minutes he isolated the source of the emissions to a pair of oversized boxes stacked near the end of the row, both of them cream colored.

Rosler took a cell phone from his pocket and punched in a number. Within minutes his supervisor, Konrad Bohl, appeared at his side. "What do you have?" Rosler turned the dosimeter so Bohl could see the display. Bohl was startled. "You are certain this is accurate?"

"I restarted it three times. Each time it gave the same reading."

"Have you notified anyone?"

"Only you."

Bohl pointed to the stack of oversized cargo containers. "And you are certain the emissions are coming from these two boxes?"

"Yes."

"Where are they going?"

"New York."

Bohl looked frightened. "New York?"

"Yes," Rosler nodded.

"We must set them aside."

"Perhaps we should call someone first."

"Why? We must not allow them to leave the dock."

"We should alert someone to investigate." Rosler glanced around with a wary eye. "Perhaps even now we have already attracted too much attention."

"You think someone is watching?"

Rosler slipped the dosimeter into his pocket. "I think we should not tip our hand until the proper authorities can determine what is really going on." He leaned close to Bohl. "These boxes were scanned earlier."

Bohl looked worried. "They went through the VACIS scanner?"

"Yes."

"And they did not detect anything?"

"That is where you should begin. If it went through the scanner, and they detected nothing, then we should be worried, not just for New York but for ourselves."

"What if the machine malfunctioned?"

"What if there is a traitor among us?"

26

CIA HEADQUARTERS
LANGLEY, VIRGINIA

KINLAW AND HOAG LEFT Winston Smith's office and walked to the elevator. When they reached it, Kinlaw pressed a button and stepped back to wait. "We should go into Operations."

"Why?"

"You have a friend there who might be able to help us."

Hoag shot a suspicious glance at Kinlaw. "I don't think so."

"She could help us," Kinlaw insisted.

"How?"

"They have access to surveillance systems around the world. We need her help."

"For what?"

"Come on, David. Don't be difficult. Everyone has cameras. Port security. Building security. We might catch a shot of those ships in port."

"What do you want to see?"

"We have…" Kinlaw glanced down at a list on the legal pad. "Fourteen ships on the list."

"Fifteen," Hoag corrected.

"Okay. Fifteen. Don't you think at least one of them was caught on a surveillance camera?"

"Maybe. What will that tell us?"

"I don't know. But I think we ought to have a look. And besides," Kinlaw smiled, "from the way you're acting, it's obvious you want to see her."

They walked to the end of the hall, where they came to a large, steel door. Unlike most others, this one had a combination dial in place of a door knob. A security camera was mounted on the ledge above. On the wall to the right was an intercom. A voice spoke. "May I help you?"

"We're here to see Jenny Freed," Kinlaw said.

"Is she expecting you?"

"I doubt it," Hoag offered.

A few minutes later the door swung open and Jenny stepped out. She grinned at Hoag. "Hey. Didn't expect to see you 'til this evening. What's up?"

"We ahhh…" Hoag blushed. "We were wondering if you could help."

"Sure." Her smile was even brighter. "What do you need?"

Kinlaw gestured toward the doorway. "Maybe we could talk someplace besides the hall."

"Sure." Jenny stepped back. "Right this way."

Beyond the door was an entryway with an opaque glass screen that blocked the work area from view. Jenny opened a door to her right, revealing a small conference room. "Come this way." She held it for them as they stepped inside then pointed toward a table in the middle of the room. "Do we need to sit?"

"I don't think it will take that long," Kinlaw replied.

Jenny closed the door and folded her hands behind her back. "So, what's this all about?"

Hoag spoke first. "We were wondering what kind of access you could get to surveillance cameras."

"Surveillance cameras?" She frowned. "Where are we talking about?"

"What about…" Kinlaw lifted the first sheet from his legal pad and glanced down at a list. "Guangzhou, China?"

"No way." Jenny shook her head. "Can't help you there. It's a really big deal to hack into the Chinese system. Last time someone tried, they got caught, and it was a huge mess. Have to get clearance from upstairs for that."

Kinlaw glanced back at the list. "Naples?"

"Probably."

"Malaga?"

"Yes," Jenny nodded. "The Spanish are very cooperative these days, in spite of what they say publicly. What else?"

"Bremerhaven."

"Probably," Jenny nodded. "That's all you need?"

"That'll get us started." Kinlaw tucked the legal pad under his arm. "Unless you can hack into installations in Iran."

Jenny gave them both a quizzical look. "What's this all about, guys?"

"Ships." Hoag flipped his notepad around to take out a copy of the list. As he did, the photograph of Nasser Hamid slipped free. Jenny caught it before it hit the floor and handed it back to him. "Thanks," Hoag smiled. He took the photograph from her and gave her the list. "We're looking for footage of these ships. We were wondering if you had access to port security cameras that might give us a glimpse of them."

Jenny scanned the list quickly. "Fifteen?"

"Yeah," Hoag sighed. "I know it's a long shot. But if it works it could really help."

"Fifteen ships," Jenny repeated.

"I know." Hoag said, sheepishly. "It's a lot to ask."

Jenny looked up at him. "You think?"

"We'd take a shot from anywhere. Not just from those ports we mentioned."

Jenny looked at him then back at the list. "Fifteen ships, out of all the ships on the seas." She pointed to the list. "You want just these fifteen at the four or five ports you mentioned."

"Yes," Hoag nodded.

Kinlaw spoke up again, "We thought maybe those particular places gave us the best opportunity."

"Okay," Jenny grinned. "I'll see what I can do."

Kinlaw stepped toward the door. Jenny caught Hoag's eye. "Seven?"

"Yeah," he nodded. "Seven."

She opened the door and held it as they walked out, then pressed a button to let them out to the hallway. As the door closed behind them, Kinlaw cuffed Hoag behind the head. "You sly little guy."

"Don't start."

"You did it."

"Yes." They reached the elevator. Hoag pressed the button. "I did it, but I'm not sure it's the right thing."

"Yes you are," Kinlaw laughed. "I can see it all over your face. You like her."

The elevator doors opened. "Yeah," Hoag grinned. "I like her."

27

FBI DATA CENTER
CLARKSBURG, VIRGINIA

TOM SINCLAIR RETURNED from lunch to find a large manila envelope lying on his desk. "What is this?" he called in a loud voice.

Melinda, one of the office assistants, came to his door. "It arrived from D.C. while you were out. Delivered by courier."

"I can see it's an envelope," Sinclair held it up and pointed to red letters stamped across the front, "but what does this say?"

"Eyes Only," she replied.

There was a twinkle in Sinclair's eyes. "And what does that mean?"

"It means access to the contents of that envelope is limited to people with a Level One security clearance."

"So, why is it lying on my desk?"

"This is a secure office," she smirked. "You can't even get on this floor without going through eight security checks."

"We have procedures for handling these documents. And get me that new kid," Sinclair shouted. "Sam or George or whatever his name is."

"Steve."

"I don't know."

"Steve Shaw."

"Yeah. That one. Ask him to come in here, please."

A few minutes later Shaw arrived at Sinclair's office. A newly-hired graduate from the University of Alabama, Shaw was working to help pay his way through law school. He appeared at Sinclair's doorway looking tired and disheveled. Sinclair looked up from the desk.

"How much are you sleeping at night?"

"Sir?" Shaw looked taken aback by the question.

"You look like you slept in your clothes last night."

Shaw glanced down at his wrinkled pants. "I probably did."

"Excuse me?"

"I was studying last night and fell asleep. Woke up late. Rushed to get in on time. Is that a problem?"

"No," Sinclair said, shaking his head. "Not a problem for me. I just don't want it to be one for you."

"Yes, sir."

Shaw turned to leave. Sinclair called to him. "Hey. Get back here. I'm not through."

Shaw turned to face him. Sinclair tossed the manila envelope to him.

"There's a memo in there requesting information on a list of eight people. Check the files on each of them, see what you can find, and write a report. Don't intentionally delay it, but be thorough. It's a request from the CIA."

"Okay." Shaw glanced at the envelope. "Am I allowed to have this?"

"Yes," Sinclair replied. "I checked it. There's nothing in there you can't know."

"Yes sir. Is that all?"

"Go," Sinclair said, dismissing him with a wave of the hand. "Get busy."

Three hours later Shaw appeared at Sinclair's office door. Sinclair looked up. "Back already? Responding to that memo should take you all week."

"I've got a little problem. I asked around. They said I should see you."

"What's up? Find something?"

"Yes." Shaw pointed over his shoulder with his thumb. "There's a message on the screen. I can't get it to go away. You want to take a look? I'm not sure what to do next."

Sinclair came from behind his desk and followed Shaw down the hall. At the far end of the building they came to a cubicle. Small and cramped, it was just large enough for a desk and chair. A computer terminal sat to one side of the desk. Shaw pressed a button on the keyboard. A screen appeared with an "Access Denied" error message.

Sinclair frowned. "You hit this with a request from that list?"

"Yes."

"Which one? Who were you looking for?"

Shaw checked his notes. "Osmani. Nabhi Osmani. Pakistan Shipping." He tucked the notepad under his arm. "I hope I haven't caused any trouble. I was just looking for files on the people on that list, and then this showed up."

"That's all right. Happens all the time." Sinclair nudged Shaw aside. "Step back for a minute, will ya? Let me see what's on the screen."

Shaw moved away from the desk. Sinclair took his seat and leaned over the keyboard to type in a pass code. The error message disappeared from the screen, and up popped a picture of Osmani. Sinclair skimmed the first page. As a young man Osmani had studied at a madrasah in Peshawar, Pakistan. Two months after turning eighteen, he and his brother, Gardez, volunteered to fight with

Osama bin Laden in Afghanistan. According to multiple sources, bin Laden made a soldier of Gardez but sent Nabhi to school in London.

With financial help from the bin Laden family, Nabhi acquired an outdated ship and developed a business in Karachi, shipping grain to the Persian Gulf. He then bought an outdated tanker and entered the oil transport business between Iran and China. That proved unusually lucrative, and with the profits from that line he expanded the business to containerized cargo, conducting business worldwide as Pakistan Shipping. At last report the company container volume had grown to over 600,000 units per year.

Sinclair groaned. Shaw glanced over his shoulder. "Find something interesting?"

Sinclair pointed to the screen. "Over the last five years, this guy's company has purchased six new ships."

"That's unusual?"

"Business has been good, but not that good." Sinclair looked back at Shaw. "They couldn't do that without some serious financial support. Building a ship is a big deal. Shipyards want to know they're going to be paid before they get into a project like that. Buying one ship is a serious undertaking, especially for a company of this size. But this guy bought six over the last five years. That's more than one a year and in several of those years he had two or three under construction at one time. That's some serious cash flow." He turned back to the screen. "These were new ships, too. They were constructed from the keel up specifically for containerized cargo."

Shaw stepped back. Sinclair gestured for him to move closer. "You can read this file."

"I don't have a Level One clearance," Shaw replied.

"I assigned you to this task," Sinclair insisted. "You can read whatever I let you read. Come on. Read this with me."

Shaw stepped closer and read the screen over Sinclair's shoulder.

The new vessels were built at shipyards in Denmark, Norway, and Greece. As they were accepted from the yards, they went into service on trade routes to China, the Persian Gulf, Germany, and the United States. All of them were registered in Panama and were named *Central Gold, Santiago, Costa del Sol, Panama Clipper, Ocho Del Rio*, and *Amazon Cloud*. Each of them sailed under a Panamanian flag.

Sinclair clicked the cursor on a tab at the top of the screen. A new page appeared. "Here we go," he said. "This is why you hit a wall." He pointed. "A counterintelligence team working from the New York office made contact with Osmani last year. Contacted him through operatives in Mumbai, India." He glanced over at Shaw. "They caught this guy some place the Indians didn't want him to be, doing something he didn't want anyone to know about. Grabbed him before the Indians found out. Gave them a lot of leverage with him." He pointed to the screen once more. "They held several meetings with him." He tapped the monitor screen with his knuckle. "This is a guy they think they can turn."

"So, he's an asset."

"Yes." Sinclair arched his eyebrows. "He's an asset. Which means we aren't telling anybody about Mr. Osmani."

Shaw folded his arms across his chest. "So, what do we tell the CIA? We're supposed to be sharing information with them from this region. Their authority over the area is primary. Ours is secondary."

"Not for this information." Sinclair scooted back from the desk. "We start giving this stuff away, you and I'll be filing paper in Hoboken."

Shaw grinned. "Do we even have an office in Hoboken?"

"You know what I mean," Sinclair smiled. "We aren't denying them the information. We're just gathering it and kicking this request back up the food chain. We'll let someone at the top make this decision. Print those screens. Write up a report and send it to me with a memo to New York." He stood and started from the cubicle. "If the CIA is asking questions, we better tell our men to watch their backs."

28

GEORGETOWN, WASHINGTON, D.C.

HOAG LEFT THE OFFICE and walked up the street along a row of townhouses toward his apartment. As he crossed Wisconsin Avenue, his cell phone rang. He took the phone from his pocket and checked the screen. He smiled. "Hello, Jenny."

"Meet me at Clyde's," she said.

"Clyde's? I thought I was coming to your house."

"Change in plans," she replied. "You remember where it is?"

"I remember, but what happened? Is something wrong?"

"We need to talk."

Hoag didn't like the tone of her voice. Talking now meant one of two things: either she was really serious about him, or she had decided she wanted to date some other guy. With their track record, he was convinced there was another guy. Suddenly he realized he had waited too long to respond to her.

"It's not that," Jenny groaned. "Honestly. All men ever think about is how long it'll be before the woman loses interest."

"Okay," Hoag sighed. "What time?"

"Seven."

Jenny ended the call abruptly. Hoag put the phone back in his pocket and spent the remainder of the afternoon wondering what she wanted.

——— (((———

Clyde's restaurant was located on M Street near Wisconsin Avenue in the heart of Georgetown. It was a restaurant with good food, and a place where people on the move came to see and be seen. Located a few blocks down from Starbucks, Hoag passed it almost every morning on his way to his office at the university, but it had been a long time since he had eaten there. He realized the last time he was there was with Jenny, on another cool autumn evening—the evening she broke up with him.

He arrived at the restaurant a little past seven. Jenny was waiting as he came through the door. From the look on her face, the conversation wouldn't be about dumping him. She stepped toward him and took his hand. "Good to see you." Without hesitating, she leaned forward and kissed him lightly on the lips. "Sorry for the change."

"That's okay."

"You remember the last time we were here?"

"Yes," Hoag nodded, "I'm afraid I do."

Her eyes sparkled. "Maybe tonight will be better."

"Maybe so."

The maitre d' led them to a table in a quiet corner, away from the main dining room. When they were seated, a sommelier brought a bottle of wine. Then they were alone.

Jenny leaned forward. "David, I wanted to talk to you outside the office."

"Okay."

"When I saw you the other day, you had a picture tucked inside your legal pad." Hoag nodded. Jenny lowered her voice. "Winston Smith gave you that picture." She gave him a knowing smile. "He got it from an FBI agent in New York named David Lansing."

"How do you know this?"

"Lansing runs the FBI's counterintelligence office in Manhattan." A smug look spread across her face. "We've been watching him for the past six months."

"Watching him?" Hoag frowned. "You mean spying on him?"

"The deputy director brought our section in to provide support for an investigation."

"Oh," Hoag replied. "That's what we call it now: not spying but investigating?"

"David." Jenny's shoulders slumped. "You were always so sanctimonious."

"I'm not sanctimonious, Jenny," he countered, defending himself. "I just think since we're all part of the same government, we ought to be working together instead of against each other."

"Look." Jenny pushed her hair back from her face. "I'm just trying to keep you and Dennis out of trouble."

Hoag took a sip of wine and glanced away. Now he remembered why he had a knot in the pit of his stomach the day he had seen her in the hallway near Winston's office. This was the reason they had never made it. The football player was just an excuse. The real reason was the way even the simplest conversation turned into an argument. He stole a glance in her direction. Still, he couldn't avoid how he felt about her. He set the wine glass on the table and smiled.

"Sorry. Old habits." Hoag cleared his throat. "You were called in to help the DDI. That must have been a huge rush, to sit at the table and become a player. Finish telling me about it."

Jenny took a deep breath. "You can be so infuriating sometimes."

"Yes, I can," he grinned. "And irresistible at others. Just like you."

She grinned back. "That part of you, I very much like."

Hoag leaned forward. "We can talk about—"

Just then, the waiter appeared. They ordered quickly. When he was gone, Hoag leaned forward once more. "Go ahead. Finish the story."

Jenny leaned toward him. "Lansing has been working with an FBI agent stationed in China named Bill Sisson. Sisson has a long history of looking the other way. Since he's been in China, he's worked out of our consulate in Guangzhou. Most of his work has been involved with assisting Customs on port security issues. Homeland Security thinks Guangzhou has become a major trans-shipment point—drugs, guns, a long list of other items. Bring it in from Germany, Russia, and France. Ship it to North Korea, Iran, Syria, wherever."

"That's an interesting combination of people and countries."

"Yes, it is."

"And you think Winston's involved?"

"Lansing was one of his students. He took him under his wing like he did you and Dennis. No one thinks Winston's involved, other than his personal relationship. But it's made him vulnerable."

"So, since Lansing gave that photo to Winston, you think there's more to Lansing's interest in Hamid than simply sharing information?"

"Hamid is a major player in the Middle East. A mysterious guy, but very well connected. If Lansing gave Winston that photograph, he did so for a purpose."

"But what purpose?"

"I don't know. But you and Dennis need to be careful."

"Does anyone else know about this?"

"About Hamid?"

"No. That I have a photograph of him?"

"No." Her eyes darted down and to the side. "No one knows but me."

"Jenny." Hoag cut his eyes at her. "Are you sure?"

She sighed once more. "I haven't told anyone."

"But you think you should."

"Yes," she nodded. "I think I should. Part of the problem we've faced since 9-11 is the failure to share information. I know something about a matter under investigation. I'm part of that investigation. I think I have a duty."

"Sure," Hoag nodded. "You have a duty, and you should tell what you know."

"Is that a snide comment?"

"No," Hoag grinned. "It's what you should do."

"This whole thing is getting crazy. And now with Iran testing a nuclear weapon ... I don't know." Her voice trailed away. "Everyone is working every possible scenario, hoping it doesn't connect to Iran, and then hoping it does and we'll find a way forward before it's too late."

"Dennis keeps telling me it has something to do with end-time prophecy."

"Yeah," Jenny nodded. "It certainly seems like it."

He looked up. "Don't tell me you're buying into this stuff, too."

"I think we should consider all possibilities."

"We have to draw a line of plausibility somewhere."

"You have no trouble considering the way Islamic prophecies influence people in the Middle East, do you?"

"That's different."

"How?"

"Islamic prophecy motivates Muslims to blow themselves up. Fly planes into buildings. Shoot people. Last time I checked, Christian prophets aren't motivating Christians to do that."

"Prophecy wasn't given for that purpose."

"You sound like you've given this some thought."

"David, I need to—"

Just then, the waiter returned. When he was gone, Jenny changed the subject.

29

BREMERHAVEN, GERMANY

DIGITAL FILES FROM THE VACIS CARGO scanner in Bremerhaven revealed little detail about the contents. Under pretense of positioning the containers for loading, agents from the Federal Police and port security created a second row of oversized containers, laying them end to end with the ones Rosler had discovered. Shielded from view by those containers, a Special Operations team slipped between the boxes. They quickly clipped the seals from the two suspicious boxes and made their way inside.

In the first box the team discovered an Iranian Shahab-3 missile resting atop a mobile launcher. Radiation levels inside the box were well beyond those considered safe. The second container held a tractor truck designed to pull the launcher. Five minutes later the team resealed the boxes and withdrew. Within the hour Federal Police notified Franz Heinrich of what they had found.

Late that afternoon Heinrich left Berlin, flew to Munich, and rode by car to Blomenburg, an estate in the Bavarian countryside that had been owned by Josef Mueller's family since the time of the Holy Roman Empire. Mueller used it often as a retreat from the hectic pace of life in Berlin.

The driver steered the car up the driveway and brought it to a stop behind the main house. Heinrich opened the rear door and stepped out. In the distance he saw Mueller strolling alone through an apple orchard. Heinrich watched a moment as Mueller, wearing slacks and a long-sleeved shirt, made his way between the rows of stark, bare trees. A chilling autumn breeze whipped past the car. Heinrich retrieved a coat from the back seat and started toward the orchard. Mueller saw him coming and waited.

"You should be inside," Heinrich called. "It is too cold out here."

"I am inside too much." Mueller gestured to his surroundings. "Here I find peace and comfort."

"At least you should put on a coat." Heinrich offered the coat he had brought from the car.

Mueller shook his head. "You wear it. I am fine." Heinrich slipped on the coat and zipped up the front. Mueller turned away and gestured to the trees. "There has been an apple orchard growing here since before there was a Germany." He glanced over at Heinrich. "Can you imagine princes of the past walking this very ground, deciding the future of a country that did not yet exist?" He gestured with a sweep of his arms. "We are those princes now."

"I don't feel like a prince," Heinrich replied.

"And perhaps there will be an orchard here, after we're gone."

"We can only hope."

Mueller laced his fingers together and stretched both arms over his head. "You didn't drive all the way out here to talk about apples or princes." He dropped his hands to his side. "What is it that you could not tell me over the phone?"

"Our inspection teams in Bremerhaven have discovered two large cargo containers on the docks. One of the containers holds an Iranian missile loaded on a mobile missile launcher. The other has a truck used to move the launcher."

Mueller stopped walking. "You are certain the missile is Iranian?"

"Yes, Chancellor. A Shahab-3."

"Where did it come from?"

"It came to us from Syria, through Jordan. No one is certain where it originated. I assume it came from Iran."

"And where is it going?"

"New York."

Mueller's eyes flashed. "An Iranian missile, on its way to New York?"

"Yes."

"Where is it now?"

"It is still sitting on the dock. Both containers are there, right where we found them. No one has seized them, but they aren't going anywhere. I assume you will want to notify the Americans, but after your comments the other day about the Foreign Office, I thought we should be as careful as possible with sensitive information. That is why I rode out here. We cannot avoid the Foreign Office on this matter, but if we coordinate our efforts we can maintain control of the situation after the news breaks. We don't want the Foreign Office spokesman taking the lead in briefing the press."

"How did we find this missile?"

"One of the workers on the dock located it with a handheld dosimeter."

"A dosimeter?"

"Yes, Chancellor."

"There was radiation?"

Heinrich looked Mueller in the eye. "Sir, the missile is carrying a nuclear warhead."

Mueller grinned. "A nuclear warhead?"

"Yes, sir."

"That is unbelievable."

"Federal Police were skeptical at first, but the Special Operations team provided photographs. The warhead is nuclear. About five kilotons, they think."

"Five kilotons," Mueller whispered. He slid his left hand into his pants pocket and let his fingers run lightly over the sun wheel medallion. "That would level New York."

"It would, indeed."

Mueller turned away, resuming his stroll among the apple trees. Heinrich walked again at his side, waiting as minutes ticked past. By the end of the row, Mueller still had not spoken. He turned left to the next row of trees and started back in the opposite direction.

Heinrich checked his watch. "Sir, it is getting late. We need to decide how to handle this situation."

Mueller looked over at Heinrich with a thin, tight smile. "Let the containers pass."

"Let them pass?"

"Yes," Mueller nodded. "Do nothing more. Let them pass."

"But, sir. We cannot let them pass. This missile… It can mean only one thing."

"Franz, we have been friends all our lives. I trust you with my life and the life of our country." Mueller rested his hand on Heinrich's shoulder. "But there are things happening about which you know very little." Mueller gave him a friendly pat. "Let the cargo containers pass. Tell no one."

"The Federal Police will want to know why. I must have an answer for them."

"Tell them the Americans have been tracking the containers and are prepared with their own response."

"Have the Americans been tracking them?"

"Let the containers pass. Do nothing more." Mueller looked away. "This is exactly the sort of thing we've been waiting for."

30

YEMEN

NASSER HAMID STEERED A 1998 VOLVO sedan across the Yemen desert. Following a hard-packed trail across the flat, dry sand, he held the gas pedal to the floor and watched as the needle on the speedometer steadily rose. The engine rumbled through a broken tailpipe with a noise that blocked out all but the sound of the hot dry wind as it blew through the open windows. Sand flew in the air behind him.

In his mind, Hamid ticked off all the things that had to happen next. The first missile was well on its way. Zahaden would see that it was loaded. But there were two more missiles, both of which were necessary for the plan to have its desired effect. Of those, he was less confident.

An hour outside Aden the car crested a hill. Down below, tucked in the folds of a dune, three buildings sat huddled against the encroaching desert sand. Palm trees grew in a cluster to the left. In their midst was a well with a spigot that trickled water into a small pool beneath. In the distance, a string of camels moved away toward the north.

Hamid lifted his foot and rested it lightly on the brake pedal. The Volvo's engine slowed to an idle and coasted down the grade. At the bottom of the hill he shoved his foot hard against the brake and turned the steering wheel sharply to the right. The rear of the car came around, putting it in a slide. The car rocked over to one side, then came to a stop between the buildings. Hamid threw open the door and climbed out.

Buildings in the compound sat at right angles to each other. A long, low building was located to the left. A square one with a tin roof stood to the right. Directly ahead was a large, steel warehouse. Hamid made his way toward a door at the far end. He pulled it open and stepped inside to a cluttered workshop.

Turbat Hoshab stood at a workbench along the front wall. He glanced up, his eyes wide, a startled look on his face. "Hamid. I was not expecting you." He stepped away from the bench. "Nabil did not tell me you were coming."

Hamid brushed dust from the front of his pants. "It's farther out here than I remembered."

Turbat laughed, "It gets shorter the more times you drive it."

"One time is more than enough for me," Hamid replied.

The two men embraced. "So good of you to join us," Turbat said.

Hamid stepped back and glanced around. "You are working alone today?"

"Yes. Suhar is in Aden. The others left a little while ago. You might have seen them as you drove up."

"On the camels?"

"Yes."

Hamid turned away. "You are ready? Everything is complete?"

"Yes," Turbat nodded. "We are ready."

Hamid glanced back over his shoulder. "May I see?"

"By all means." Turbat gestured with his hand. "Come this way." He led Hamid through a doorway to a large room in the central portion of the building. Two standard cargo containers sat side-by-side. One was a typical forty-foot box. The other was a larger, sixty-foot box. Hamid walked around them, checking their appearance. A small, red, crescent moon was stenciled in the upper left corner of the door on each one. He gestured toward them with a nod. "What are these? On this container and the other."

"What?"

"That crescent." He pointed to first one then the other box. "Why is it there on the door?"

"Nabil suggested we should mark them. The two containers must be stacked together. All containers look the same," he shrugged. "I think he wanted to make certain they could find them on the loading dock and get them in proper position on the ship."

Hamid frowned. "That's why we were careful about the numbers on the outside." He stepped to the corner of the nearest box and pointed. "Right there."

"I know," Turbat nodded. "But Nabil said to do it this way. He didn't want any mistakes."

Hamid didn't like the crescents. He had specifically instructed Osmani to make certain that all of the containers had only standard markings. There was to be nothing different or unusual about them. That Nabil made such a decision on his own struck Hamid as the kind of arrogance that had led to the failure of previous missions. He wanted the symbols removed but saying something now would place him at odds with Nabil, and right now he needed Nabil. He gestured to the cargo container once more. "Open the door," Hamid said, gesturing toward the smaller box.

"They are sealed already," Turbat countered. "Nabil said you wanted them that way."

"Open the door," Hamid repeated. "You can reseal them later."

"Yes," Turbat replied. "As you wish." He turned away and found a pair of snips, then clipped the wire seal from the door. With the seal removed, he lifted the latch and opened the forty-foot container. Inside was a tractor truck designed to tow a Soviet-built missile launcher. Hamid leaned inside the box and let his eyes scan the truck.

"The truck will remain in place while the box is moved?"

"Yes. They are quite heavy."

Hamid glanced back at Turbat. "They swing those boxes around when they load them. They don't care what it contains."

"Yes," Turbat nodded. "I have seen them many times. They move quite rapidly and in an erratic fashion. Nabil said that was not a problem."

"You asked him?"

"Yes."

"So, you thought of it, too."

"Yes," Turbat nodded. "I did."

"Hmm." Hamid thought for a moment, then he gestured toward the second box. "Open the next one."

The larger box sat a few feet away. Turbat clipped the seal from it and swung open the door. Inside was a Soviet-built MAZ 534 missile launcher. An oversized trailer, the launcher was loaded with an Iranian Shahab-3 missile. Almost fifty feet long and about four feet in diameter, the missile and launcher filled the box from end to end. At the top of the missile was a small gold cone, an indication that it was armed with a nuclear warhead. Hamid smiled when he saw it.

"What have you done to contain the radiation?"

Turbat stepped closer and pointed. "We lined the box with a lead insert."

Hamid moved to the left for a closer look. "I cannot tell by sight."

"That is good," Turbat grinned. "It is as it should be."

"Yes," Hamid smiled and nodded. "I suppose so." He rapped the wall with his knuckle. "Solid. What about the floor?"

"It is lined also."

"And the frame of the box will hold the extra weight?"

"Yes. We made sure of that."

A broad grin stretched across Hamid's face. "The missile is ready to go?"

"Awaiting target coordinates and the launch code."

"Good," Hamid backed away from the container.

Turbat grasped the latch handle and swung the door closed. "We have been exposed long enough," he warned.

Hamid moved aside and watched as Turbat sealed the doors. "You have arranged to transport both boxes to the dock?"

"Yes," Turbat nodded. "It has been arranged."

31

FBI COINTEL OFFICE
MANHATTAN, NEW YORK

DAVID LANSING SAT AT HIS DESK and stared out the window. From
his office on the sixteenth floor of Federal Plaza, he looked down on
the Manhattan streets below. After ten years with the FBI, Lansing
had served in six countries, working counterterrorism details from
Beijing to Frankfurt. Five months ago he had been assigned to the
New York office. With a wife and three children, he was glad to be
located in one place for a while, especially when that one place was
in the United States. He bought a house across the Hudson River in
Bound Brook, New Jersey, enrolled his children in school and, for all
appearances, settled down to a regular routine.

Beneath the calm exterior, however, Lansing's mind raced and
his stomach roiled. What had begun years before as a way to make a
few dollars had now grown far beyond his control. Two years out of
law school and new to the Bureau, he had gotten in over his head,
first at the blackjack table, then with houses and trips. Before he
knew it, he owed big money to people with little patience, even for
an FBI agent. When he couldn't repay, they offered to let him work
it out. That was when he found Bill Sisson.

Like Lansing, Sisson was an FBI agent already working both
sides of the street. Together they turned the art of ignoring the facts
and the law into a lucrative business. Only now it was far beyond

that. They were into something much more serious than anything they had ever seen. And they had both seen a lot.

Today Tajik al Shahan, a wealthy Saudi Arabian, controlled their every move. With the help of Lansing, Sisson, and others, Tajik used China as a staging ground for shipments of contraband to rogue nations banned from doing business with the West. Once in China, with the right officials on the take, anything was possible. Industrial equipment, weapons, and even parts for nuclear reactors could be shipped anywhere in the world.

For Lansing, what had begun with the bending of a few rules eventually mushroomed out of control. Extortion and bribery were Tajik's favorite tools. Lansing was expected to make certain no one noticed. "We are like the new Lords of Alamut," Tajik had said, "ushering in the great age of the Mahdi." Not that anyone took him literally. No one in the Middle East meant anything the way they said it. But the trail of dead bodies spoke volumes.

Last month Lansing had broached the subject of slowing down, of not moving things so aggressively. They were transporting shipping containers through China so fast, he was certain Chinese officials would raise an objection in spite of the money they were being paid. Tajik had dismissed his concerns with the wave of a hand.

As he stared out the window, Lansing's mind turned to the clues he had left. He thought surely someone would discover what they were doing. He had begun leaving these hints months ago. Wasn't anyone watching? Bank accounts. Financial transactions. A simple review would have raised immediate questions about how someone on his salary could move that much money through that many accounts. He stared out the window at the Manhattan skyline and gently rocked his chair as he thought about what to do next.

Seated at a desk a few feet away was Russell Cooper. A graduate of Harvard Law School, Cooper had worked a stint with a Wall

Street investment firm then joined the FBI. Initially assigned to an organized crime task force, he began his career monitoring bank accounts of the most notorious crime bosses in the country. His work proved critical in the arrest and conviction of Sonny Callitore, head of the Santoretti crime family.

Cooper's expertise became instant legend in the Bureau. Then, when terrorists attacked the World Trade Center on September 11, he was transferred to the Counterintelligence Office. Only days after the attack he began to monitor international banking systems in an effort to discover the money trail that funded key terrorist networks. That work had developed into an ongoing operation that sought to preemptively discover the existence of new terrorist cells based on patterns of financial transactions.

As Lansing and Cooper sat at their desks that day, a two-page memo arrived from the Clarksburg Data Center. Lansing picked it up from the in-box and scanned it. His heart skipped a beat when he saw the memo came from Winston Smith. *He took it*, Lansing thought. He spun his chair sideways to face Cooper. "Hmmm," he groaned as he looked over the first page again. "This looks like it was meant for you."

Cooper looked up, "Something interesting?"

Lansing flipped over to the second page. "CIA is asking for information about a list of people. At least one person they're interested in is one of our sources. A guy in Pakistan named Osmani. Someone has to respond to the request. Clarksburg thinks we should do it."

"Respond to a memo?" Cooper was puzzled. "What's that got to do with me?"

"Not much, actually." Lansing scooted closer to Cooper's desk. "I was just buttering you up. Look at this." He pointed to a list of names on the second page of the memo. "The CIA sent this request to Clarksburg. They're looking for information on all these people. What do you suppose they're up to?"

"I don't know." Cooper leaned over and scanned the list. "Recognize anyone else on there?"

"Not really. You?"

"No," Cooper shook his head. "I don't think so." He tapped the memo with the back of his index finger. "Couple of these names sound vaguely familiar. Why'd they send it to us? What are we supposed to do with it?"

"Draft a response." Lansing folded the top sheet over and handed the memo to Cooper. "You write the response. I'll contact the field and see if anyone knows what's going on. Write up a memo and get it over to Langley."

"What do I say?" Cooper had a blank look on his face. "I've never responded to one of these."

"Do a quick check of our files and see what else we have, then say as little as possible."

"Thanks," Cooper mumbled.

"Don't mention it," Lansing grinned.

Cooper spent most of the following day combing through the FBI database for information about the men on the list, retracing much of what Steve Shaw had done at the Data Center in Clarksburg. Not surprisingly, he found they had extensive files on all eight men. Two were under surveillance in Malaga, Spain. Three had made visits to North Korea. One had recently visited New York. Another had made four trips to Tehran in the past two months. Five had been the subject of previous requests from federal agencies—CIA, ATF, and DEA among them. But by far, the most interesting man on the list was Nabhi Osmani.

According to a file buried deep in the database, Osmani made contact with a U.S. Customs agent in Mumbai. The initial meeting dealt with questions about pre-certification of cargo at the port in Karachi. Osmani was interested in shipping cargo to the United States that would be pre-cleared through Customs prior to loading it on his ships. Doing that meant Customs questions about the cargo could be addressed and corrected in Karachi rather than at a port in the United States, half a world away. In the course of that discussion, Osmani asked about establishing a similar relationship and procedure at all of the company's locations. He even suggested his company would cooperate in establishing cargo scanning facilities at each of those ports.

The idea and subsequent discussion struck the officer with whom Osmani spoke as more than a mere inquiry about Customs issues. Acting on that suspicion, the officer turned the information over to an FBI agent working from the U.S. Embassy in New Delhi. Several more meetings with Osmani followed, with FBI agents posing as Customs officials. During each meeting Osmani seemed to indicate he had more to say, but each time the meeting ended abruptly. At the same time, FBI agents uncovered intriguing pieces of his background, especially his relationship with Osama bin Laden and the financing provided by the bin Laden family.

Cooper developed the information for Lansing and briefed him that afternoon. Lansing listened attentively then leaned away. "That's an interesting guy." He rubbed his eyes and feigned ignorance. In fact, he knew far more about Osmani than was contained in the FBI files. "What's the name of the company?"

"Pakistan Shipping," Cooper replied.

"Think you can find out anything about it?"

Cooper raised an eyebrow. "Do I think?"

"Yeah," Lansing chuckled. "I suppose you can." He turned back to his desk. "Work on Pakistan Shipping and see what you can find." In the short time he had known Cooper, Lansing had learned that keeping him busy was the best way to handle him. "Might be something there that breaks that whole thing wide open."

"Break what wide open? What am I looking for?"

"I don't know," Lansing shrugged. "Anything interesting."

"What do I do about replying to this memo?"

"Give them some stuff on two or three of those other guys. Nothing too critical. But don't give them anything on that guy... Oss-whatever."

"Osmani," Cooper corrected.

"Yeah. Osmani. Don't give them anything about him."

Late that afternoon Cooper turned to the task of preparing a response memo. As he glanced over the CIA's request once more, he noticed the original inquiry had come from Winston Smith, but in the memo history he found the names of Kinlaw and Hoag. Seeing Kinlaw's name brought a smile to Cooper's face.

Cooper had been classmates with Hoag and Kinlaw at Harvard. He and Hoag never quite hit it off but Kinlaw had spent Saturdays tutoring Cooper during their first year. As a result the two became good friends. They saw even more of each other when Cooper began dating Kinlaw's sister. Though that relationship did not last, he and Kinlaw remained close. They spoke frequently by phone, and just last year he had stayed at Kinlaw's home while in Washington for a conference.

When Cooper saw Kinlaw's name on the memo, he felt compelled to find a way to send him a message, one that would let Kinlaw know the FBI knew more than it was willing to divulge, but one that would keep him out of trouble with Lansing. As he glanced back at the list of names, he realized why one or two of them had seemed familiar earlier. They had been the subject of an earlier inquiry by the CIA, one to which the FBI had responded in a much different way.

Cooper smiled as he turned to the keyboard and began to type. "Kinlaw thinks he's so smart," he chuckled to himself, "let's see if he gets this message."

32

GUANGZHOU, CHINA

BILL SISSON SAT AT HIS DESK at the U.S. Consulate in Guangzhou. With his chair turned to one side, he stared out the window at the Pearl River and watched as it slowly drifted past. His eyes followed a boat moving with the current, but his mind was far away.

He had first been approached while stationed in London. Someone wanted a favor, an uncle from Vienna who needed assistance getting past Customs in New York. Could he make a call, put in a word? He didn't remember the man's name or what his problem was. All he remembered was the feel of the twenty-dollar bills in his hands that evening, a stack of twenties in each hand and more lying on the bed. It seemed like all the money in the world. That was the beginning. By the time he left London, he was the man to see. The fixer. The Bureau offered him an office in Los Angeles, but he turned it down for a post in Spain, and the game continued. Now he was in China, the last stop before retirement, and wondering what he would do next.

Just then, an assistant leaned over to drop a single-page memo on his desk. "New York sent you this," she said.

Sisson glanced at the paper. "Great," he grumbled. "Just what I need."

Though assigned to an office in the consulate, Sisson was part of the FBI's counterterrorism unit and accountable to the office in New York. David Lansing was his supervisor. Sisson, more than ten years Lansing's senior, regarded the FBI hierarchy with disdain, routinely ignoring their requests and instructions. A memo from Lansing, however, was a different matter.

When Lansing and Sisson first began working together to cover Tajik's operation, they were careful to communicate by surreptitious means. Later, as they grew more confident, they sent each other messages in official memos, conveyed subtly through innuendo and implication, relying on each other to fill in the blanks of what had gone unsaid. Sisson's eyes wandered down the page. They came to a halt at Pakistan Shipping.

A few minutes later Sisson left his desk and walked down the hall to the Customs attaché. There, he found Henry Vogrand, an assistant in the port inspection office. Henry sat at his desk, eyes focused on the screen of a laptop.

Sisson leaned against the doorframe. "Henry, you got a list of ships for the week?"

Henry opened a desk drawer and took out a thick, loose-leaf binder. A label across the front identified it as the Ships Log. He set the book on the desk without replying. Sisson picked it up. "Thanks."

"Don't leave the room with it," Henry growled.

Sisson took a seat at a vacant desk nearby and opened the book. He scanned through the first few pages and found an entry for a ship named the *Santiago*. He knew from memory it belonged to Pakistan Shipping. It was docked at the container port south of the city and scheduled to sail the following day. Kubachi Logistics was agent for the cargo. Sisson glanced over his shoulder to see Henry, still hunched over the screen of his laptop, then turned back to the log book. He grasped the edge of the paper and coughed. As he did, he ripped the page from the binder, folded it in half and tucked it under his jacket. He flipped through a few more pages, then closed the book, leaned over Henry's shoulder, and dropped it on his desk. It landed with a loud thud.

Henry glared at him. "It would be nice if you didn't do that."

"Sorry."

From Henry's office, Sisson made his way downstairs and signed himself out of the building. On the street, he took a cell phone from his pocket and entered a text message. "Lunch. White Swan."

Almost immediately he received a response. "Yes."

Twenty minutes later he entered the hotel lobby. Wang Deng Yua was waiting for him.

About Sisson's height, Yua was lean and taut, a result of years spent studying wushu, the Chinese art of boxing. He smiled as Sisson approached. "Glad you called. I was wondering who would buy my lunch today."

"You have expensive tastes," Sisson replied. "If you ate a little cheaper, maybe you'd get more invitations."

"I do not go lacking for offers," Yua smiled as they started across the lobby. "Are you certain it is safe for us to meet so close to your embassy?"

"No time to go across town."

Sisson and Yua walked past the tourist shops to the dining room. A waiter seated them at a table near a window overlooking the river. They ordered lunch and talked while they ate.

Yua glanced around cautiously. "I assume you had some reason for contacting me?"

"You have the *Santiago* in port. Right? You're the agent?"

"Yes."

"What's it loading?"

"Construction material."

"Construction material?"

"Manufactured wood beams."

"Where is it headed?"

"Los Angeles."

Sisson looked skeptical. "We have to come all the way to China to get wooden beams?"

"It would seem so." Yua wiped his mouth with a napkin. "You are interested in these products?"

Sisson ignored the question. "The ship's sailing tomorrow."

"Yes," Yua nodded. "It will sail by the afternoon."

Sisson cut his eyes at Yua, "Assuming you pass inspection?"

Yua stopped chewing. "Inspection? I have heard nothing of an inspection. These are harmless wood products. Who has called for an inspection?"

"Henry has the ship on a list."

"You saw this list?"

"He keeps it on his desk."

"I have heard nothing of any inspection. They have not notified us. We always are notified in advance." Yua chewed slowly. "Why would they do that? Why would they inspect without telling us?"

"It is bound for the United States."

"Yes, but it's building material," Yua retorted. "It was previously cleared at the factory. By your Customs officials. The containers are sealed."

"You know Henry," Sisson shrugged. "Once he gets something in his mind, he's hard to dissuade."

"Okay." Yua had a look of resignation. "How much do you need?"

"How much?" Sisson looked perturbed. "We never talk like that."

"We always talk like that," Yua scowled. He patted the front of his jacket. "Why do you think I brought this envelope in my pocket? How much is it going to take this time?"

"I don't want money. I want information."

"Oh," Yua chortled. "You are playing it straight now?"

Sisson ignored the tone of Yua's voice and asked again. "What do you know about Nabhi Osmani?"

"Someone from your Homeland Security Office was asking about him last week."

"Asking you?"

"No. Just asking."

"What do you know about him?"

"No one knows much of anything. He lives in Karachi. That is all."

"Does he come here?"

"Sometimes."

"Anytime recently?"

"I do not think so."

"How did you come to be agent for his ships?"

"That is a long story."

"I have plenty of time."

"You are coming to the docks tomorrow? For this 'inspection?'"

"Yes."

"I will show you the ship then."

When Sisson and Yua finished lunch, they left the dining room and walked back across the lobby toward the front of the building. As they stepped outside, Yua slipped an envelope into Sisson's hand.

33

ALEXANDRIA, EGYPT

NASSER HAMID SAT ALONE AT A TABLE in Kushari Bondo, a crowded café in the Smouha section of Alexandria. Located just blocks from the Mediterranean shore, the café was popular with tourists and locals alike. From the corner where he sat, Hamid had a view of the street through a front window. While he sipped tea and waited, his eyes darted from the window to the door and back to the window.

A middle-aged man appeared on the sidewalk outside. He glanced through the window and entered the café. Hamid recognized him from his photograph. He was Abdul Al-Jawad, not quite as old as Hamid's father, with graying hair. Wearing rumpled cotton pants and a white shirt, he was slender and wiry and looked like many men in the region—accustomed to hard work, long hours, and never enough to get by.

Al-Jawad stood just inside the door and glanced around nervously. Hamid caught his eye and gestured with a nod of his head. Al-Jawad crossed the room to the table.

"You are the one who called me?"

"Have a seat." Hamid pointed to a chair on the opposite side of the table. "Would you care for something to eat?"

"No," Al-Jawad replied as he slid onto the chair.

"Perhaps something to drink? Some tea?"

"If you insist," Al-Jawad conceded.

Hamid motioned for a waiter. "Some tea for my friend," he smiled. "And perhaps some bread for us, while we talk."

The waiter disappeared. Al-Jawad's eyes darted from side to side, as if checking the room. "You are looking for a driver?"

Hamid rested his hands in his lap. "I have some freight that needs to be delivered. They tell me you are a truck driver."

"Yes."

"And you have your own truck?"

"Yes." Al-Jawad nodded. "It is a fine truck."

"You keep it in good repair?"

"Certainly. It is my life."

The waiter returned with tea for Al-Jawad and a plate of bread. He set it on the table and stepped away. Hamid gestured toward the plate. "Please. Have some bread. It's very good here."

Al-Jawad slipped a piece of bread from the plate and took a bite. "Where would you like the cargo delivered?"

"The Egyptian border. Near Gaza."

"The cargo is here? In Alexandria?"

"Yes."

Al-Jawad took a sip of tea. "Gaza is a long way."

"You have been there before?"

"Yes," Al-Jawad nodded. He took another sip of tea. "I have been there many times."

"So, you can do it?"

"Perhaps. What will you pay?"

Hamid took an envelope from his pocket and slid it across the table. Al-Jawad hesitated. Hamid tapped it lightly with his finger. "For your time in considering this offer."

Al-Jawad picked up the envelope, leafed through its contents, and placed it in his pocket. "You will always pay in dollars?"

"Yes," Hamid replied. "Or any other currency you wish."

"U.S." Al-Jawad took a sip of tea. "I prefer dollars."

Hamid smiled. "We have grown to trust it."

"Yes."

Hamid checked the window then looked back at Al-Jawad. "There will be another payment when you pick up the cargo, and another when it is delivered."

"And what is the nature of this cargo?"

Something inside Hamid bristled at the question. He would have asked the same question if their roles had been reversed; nevertheless, he did not like it. Hamid smiled. "It is for the Mahdi."

Al-Jawad grinned. "I have been waiting a long time for the Mahdi."

34

MOSSAD OPERATIONS CENTER
ASHDOD, ISRAEL

EFRAIM HOFI SAT IN A CONTROL ROOM at the Mossad operations center at Ashdod. At the opposite end of the room was a flat screen that covered the wall. Images from the café in Alexandria appeared on the screen.

At sixty-one, Hofi had enjoyed a long career. He joined the Israeli Defense Force after college and rose quickly through the ranks, eventually attaining the rank of colonel. Then, in a battle at Bint Jubail during the First Lebanon War, a grenade exploded near his bunker. Shrapnel from the blast damaged muscles in his leg and left him with a limp. Forced to walk with the aid of cane, he was unable to return to combat. As a result, he was assigned to Mossad, where he became an operations officer. Later, in an administrative shakeup by Benjamin Netanyahu, Hofi was elevated to director. Now he was responsible for all of Mossad's operations.

Hofi folded his arms across his chest, leaned back in his chair, and watched as events unfolded in the café. From a speaker near the screen he listened to the operatives on the scene.

"Visitor is leaving," someone whispered. "Subject is seated at the table alone."

A unit commander on sight spoke up, "Confirm target is in range."

A third voice broke in, "Target is in range."

An operator in the control room responded. "Nevi One do you have a status on collateral damage?"

The unit commander replied, "Collateral would be minimal."

The operator spoke again, "Stand by for authorization."

Hofi watched as Hamid slid his chair back from the table and stood. While he waited at the table, a second man entered the picture. Hofi pointed to the screen.

"Who is that?"

The operator pressed a button on his console. "Nevi One, can you confirm identity of the second visitor?"

Hofi rose from his seat and stepped to a technician seated at a nearby work station. He leaned over the man's shoulder. "Tighten the image on the table."

"Negative identity on the second visitor."

The picture on the screen zoomed in on the table. Hofi leaned away from the work station and stared at the screen. He placed his hands on his hips and said with a stern voice. "Hold your position."

A message crackled through the speaker as the order was relayed to the field. "This is Solomon. Stand down on the primary target. Observe only."

"Roger. Observe only."

Hofi leaned over the technician's shoulder again. "Can you get us audio from the café?"

The technician nodded and pressed a button. Voices in Arabic came over the speaker. After the first few sentences, Hofi called out. "Can we get a translation?"

Someone overdubbed the translation.

"You are certain they will not interfere?"

"I am certain."

"We cannot have American Customs snooping around the port when the ship is loaded."

"The FBI agent will see to it that they do not interfere."

"This FBI, they are reliable?"

"Yes. We have their agent 'in our pocket' as the Americans like to say."

"I don't have to remind you what is riding on this."

"No. You do not have to remind me. I am not a schoolboy."

"And you will make certain there is no one to talk about it?"

"That goes without saying."

The visitor stood and stepped away from the table. Hamid sat at the table alone. He took a sip from his cup and then another. When the visitor was gone, he rose from the table, made his way to the door, and disappeared outside.

Hofi watched the screen a few minutes longer then turned to those in the room. "We need a voice match on the audio from the café. And we need a translation that matches the conversation with the voices."

"Shouldn't we warn the FBI?"

"Not yet. We need to assemble the information first."

"You will need to request permission from Langley to use their voice database."

"No." Hofi shook his head. "We will use only our own database. Do not share this information with your American counterparts. We need to know what we are dealing with before we start talking to anyone." The room fell silent. Hofi glanced around. "Get busy."

35

BREMERHAVEN, GERMANY

THE CONTAINER SHIP *Panama Clipper* was docked in Bremerhaven, one of the largest ports in Europe. Overhead cranes lifted cargo containers from the staging area onshore and whisked them to their places aboard ship. Blue, red, and white containers slowly filled the ship's hold and rose above the deck.

Ephraim Zaheden stood near the far side of the ship and watched as the stack of containers on the deck slowly took shape. While he watched, the crane lifted an oversized cream-colored box and brought it toward an opening in the stack. Carefully, the operator lowered the box into the stack and rested it on the ship's deck. As it settled into place, Zaheden glanced to the left. A tall, slender man came from behind a vent shaft. He leaned against the vent and tilted his head back to watch. When the box was in position, the man glanced over at Zaheden. A smile flickered across his face.

A motor on the crane whined. Zaheden turned to see a second box rising in the air. Carefully, it made its way toward the ship, dangling perilously from cables attached at the corners. As the box passed beneath the crane, a crewman on the deck keyed a radio and called out instructions. Slowly, the crane operator turned the box in midair, then lowered it toward the deck. Using a guideline, crew members on board the ship brought the box to a spot directly behind the first, setting the two end-to-end.

Zaheden glanced to the left again. The man by the vent shaft was gone.

36

THE WHITE HOUSE WASHINGTON, D.C.

JACK HEDGES SAT AT HIS DESK in the Oval Office, twirling a pen between his fingers. Across from him was Braxton Kittrell, his chief of staff. Secretary of State Lauren Lehman stood to the left. They had been in that position for twenty minutes, engaged in heated debate.

"We must meet with Kermani," Lehman insisted. "We have no choice. It has to be a neutral site, but we have to meet with him." She shifted her weight with a sigh. "Mr. President, Iran is now a nuclear power in a critical area of the world. Our economy runs on oil. The price has skyrocketed since their test. The only thing holding prices down at all is the fact that you suggested talking to them. We have longstanding commitments to allies in the area. They rely on us for support and leadership. We cannot—"

"That's right, Mr. President," Kittrell said, interrupting her. "The moderate, sensible, decent countries in the region look to us for leadership not appeasement. We cannot appear to be caving to the Iranians, especially not at the point of a nuclear pistol."

"Mr. President," Lehman argued, "you announced this opportunity at your press conference. This was our idea. Your idea. The world heard you. They are expecting—"

"He's not president of the world," Kittrell snapped. "He's president of the United States of America. Third World countries have the luxury of being magnanimous. We do not."

Lehman ignored him and focused on Hedges. "Mr. President, your instincts at that press conference were correct. The wisdom of the offer you made then still holds now." She tapped her finger against the desktop for emphasis. "Meet with the Iranians. Talk to Kermani. See what he has to say. You can only look bigger by going. If you back away now, you'll appear weak and indecisive, and you'll turn a tense moment into an international crisis."

Kittrell growled at her, "You don't know—"

"Enough," Hedges said, waving his hand. "I've heard enough." He dropped the pen he had been twirling and leaned back in his chair. The room grew quiet as he stared past them. After a moment Hedges' eyes darted to Lehman. "Where did you have in mind?"

"Dubai will host the meeting," she replied.

Kittrell shook his head. "Mr. President. Really." His voice had a dismissive tone. "I don't think Dubai would be interested. They're not a significant political player in the region. I don't think they would take the risk of—"

Hedges cut off Kittrell with a frown. He turned back to Lehman, "You've talked to someone in Dubai already?"

"Yes, Mr. President. If asked, Bandar Al Maktoum will agree to host the meeting."

"Okay." Hedges took a deep breath. "Dubai it is. How soon?"

"Two weeks. Maybe three. We'll need time to negotiate some preliminary issues with the Iranians first."

"Like what?"

"Like the topics you'll discuss with Kermani."

"I hate these things." Hedges shook his head. "We negotiate to negotiate?"

"Yes, Mr. President."

Hedges leaned forward and propped his elbows on the desk. "I want them to agree not to supply nuclear weapons to Al-Qa'ida and other terrorist groups."

"We'll need to define those groups as narrowly as possible."

"Al-Qa'ida. Hamas." He folded his hands together and rested his chin against them. "And whoever is causing the most trouble between Turkey and Iraq. Pick one."

"Yes, Mr. President," Lehman nodded.

"They need to concentrate their technology on peaceful use," Hedges continued.

Lehman raised an eyebrow. "Agree to the Nuclear Nonproliferation Treaty?"

"Will they?"

"I don't know," Lehman shrugged. "We can always ask."

"Ask."

37

PORT FACILITY, GUANGZHOU, CHINA

SISSON LEFT HIS OFFICE and rode down to the container port just south of Guangzhou. A sprawling facility on the banks of the Pearl River, the port was located halfway between Guangzhou and Hong Kong. Containers stacked two and three high covered acres and acres on either side of the river, the product of the area's prosperous and lucrative manufacturing business. Anchored in the warm autumn sunshine was the *Santiago*, one of Pakistan Shipping's newest container cargo ships.

Cranes moved back and forth, lifting containers from the staging area and whisking them to the *Santiago's* hold. Up the dock a little way Chinese port officials watched and waited, binoculars dangling from their necks, clipboards at their sides. Wang Deng Yua, Henry Vogrand, and several technicians from the U.S. Department of Commerce stood nearby. With them was Shang Li, deputy director of the Port of Guangzhou. Bill Sisson stood a few feet away and waited.

An hour or two later, a crane lifted an oversized cargo container and swung it toward the ship. Yua pointed to it. Officials watching the process were suddenly alert. They grabbed their binoculars and trained their eyes on the container, tracking its every move. When the container was safely aboard the ship, one of the officials leaned forward and said something to Yua. Customs' technicians nodded in agreement. They started forward as a group and made their way up the gangway toward the deck of the ship. Sisson trailed behind.

When they reached the deck, Chinese inspectors accompanying Li confronted the ship's captain and demanded to see inside one of the containers. Henry checked the clipboard, a bewildered look on his face, then glanced back at Sisson. Sisson stepped forward, pointing, "It's the big one. The white one over there."

Henry turned to the captain. "The white one. The oversized one." He pointed. "Over there."

"Where?" The captain frowned.

"Come on," Sisson said. "I'll show you."

Sisson led the captain toward the container that had just been loaded. On the upper right corner of the door was a small Star of David stenciled in blue with a circle around it. Li moved slowly around the container, one hand thoughtfully stroking his chin, as if he knew exactly what he was doing. Sisson knew it was all an act.

As deputy director of the Port of Guangzhou, Li was responsible for inspection of cargo. He also supervised cooperative inspection programs with foreign governments. He had a longstanding relationship with Henry and every other customs and export official from countries using the Guangzhou facility. More important for the moment, however, Li was married to Yua's sister.

Li nodded and pointed toward the container. Yua turned to the captain. "He wants to see inside this container."

"It's sealed," the captain protested. "I have no authority to open it."

"He has authority," Yua replied, gesturing toward Li.

The captain looked at Henry then at Sisson. Sisson nodded. Reluctantly, the captain turned to a tool locker and took out a pair of wire clippers. "Here." He thrust the clippers toward Yua. "You want to see inside the container, you clip the seal."

Yua stepped to the container. Li pointed again toward the door, gesturing impatiently with his finger. Yua clipped the wire seal, unlatched the door, and swung it open. Inside, the container was packed with I-beams made from manufactured wood material. Yua glanced in Sisson's direction. Sisson nodded again.

Li moved closer and leaned through the doorway. The container was filled to the roof. He shook his head and said something Sisson could not understand. Yua moved closer, gesturing to the beams and pointing to something inside the container. After a moment, he and Li stepped back. Yua pushed the door closed and latched it in place, then turned to the captain.

"As you can see, he only wanted to view the contents."

"What about the seal?"

"Not a problem," Yua smiled. He took a red tie-wrap strap from his pocket, threaded the wires through holes on the latch and door frame, then pulled it tightly closed. A small, red medallion bearing the government seal dangled from the red strap. When it was in place, he looked at Sisson. "That should do it."

38

WASHINGTON, D.C.

HOAG LEFT THE OFFICE and walked across campus to Yates Field House, a Georgetown athletic facility. He was sweating his way through a workout when his cell phone rang. The call was from Jenny. He answered the phone between gasps for breath.

"Am I interrupting something?"

"At the gym," he replied. "What's up?"

"I have something you need to see."

"Where?"

"At the office."

Hoag checked the clock on the wall. It was already after two. "I'll have to shower. How late are you working?"

"I'll wait. Get over here. You need to see this."

An hour later Hoag entered CIA Headquarters at Langley and made his way downstairs. Jenny met him in the hallway and escorted him to a room in the operations section of the building. When the door was closed and locked Hoag turned to her.

"What's so important?"

"We located some surveillance footage," Jenny replied. "I think you'll find it interesting." She led him across the room to a monitor and pressed a button on the keyboard. On the screen were images of a ship, moored to a dock.

Kinlaw leaned over Jenny's shoulder, looking closely at the screen. "That's a self-loading container ship. Is it one from the list?"

"Yes."

"Which one is it?"

Jenny pointed to the right. "Get a chair." Hoag took a seat beside her. She pressed a button to tighten the frame of the picture. "This is the *Panama Clipper*." The image zoomed in on the bow. The name appeared in clean white letters.

"Where was this taken?"

"Bremerhaven, Germany."

As the tape played, a cargo container swung through the air above the dock. Suspended from a crane, the container paused in midair and slowly lowered onto the deck of the ship.

"When was this taken?"

"A few days ago. I can check the exact date."

"The ship has sailed?"

"Left there the day this was taken."

"Where was it going?"

"New York. I think."

"So." Hoag bounced his knee up and down as he thought. "They aren't quite halfway."

"I don't know."

"It's usually a fourteen-day trip for freighters crossing the Atlantic from Germany." Hoag pointed to the screen. "Can you get closer on the containers?"

"Yes." Jenny turned back to the console. "You sure about the crossing time? Seems a little long."

"What?"

"For ships. Is it really a fourteen-day trip?"

"That's the advertised time. They can make it quicker." He pointed to the screen. "Tighten up so I can see the containers."

The image focused on the stack of cargo containers sitting on the ship's deck. Hoag moved his chair closer. "Can you get the image any sharper?" Jenny pressed a button. A single box filled the screen. Hoag pointed. "Now, pan along the sides and around the ends."

"This is a tape not a camera," Jenny explained. "What you see is all there is. I can only give you what we already have."

The image panned slowly to the end of the stack. Something caught Hoag's eye. "There," he pointed. "On the end of that container." He tapped the screen. "What is that logo? None of the others have that on them."

Jenny pressed another button, moved the cursor to the spot on the screen, and tapped the mouse. The image slowly tightened on a close-up showing the container door, but the angle was extreme and the picture grainy.

"Can you sharpen that up?" Hoag pointed to the screen. "Enhance it?" Jenny hit several keystrokes on the keyboard. The image sharpened. Hoag leaned closer to the screen. "What is that? I still can't quite make it out."

"Scoot back," Jenny replied. "It'll help if you're farther away, like looking at a Monet. Too close and it's just pixels."

Hoag slid his chair back and squinted. "Hey. That is better."

"What do you see?"

"Looks like a star. With a circle around it. Only the circle doesn't quite close."

"What does it mean?"

"I don't know." Hoag's voice trailed away, his mind deep in thought. "But it looks familiar. I've seen it before, only I can't remember where."

"Want a print?"

"Yes." Hoag folded his arms across his chest and rocked back in the chair. He pointed at the monitor screen. "I know I've seen it before, or something like it."

Jenny pressed a button on the keyboard. "It'll take a minute to print." Hoag didn't respond. She nudged him. "Are you finished with this tape?"

Hoag sat up straight. Still focused on the image of the cargo container, he gripped the edge of the chair with both hands and leaned forward. "Any way I could get a copy of that tape?"

Jenny smiled and took a DVD case from beside the monitor. She held it up, grinning playfully. "Dinner?"

Hoag looked distracted. "What?"

Jenny grinned at him and waved the DVD case again. "Is it worth dinner?"

"When?"

"Tonight," she frowned, teasing him. "When did you think?"

"Okay," Hoag grinned. "Where?"

"Citronelle's."

39

GUANGZHOU, CHINA

MARK WHITE, A SPECIAL AGENT in charge of the embassy's FBI detail in Guangzhou, received a phone call from Chin Lai, chief of the Guangzhou police department. Bill Sisson had been found dead in his apartment. Though by then it was seven o'clock at night White swung into action. Within the hour he assembled an investigation team and dispatched them to Sisson's apartment. Darrell Driskell was the ranking agent on the team.

When Driskell arrived at the apartment, Guangzhou police were already on the scene. Driskell was stopped at the door by a uniformed policeman.

"No, no." The policeman waved his hands in Driskell's face. "Out!" he shouted. "Out!"

Driskell reached his hand inside his jacket for his badge. Startled, the policeman stepped back and placed his hand on his pistol. Before he could draw it, Chin Lai nudged him aside. "Mr. Driskell, I believe?"

"Yes," Driskell replied. He drew his badge and ID from the inside pocket of his jacket. The policeman grinned sheepishly and backed away.

Chin gestured toward the interior of the apartment. "Right this way. My men are going over the scene now."

"Has anyone moved the body?"

"No. It is just as we found it."

Driskell followed Chin down a short hallway. To the left was a galley kitchen. To the right was a bathroom. A few feet farther, the hall opened into a small living room. A sofa sat along the wall to the right. Sisson lay sprawled across it. Blood was splattered on the wall above his body and across the cushions on the sofa. A man leaned over the body, checking the pockets. Another stood to one side, camera in hand. Driskell stepped closer. Chin said something to the two men. They glanced at Driskell and backed away.

Sisson was fully clothed. Even his tie was carefully knotted and snug against the collar of his shirt. He still wore both shoes and his watch was on his wrist. His forehead bore an entry wound which appeared to be the only wound to the body. From the amount of blood seeped into the sofa, Driskell was certain the body had not been moved.

A small table sat in front of the sofa. It was turned at an odd angle. Driskell glanced up at Chin. "Did anyone move the table?"

Chin said something to the two men with him. They both shook their heads. Chin turned back to Driskell. "They do not think so."

"This is the way it was when they arrived?"

"Yes."

Driskell gestured toward the man with the camera. "Did he take pictures of the scene before they approached the body?"

"Yes."

"Think I could have a look at them?"

"Certainly."

Driskell glanced back at the table. Two magazines lay there. He leaned over them a moment, then he pointed to a picture on the cover of one. "She is beautiful," Chin said.

Driskell looked up with a frown. "What?"

"The woman." Chin pointed to one of the magazines. "Hoa Ching. One of our most beautiful models."

Driskell looked again. "Yes," he smiled. "She is pretty. What is that red spot?"

Chin leaned closer. "It appears to be a drop of blood."

"Can you have a lab check that out?"

Chin leaned forward for a look. "You think it is Mr. Sisson's blood?"

"I think it might be," Driskell said. "And if it is," he turned to face the opposite direction, "perhaps he was standing when he was shot."

"Which means?"

"I don't know," Driskell shrugged. "Might mean he knew the person who shot him."

"Or that he did not."

"Yes." Driskell moved around the table. "If that's his blood on the magazine, then he could have been standing out here, near the middle of the room. Takes a shot to the head, falls backward, over the table, and lands on the sofa."

Chin backed up toward the kitchen and stood in the doorway at the end of the hall. "Which means the shooter would have been standing here."

"Which means," Driskell pressed, "he either knew the shooter or the door was open."

"Or the shooter opened it."

"Yes. Did you check the door?"

"Not yet."

Driskell and Chin moved to the entry door and pulled it open. They both leaned around to inspect the bolt and strike plate.

"I don't see any scratches," Driskell said.

"No," Chin replied. "There are none. No sign it was forced open."

Driskell pushed the door closed. "We need to check this place for fingerprints."

"Yes," Chin agreed. "We were waiting for an evidence technician when you arrived."

"My team is prepared to process the scene, if you like."

Chin nodded and backed away, gesturing with both hands open. "As you wish."

Driskell nodded to the men who had accompanied him. They moved across the room and went to work. While they processed the living room, Driskell wandered to the bedroom. Chin followed him.

"We have not been in here."

Driskell glanced around. "Doesn't look suspicious."

A bed occupied the middle of the room and filled it almost wall-to-wall, leaving just enough space to slip around it on either side. A closet was located to the right of the door. The bed was unmade. A pair of socks lay on the floor. House slippers sat nearby.

"I don't see anything amiss," Chin replied. One of the men in the living room called to him. He backed away and stepped outside, leaving Driskell alone.

With Chin out of the way, Driskell pulled back the sheets and slowly moved around the bed. Finding nothing there, he opened the closet door. Six business suits hung neatly in place. A stack of white shirts, pressed and folded, rested on a shelf to the right. Beneath the shelf was a drawer. Driskell quietly slid it open and looked inside. It held underwear, a belt wound tightly in a coil, and two pair of white socks. He pushed them aside and worked his hand down to the bottom of the drawer. As he felt along, his fingers touched something. Carefully, he pulled out a linen envelope. It was filled with U.S. twenty dollar bills. On the back flap was a blue Star of David with a circle around it. Driskell slipped the envelope into his pocket and closed the drawer.

40

WASHINGTON, D.C.

AS HOAG STEPPED FROM THE TOWNHOUSE he was met by a crisp, clear autumn morning. After a stop at Starbucks for coffee, he picked up Jenny at her apartment. When they were seated in the car, Jenny glanced over at him. "Are you sure this is a good idea?"

"Yeah," Hoag nodded. "Why not?"

"It's a little cool for a boat ride."

"The sun's out." Hoag gestured through the windshield. "There's not a cloud in the sky." He smiled at her. "It'll be great."

From Jenny's apartment they drove downtown to the Washington Marina. Situated along the Potomac River and just beneath the Fourteenth Street Bridge, it was only blocks from the Capitol and even closer to the White House. Hoag parked the car in a space near the building and led her toward the docks.

Jenny shielded her eyes against the morning glare and looked around, squinting. "When did you buy a boat?"

"I didn't."

"Well, whose boat are we using?"

"It belongs to a friend," Hoag replied.

"Nice friend to let you use his boat."

"Yes," Hoag nodded with a smile. "He is."

By then they were near the end of the pier. Jenny surveyed the boats moored in the slips. "So, which one is it?"

"Down here."

Hoag took her hand and led her past the berths. A yacht tied off the end of the pier caught her eye. "That's a nice one," she said, pointing.

"Yes, it is, but it would take a five-man crew to operate it." Hoag looked back at her with a twinkle in his eye. "And we'd get arrested if we used it."

"Why?"

"It belongs to one of the Saudi royals."

"How'd they get that in here, anyway?"

"Very carefully."

A little farther down the pier they came to a sixteen-foot Chris-Craft Runabout. Made of cedar and mahogany, it was fully restored and in pristine condition. Jenny's eyes were wide with amazement. "David, this is a beautiful boat."

"Yes," he beamed. "It is."

Hoag climbed aboard, then he reached up and helped her into the boat. She took a seat on the left. He settled in behind the steering wheel on the right. The air was cool, but the leather upholstery felt warm from the sunshine. He turned to her. "Ready?"

"Yes," she nodded. "I'm ready."

With a turn of the ignition, the boat's six-cylinder Chrysler inboard motor came to life. It idled smoothly as Hoag reached over the side, untied the lines, and slipped back into his seat. "Okay," he smiled, as he put the engine in gear. "Here we go."

The boat moved smoothly through the water as they made their way from the marina into the Washington Channel. Hoag steered to the right and slowly passed beneath the Fourteenth Street Bridge. As they emerged from underneath it, the Jefferson Memorial came into view on the left. Hoag guided the boat to the left, glided under the bridge at Ohio Street, and came into the main channel of the Potomac River.

Hoag eased forward on the throttle. The engine roared as the boat picked up speed. They turned upstream and rode as far as the Key Bridge, rounded Roosevelt Island, and then headed downstream. The sound of the engine made it difficult to talk, but neither seemed to mind. Above them was a cloudless blue sky, and on either side they had a view of the nation's most treasured monuments. Hoag stole a glance in Jenny's direction once or twice. Each time she smiled back at him with a pleasant, relaxed look on her face.

About noon they reached Alexandria. They tied the boat at the foot of Cameron Street and walked up to Charthouse for lunch. As they sat at a table overlooking the water, Hoag looked at Jenny. "I have to attend a function at the school Wednesday evening. Would you like to join me?"

"Sure," Jenny answered. "What kind of function is it?"

Hoag smiled. "I like the way you said yes before you knew what it was."

"I've always said yes to you before I knew what it was."

"Yes," he nodded. "You have." He took a drink. "It's a reception for Vic Hamilton, one of the professors in the department. He's retiring. It's not a big deal, but I have to attend." He looked at her and shrugged. "Might be fun."

"Great." She took a bite and swallowed. "Do you actually teach there?"

"Taught a full load last year."

"And this?"

"Not so much. Other things have kept me busy."

As they continued to eat and talk, Hoag brought the conversation around to the unspoken issue between them.

"I'm wondering, Jenny." She looked up at him, expectantly. He felt his cheeks grow warm as he continued. "Where is this going?"

"Where is what going?"

"Us," he replied. "You. Me. Us."

"I see you haven't changed." She smiled at him. "Always direct."

"Well, it's not like this is the first time we've been through this."

"No, it's not." Her face softened. "It's much better this time." She took a deep breath. "I like my job, David. I like the location. I like what I do. I like knowing things no one else knows. That's good for me, but it makes it difficult to be with someone else."

Hoag nodded. "I can understand that."

"Can you handle me liking my job?"

"Yes. Can you deal with me being here sometimes and gone others? And not being able to tell you why?"

"Isn't that the life we both lead?"

"Yes," he nodded. "I suppose it is."

"I know this much." She gave him a warm smile. "When I'm with you, I feel like me. When I'm not, I don't. I haven't felt like me for a long time."

"I didn't like being dumped." Hoag took another sip of tea.

"I didn't handle that situation well."

"Why did you do it? I thought things were going great with us."

"They were, and that was the problem."

"Things were going great, and that was a problem?" Hoag was puzzled. "I don't understand."

Jenny leaned back in her chair and folded her hands in her lap. "When I was in high school, my family attended a church in New York. Redeemer Church. I think it was Presbyterian, but no one really cared about labels. It was very alive. Serious people attended, with serious thoughts and serious intellect, but also with a serious commitment to serving God." She paused a moment, as if searching

Hoag's face for a reaction, then continued. "The summer before my senior year in high school, I got serious."

"You were always serious."

"I got serious about believing in God. I began to look at my life, not for what I wanted to do but for what I thought God might want me to do, or be, or become."

"A calling."

"Yes. A calling. Don't make fun of it."

"I'm not making fun. I'm familiar with the term. But you weren't like that in college. You never talked about it. You never went to church."

"Exactly."

Hoag wiped his mouth on the napkin. "I'm afraid I'm not following you."

"Our sophomore year, Monica and Kelley—you remember them?"

"Yes."

"They invited me to a retreat. We went to New Hampshire. Stayed at a cabin near Manchester. I told you about it. A friend of Monica's dad owned it."

"Yeah. I remember something about it."

"While we were there, I found that part of me that had gotten lost during those first two years at college. I got serious again about being a Christian."

"Why did that mean breaking up with me?"

"At first I didn't think it would, but I was different, and I wasn't going back to the way I had been. There was this whole area of my life I couldn't discuss with you."

"Couldn't discuss?" Hoag frowned. "What do you mean? We talked about everything. Why couldn't you discuss it with me?" Jenny's eyes darted away. Hoag pressed the point. "Why? Why couldn't you talk to me about this?"

She looked over at him. "You tend to be cruel about that issue."

"Cruel? I've never been cruel. What are you talking about?"

"You remember Carol Westbrook?"

"Yeah," Hoag nodded. "I remember Carol."

The corner of Jenny's mouth twisted in a wry smile. "Remember that day in Union League Café?"

Hoag felt his face blush. "She was being a jerk."

"All she said was, 'What if God is real, and He really does mind what people say and think?'"

"And what did I say?"

"You said, 'Carol, if you were half as smart as you think you are, you'd be really intelligent. But you aren't. You're half as smart as *I* think you are. Which means you're an idiot.'"

Hoag felt his cheeks grow warm with embarrassment. "I said that?"

"You screamed it, actually." Jenny was unflinching. "I knew if I told you I was a Christian, you'd think the same thing about me. And I was already getting some of that from other people I knew. So, instead of telling you, I broke up with you." They stared at each other a moment, then Jenny continued. "I want to see you, David, but we can't get very far until we get past this."

Hoag glanced at her and smiled. "I want to kiss you."

"Always direct."

"You don't mind, do you, that I want to kiss you? That doesn't bother you or throw you off track, or take you some place you shouldn't go, does it?"

Jenny's face turned cold. She leaned forward. "This right here." She tapped the table with her index finger to emphasize the point. "This is what I'm talking about. This is what you do."

"Okay," Hoag said, apologetically. "I won't be a jerk."

Jenny wagged her finger. "You can't fake your way through this, David."

"What do you mean?"

"I mean, you can't hold your breath. It won't work. I want to see you. I wasn't lying when I said being with you makes me more myself." She leaned back. "But this relationship isn't going very far until we work this out."

Hoag looked away. "Okay," he sighed.

41

LOS ANGELES, CALIFORNIA

JABBAH ILMIR AWOKE well before dawn. He showered and dressed quietly so as not to wake his family, then walked to the living room of their modest apartment. There, he spread his prayer rug on the floor, knelt facing the east, and began to pray. An hour later he stared at his wife as she lay sleeping in their bed. Tears filled his eyes at the thought of not seeing her again. *These things must be done*, he thought to himself. *Allah has chosen me. I must be willing to sacrifice*. After a moment, he walked across the hall and looked in from the doorway at his two sons. Ilmir glanced at his watch. It was time to go. Perhaps one day, after the Mahdi appeared, they would understand his great courage. With a heavy heart, but deep resolve, he turned away and started toward the door.

Outside the building Ilmir made his way down to the parking lot. He forced his mind to think only of what to do next. Find the car. Open the door. Drive to the street.

The sky was still dark as he arrived at the warehouse. Located two blocks off Crenshaw Avenue, the building once had been used as storage for a furniture company two blocks away. Now the furniture was gone. The building had been empty for most of the year. When Ilmir rented it two months earlier, the owner had been all too willing to accept payment in cash and equally eager to avoid any probing questions or onerous background checks.

Ilmir walked around to the back of the building, opened the door, and stepped inside. Using a flashlight, he found the button for the rollup door and pressed it. The metal door clanked and rattled as it wound its way up to the ceiling. A few feet inside the building, a truck loomed in the shadows.

The one-ton delivery truck had been stolen three weeks earlier from the parking lot outside an appliance store in Tustin. It had remained hidden in the warehouse ever since. Late last night a crew took the license plate from the truck and swapped it for the plate on a truck parked at a store in Orange.

Ilmir opened the door on the driver's side and climbed into the cab. The key was already in the ignition. A small garage door remote was jammed in the ashtray. Ilmir adjusted the seat position and checked the mirrors, then he rested his hands on the steering wheel and looked out into the predawn darkness. His mind was clear, but his heart raced and his skin tingled. This was the day for which he had trained, the day for which he had waited. No more practice runs. This was the final moment. He was nervous but not afraid.

He reached for the key and turned the ignition. The engine came to life. When the engine idled smoothly, he put the truck in gear and eased it out the door. He steered it into the lot behind the building, brought it to a stop, and jumped out. Moving quickly but not running, he returned to the building, lowered the rollup door, and then jumped back into the truck.

From the warehouse in Mesa Park Heights, Ilmir drove to Crenshaw Boulevard and turned south. Traffic was light. He made good time. At Century Boulevard he stopped for the traffic light. As he pressed the brake to slow the truck, a car cut in front of him and darted into the gas station on the opposite corner, narrowly missing the bumper of the truck. Ilmir gasped as the car whizzed past, but it was there and gone before he could do more. When the traffic light turned green, he turned the truck to the right onto Century Boulevard and drove west, past Hollywood Park. He checked his watch. It was five-thirty. Too early for what he had planned.

A block past Hollywood Park, he came to a McDonald's. He turned into the parking lot and went inside to order breakfast. He ate it in the truck as he continued down Century. His stomach churned with every bite, but he swallowed hard and held it down.

As he drove along, his mind wandered back to childhood. He had been born in Pakistan, but when he was two years old his family crossed the mountains into Afghanistan. Traveling on horseback, they made most of the trip at night to avoid the armed militia that patrolled the mountain passes.

When Ilmir was twelve, Russian soldiers burned the family's poppy fields. His father kept them alive that winter by robbing Russian supply trucks. When that proved difficult, he turned to murdering the soldiers, one by one, and taking their money. Eventually, he was caught and hanged. His rotting corpse dangled for days from a tree near their house. The night he was killed, Ilmir left home to join the Mujahedeen. An uncle stopped him before he reached the mountains. Three weeks later Ilmir was sent to Egypt. Later, a cousin in England helped him gain admittance to college. After graduation he traveled to the United States, where he studied computer programming at Los Angeles City College. All the while, he waited for a message. Now that wait was over.

Three miles later a traffic light caught him. He brought the truck to a stop and glanced to the left. A Volkswagen Beetle came to a stop beside him. He looked down through the passenger window. A woman sat behind the steering wheel. She was a blonde, wearing a black dress. Ilmir stared at her.

The light changed and the Volkswagen started forward, jerking Ilmir back to reality. He moved his foot from the brake and pressed the gas pedal. A pang of sadness swept over him as he thought again of never seeing Elana again. His mind raced ahead to a moment later that day when she would find out. Nazwa said he would tell her all about it.

Nazwa. His thoughts turned dark. *He'll tell her about it, all right. While he's holding her close and whispering in her ear.* He pushed the thought from his mind and took a sip of Coca-Cola. Allah had assigned him a mission. He must not fail.

Ten minutes later Ilmir crossed beneath the 405. Los Angeles Airport loomed ahead. Traffic became heavier. Cars merged from left and right, filling the lanes on either side. He steered the truck into the far right lane and followed the signs for departing passengers. He had done this in practice runs many times before. He knew exactly what to do.

The truck's automatic transmission downshifted as it climbed the ramp to the upper level. Ilmir inched along with traffic, working his way to the exact, predetermined point. As his eyes darted left and right, he saw a man step from a Mercedes and kiss a woman seated in the car. The man glanced up at the truck. On his face was a puzzled look. A little farther a policeman gazed at the truck as it rolled past. Ilmir felt his heart race. His fingers nervously tapped the steering wheel. His left leg bounced up and down. The garage door remote rattled in the ashtray.

Halfway down the upper deck, he came to a stop behind a knot of cars and shuttle vans parked in the two right lanes. Passengers scrambled to unload baggage, husbands and wives said goodbye, a family with small children scampered from a van. Up ahead, a policeman directed traffic. The shrill sound of his whistle echoed against the buildings.

To the right a cab driver stuck his hand out the window of the cab and pointed to the lane in front of the truck. Ilmir motioned to the driver. The cab darted in front of the truck, moved over two lanes and sped away. Ilmir turned the truck into the space where the cab had been.

Cocked sideways, the truck sat at a precarious angle with the front facing toward the curb and the back stuck out in traffic. Ilmir took the garage door remote from the ashtray and placed it in his left hand. At the same time, he pressed the gas pedal to the floor. The engine revved as the truck lurched forward. It jumped the curb between two large concrete columns and plowed ahead. Luggage and people flew to the sides. The bumper struck a woman and knocked her forward, sending her sailing into a plate glass window. Blood splattered on the sidewalk.

Inside the building, people crowding the ticket counter turned to see what was happening. Their eyes grew wide with fright. A policeman started toward the truck, one hand pointing, the other reaching for his pistol. Ilmir moved his thumb to the button on the remote.

"All praise to Allah, who saved me from this life, and who will meet me in eternity." He pressed the button with his thumb.

Instantly, searing, hot flames burst through the rear wall of the cab and swirled around Ilmir's head. The seat pushed forward against his back then broke free of its mounting and shot forward, carrying his body with it. Instinctively, Ilmir covered his face with his hands as his head hit the frame of the cab above the window. Then everything turned black.

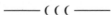

While Ilmir had driven west toward the airport, Minab sat at the kitchen table in the house in Mesa Park Heights. On the table before him was a backpack, stuffed with cakes of C-4 explosive that had been neatly wrapped in brown paper. Minab watched as Kun-di Mastung carefully slipped a detonator into each package then twisted the lead wires into the controller. When that was finished, he took a 9-volt battery from a shopping bag and twisted two wires from the controller onto the terminals. Once finished, he packed it all neatly in place and looked at Minab.

"The backpack is ready. Are you?"

"Yes," Minab nodded. "I am ready."

"This is your last opportunity," Kundi said, grimly. "If you go forward from here, there is no way back."

"I understand," Minab nodded. "I am ready."

"Allah will be pleased," Kundi smiled. He threaded wires from the trigger through a hole in the main compartment of the backpack and tucked it out of sight in a zippered pocket. "When you are ready, unzip this compartment and take out the trigger. Hold the plunger down with your thumb and pull the safety pin free. To detonate, just release your thumb."

Minab smiled. "Simple as that?"

"Simple as that," Kundi nodded. He zipped the backpack closed and stepped away from the table.

Minab stood, tucked the tail of his shirt into his pants, and hung a strap of the backpack over his right shoulder. He took one last sip of coffee and started toward the back door. An hour later he arrived in Anaheim. He steered the car into a parking deck and brought it to a stop alongside a Ford Explorer. A young family, husband and wife with three children, were walking away as Minab arrived. He heard their laughter and excited chatter as he stepped from the car.

Ten minutes later Minab emerged from the parking deck and started toward the central plaza near the entrance to Disneyland. Even at that early hour a crowd was gathering. He took a seat near the fountain, slipped an iPod from his pocket, and placed the ear buds tightly in his ears. With the press of a button, music transported him to another place and time. Thoughts of what he was about to do faded from his mind.

In an hour the plaza was filled with people. By then word of an explosion at the airport had reached some. Everyone seemed concerned. No one appeared alarmed. At eight o'clock the windows in the ticket kiosks opened. Lines formed at the park entrance. Minab set the backpack on his lap, unzipped the pocket that held the trigger, and took it out. With the trigger tucked out of sight in his hand, he zipped the pocket closed against the wires and slung the backpack over his right shoulder. He adjusted the ear bud in his left ear and started toward the entrance.

As Minab walked, he tucked the iPod in the waistband of his blue jeans and reached with this left hand to pull the safety pin from the trigger. He felt the end of the plunger press against his thumb. At the park entrance, he waded into the crowd and threaded his way to a place halfway between the entrance and the nearest ticket booth. He knew precisely where to stand. He had practiced this many times.

His heart raced as he thought about all he had done and all he had planned to do. What he had accomplished seemed so small against what he had hoped to achieve. Still, Allah required the most of only a few. Others had the luxury of living life to a natural end. A chosen few had the privilege and honor of participating in the work of true religion.

Minab slid his thumb to the right and released the trigger.

42

WASHINGTON, D.C.

THAT EVENING HOAG ESCORTED JENNY from the car. They walked across campus and up the steps of Healy Hall. Inside, they made their way to the Hall of Cardinals. A crowd already had gathered there when they arrived. Hoag introduced her to Vic Hamilton, then Kinlaw and his wife Debby appeared.

"Wasn't sure you'd make it," Kinlaw quipped.

"Man, what a day," Hoag sighed. "I can't believe somebody did that."

"Homeland Security has been after them to change the configuration on that airport."

"And Disneyland. That's getting close to the heart of America."

"I remember the first Disney movie I saw."

"What was it?"

"*Swiss Family Robinson.*"

Jenny and Debby had been talking, but now they nudged in between them. "You two get to see each other every day," Debby needled. She turned to Hoag. "How have you been, David?"

"Good, until today."

"That was so sad." She leaned against Kinlaw. "I hear Vic has a trip lined up to Jordan."

"Israel."

Jenny frowned. "How did he swing that?"

Hoag grinned. "A few calls to the right place, I suppose."

"You think he'll get to take it now?"

"I don't know. We'll see."

They talked and visited for a little while, then a murmur swept over the room. Jenny glanced at Hoag. "What's going on?"

"Just wait." He had a sheepish grin. "You'll see."

A moment later the crowd parted and Jack Hedges appeared. Jenny's mouth fell open. She slapped Hoag playfully on the shoulder. "You didn't tell me the president was going to be here."

"I thought you'd enjoy the surprise."

"I would have worn something else."

"What?"

"I don't know," she laughed. "But something else."

"Have you ever met him?"

"No."

"Would you like to?"

"Well… I suppose. I mean…" She caught the twinkle in his eye. "How could you do this to me?" She laughed and slid her arm in the crook of his elbow.

"I wanted to surprise you." Hoag started forward with Jenny holding his arm. She tugged on it to stop him. Hoag hesitated. "What's wrong?"

"You can just walk up to him?"

Ahead of them, Hedges shook hands with Vic Hamilton and turned to a couple standing at his left. Hoag nudged Jenny forward. "I can now." He looked back over his shoulder and nodded to Kinlaw. The four of them moved in Hedges' direction.

When they were a few feet away, a man in a dark grey suit smiled at Hoag. Jenny leaned closer and whispered. "Who is he?"

"Ben Warren."

"Do I know him?"

"No."

Warren thrust his hand toward Hoag. The two men shook hands. "Ben," Hoag said, greeting him warmly. "How are you tonight?"

"Except for the trouble in California, I'm doing great, David." Warren reached around Hoag to shake hands with Kinlaw. "Dennis. Good to see you." He turned back to Hoag. "We got the clearances for Vic yesterday. Did they tell you?"

"Yes. Thanks for doing that."

"No problem. He and the president have been friends a long time. Thanks for suggesting the trip."

"Will he get to do the dig at the site he wanted?"

"Oh, yeah." Warren nodded. "All lined up. Did the boat work all right?"

"Yes. Worked great. Thanks."

Warren cut his eyes at Jenny then back to Hoag. "Always glad to help out. He saw you from the Oval Office, when you rode through the Tidal Basin around the Jefferson Memorial. Wondered why it was out. I told him they were running it to keep everything working."

Just then Hedges stepped forward. Warren turned to him. "Mr. President, may I present some of our friends." He gestured toward Hoag. "David Hoag and Jenny Freed."

Hedges shook their hands then gave Hoag a pat on the shoulder. "Thanks for helping us with the trip for Vic. Great idea."

"Yes, Mr. President. My pleasure."

Warren stepped aside and gestured toward the Kinlaws. "Mr. President, this is Dennis Kinlaw and his wife, Debby."

Hedges had a tight smile. "Dennis Kinlaw. I've heard great things about you." He turned to Debby. "My wife read your article in *The Washingtonian* last month."

"Thank you, Mr. President. I hope she enjoyed it."

"When she heard you would be here, she asked me to tell you she loved it."

Warren spoke up. "Mr. President, Ms. Freed is Alex Freed's daughter. He was at the dinner in New York last week."

"Yes." Hedges brightened as he turned in Jenny's direction. "We were there with Mickey Milanhour and a group from Black-ledge Capital."

"Yes, sir," Jenny gushed. "My father works with them on their securities offerings."

"Your father is in finance?"

"He's an attorney."

"Which firm?"

"Milbank, Freed & Inge."

"Oh, my. Of course. He's in the thick of it then. I've known Johnny Inge since college."

Another couple stepped up. Hedges turned to speak with them. Warren gave Hoag a nod and moved on. Hoag turned to Kinlaw. "That went well."

"Yes. Rather. I don't know how Ben kept all that straight. We haven't seen them in years."

"I haven't seen him since before the campaign," Debby offered.

Jenny had a blank look on her face. "How did he know my name?"

"You're on the guest list," Hoag said.

"The guest list?"

"You don't think they would let the president attend an event without knowing who's going to be there, do you?"

"I suppose not." Jenny tugged on Hoag's arm. "You should have told me."

"It would've spoiled the fun," Hoag laughed. Jenny grinned at him and squeezed his arm again.

43

SOCHI, RUSSIA

JOSEF MUELLER AND FRANZ HEINRICH boarded a plane in Munich and flew to a small airport outside Sochi, a Russian resort city located on the coast at the eastern end of the Black Sea. Once on the ground, the plane taxied past the public facilities and into a hangar across the runway from the commercial terminal. When the engines shut down and the hangar doors closed, Mueller and Heinrich emerged from the plane and started down the steps. They were met by a small security detail and Vladimir Vostok's chief of staff, Anatolyn Luzhkov. Moving quickly, Luzhkov guided them to a Mercedes sedan parked a few feet from the airplane.

Mueller took a seat in back. Heinrich crawled in beside him. Mueller glanced out the window. "You are certain no one will know we are here?"

"The airplane bears a registration number assigned to Krupp Manufacturing," Heinrich replied. "The car in which we are riding is registered to a wealthy businessman in Moscow." He tapped the window beside him. "The windows are tinted. And we have a limited security detail. We have done all we can to insure secrecy and security."

"Let us hope it is enough."

"I did as you instructed."

Mueller watched out the window. "Where is Luzhkov?"

"He is—"

Just then, the front passenger door opened. Luzhkov leaned in with a smile. "We are ready now." He took a seat up front on the passenger side. "The drive won't take long. Have you been to Sochi before?"

"No," Heinrich answered. "This is our first trip."

"Well then, you should enjoy the scenery." Luzhkov said something to the driver. The car started forward.

Forty-five minutes later they turned into a compound overlooking the water, twenty miles north of the city. The driver steered the car toward a garage located behind the house. As the car approached, a garage door opened. The car rolled quietly into an open stall and came to a stop. While the door closed behind them, Luzhkov leaned over the seat once more. "We will go inside now. The president is awaiting your arrival." An aide opened the car door. Mueller hesitated. Luzhkov nodded. "It is okay. We are safe."

The house, a three-story rambling structure, sat atop a bluff overlooking the Black Sea. Built in the 1990s by Boris Yeltsin, it had been seized in the reactionary economic realignment that followed the end of his reign. Now it was owned by the Russian government and used as a presidential retreat.

Luzhkov led Mueller and Heinrich to a room facing the water. On one side windows stood floor to ceiling and afforded a commanding view of the sea. Nearby was a table with straight-back chairs. On the table was a tray that held a container of crushed ice and four bottles of water. Along the opposite wall, well back from the windows, a sofa and three overstuffed chairs were arranged around a coffee table. Luzhkov turned to Mueller and gestured to a chair at the table near the windows. "You may sit here, Chancellor. President Vostok will be out in a moment." He pointed across the room. "There is a restroom just down the hall, and if you would like, we can arrange for some fruit or cheese. The president was planning to eat a late lunch with you after you have talked."

"Thank you," Mueller replied. "I am fine for now."

"Very well." Luzhkov turned to Heinrich. "Come with me, Franz. I will show you to a room. You may rest while they talk, perhaps take a nap. We will awaken you in time for lunch."

When Luzhkov and Heinrich were gone, Mueller moved to the sofa, out of sight from the windows. He sat down, crossed his legs, and waited. In a few moments, Vostok entered the room. Mueller stood. Vostok embraced him. "Josef, so good to see you."

"Yes," Mueller nodded. "Thank you for accommodating me."

"By all means." Vostok gestured toward the table near the windows. "We could sit over here. The view is marvelous, especially this time of day."

Mueller shook his head. "I prefer the sofa."

"Oh." Vostok had a polite smile. "Very well. The sofa, then." He took a seat at the opposite end and settled into place. "So, Franz Heinrich said you wished to speak to me. He mentioned something about Radinsky. I suppose you have read his book."

"Yes. I was hoping you had as well."

"Interesting, his treatment of Stalin and Hitler. I did not know they had met in person before their incursion into Poland. I assumed emissaries handled their negotiations."

"They dealt with the fate of the world, not unlike what we face today. I suppose it should come as no surprise that they met face-to-face."

"And so, here we are, like Stalin and Hitler. Are we to discuss the fate of Europe?"

"It is far more serious than that." Mueller shifted positions. "Hitler was stupid in the way he prosecuted his war, but he was right about one thing. Europe must determine its own fate."

"You are worried about Iran?"

"I am worried about Iran," Mueller nodded, "but I am more concerned about the Americans."

"Oh?" Sarcasm dripped from Vostok's voice. "Are they not the world's superpower? Insurers of the peace?"

"They act as if the fate of the world rests in their hands, as if we have no say in the matter; yet, they are powerless."

"They do not see themselves as powerless."

"They are blinded by the luxurious life they have lived. A life we and others have financed. And for what purpose?"

Vostok rose from the sofa and walked to the table near the windows. "We buy their bonds so they can purchase our oil." He filled two glasses with ice and water. "In return, they insure a stable environment which enables us to earn more money to buy more of their bonds." Vostok glanced back at Mueller. "Would you care for something stronger than water?"

"No." Mueller shook his head. "Not now." He folded his hands in his lap. "You make my point precisely. When we buy their bonds, we prop them up and facilitate their arrogance. That was fine in the past, but they are no longer capable of providing the stability we need to prosper."

Vostok crossed the room with the glasses and handed one to Mueller, then he returned to his seat at the end of the sofa. "This is nothing we haven't discussed before, Josef. Why the urgency now?"

"Iran's nuclear test has changed things." Mueller took a sip of water. "The Americans will not wait for Iran to develop a nuclear arsenal. They will strike, and the world will be plunged into war."

"Isn't that a rather extreme assessment?"

"China has an army of over two million men. Iran is their primary source of oil. The Middle Eastern countries have no economy except that of oil. United States policy in the Middle East, however, is focused on one thing—Israel. The Americans have become trapped in the Christian-Jewish-Islam conflict. They see this as a religious war and are obsessed with Islam as the villain. Now Iran, with its nuclear capability, will become their primary target. The Americans are free to pursue this policy because they have no economic interest in Iran. They don't buy Iranian oil. The success or failure of Iran means nothing to the American economy. However, it means much to ours and to China's."

"A religious war." Vostok looked over at Mueller. "Aren't all wars religious?"

"They have been. That is why Stalin sought to eliminate religion from Russian culture."

"And he was almost successful." Vostok took another sip of water. "The Chinese are concerned about the Americans?"

"Yes. Very much so."

"You have spoken to them already?"

"They approached me. In Berlin. They are in agreement. We can no longer look to America for our military or economic security."

"What do you propose we do to change the situation?"

"Stop buying American debt obligations."

"Stop buying their bonds?" Vostok had a puzzled look. "Wouldn't that be at least as catastrophic as armed conflict?"

"Only for the United States. The European Union will pump enough liquidity into our economies to make certain there is no European collapse."

"Russia is not a member of the European Union."

Mueller smiled. "We are all Europeans."

"But you do not own much U.S. debt. We and China own quite a lot."

"We do not own many of their bonds. This is true. But we have not much oil either. And Russia is a short distance away."

"And what would Russia receive in return for its cooperation? More access to European markets? You have promised that before."

"Not just European markets," Mueller replied. "But the world." Mueller's eyes sparkled. "The collapsing American economy would neutralize their military power. Russia, the world's largest producer of petroleum, would return to its rightful place as the remaining superpower not the United States."

A smile spread across Vostok's face. "Superpower." He took a loud, deep breath. "It sounds like…destiny."

"Yes," Mueller nodded. "A truly Russian destiny." He gestured with a nod. "And it is all yours, once we have neutralized the Americans." He took a sip from the glass. "We can do that without firing a shot."

44

PORT FACILITY, YEMEN

THE CARGO BAY OF THE *Amazon Cloud* was filled to capacity. The overhead crane fell silent as workmen slid sections of moveable decking over the top and secured it in place. When it was prepared and ready, the foreman signaled the crane operator and loading continued on the main deck.

Turbat Hoshab watched from the dock. His young grandson, Taizz Bajil, stood beside him.

Taizz glanced up, "This is the ship for the Mahdi?"

"It is," Turbat smiled. "But we must not tell anyone."

"I thought the coming of the Mahdi was a great day."

"It is a great day, but we must let him proclaim his own arrival."

"Oh."

Taizz pointed to the ship. "What are those tall things standing up on the ship?"

"Cranes."

"Why doesn't it use them today?"

"The overhead cranes are much faster. They use the cranes on the ship when they are at a port that doesn't have its own." Turbat smiled down at the boy. "You have many questions today."

"Mother says I have many questions all the time."

Turbat chuckled in reply then turned back to watch the loading continue.

In a little while a man appeared at the ship's rail. He leaned over the side, as if looking, then threw up his hand in a wave. Turbat waved back.

Taizz looked up at Turbat once again, "You know him?"

"Yes," Turbat replied. "I know him."

Taizz leaned closer and lowered his voice to a whisper. "Does he want to see the Mahdi too?"

"Yes," Turbat nodded. "He wants to see the Mahdi." He pointed. "Watch the cranes now. They are loading the ship."

"They have been doing that for a long time."

"It takes most of the day to load a big ship like this."

Just then a cargo container moved overhead. Hoisted aloft by the crane, it sailed through the air against the clear blue sky. Even from far below, Turbat could see a small, red, crescent moon in the upper left corner of the door. He watched as the container settled aboard the ship's deck.

Minutes later a second box, a sixty-foot container, came through the air. The crane operator swung it around and lowered it toward the ship. Sirjan Odeh stepped forward to make sure it lined up end-to-end with the previous one. Born in Liverpool, England, Sirjan was the son of Anwar Odeh, a wealthy businessman who made a fortune trading commodities on the London Exchange. Sirjan grew up in the lap of luxury. He wore the best clothes, ate the best foods, attended the finest schools, and enjoyed vacations to the world's most opulent resorts. Anwar, anxious for his son to fit in with traditional English society, eschewed the mosque and had forbidden his wife and son from publicly practicing any form of Islam.

At the age of eighteen, Sirjan visited a cousin in the Wakhan District of northeastern Afghanistan. For three months he was schooled by members of the Taliban in the most radical Deobandi expressions of Islam. When he returned to Liverpool he joined a mosque, adopted traditional Islamic dress, and spent his days reading the Qu'ran. When Mullah Omar agreed to set aside Taliban disagreements with the Shi'a and allowed cooperation with Nasser Hamid, Sirjan had been one of the first to volunteer. Hamid found a job for him with Pakistan Shipping, where his education and motivation gained quick recognition.

When the container was securely in place, Sirjan returned to the rail and gave Turbat a thumbs-up.

Turbat lingered on the dock a moment with Taizz, watching the cranes lift the boxes and place them aboard the ship. After a few minutes he turned away. "Come along." He straightened his karakul. "We should be going."

Taizz ran after him. "Don't you want to see it sail?"

"No." Turbat shook his head. "I am hungry."

The boy's eyes brightened. "We can have some cassatella?"

"I was thinking of something more," Turbat chuckled. "How about couscous?"

"Couscous," Taizz giggled. "It sounds like something you did in your pants."

"Hush. You shouldn't talk that way."

"Couscous," Taizz repeated.

Turbat laughed. "Where do you learn such things?"

"From you," Taizz giggled again. "I learn it from you."

45

RIGGS LIBRARY
GEORGETOWN UNIVERSITY

HOAG STOPPED BY STARBUCKS for a cup of coffee and sipped it as he walked across campus to the Riggs Library. Steam from the coffee rose in the crisp morning air. Every sip felt warm on his cheeks.

As he walked along, he thought of Jenny. Things were different than before, and yet they were also much the same. Their conversations left him tired from talking and always with the nagging feeling that no matter what he said, she would have one more comment to top his. And now, there was the religious issue. *Christianity*. The thought of it made him bristle and left him restless and unsettled. Still, thinking about her made him smile. A grin spread over his face as he saw her in his mind, her brunette hair falling just below her ears, cut at an angle that framed her face perfectly. It looked smart and neat and cute, which was an apt description of more than her hair.

Located not far from the Hall of Cardinals, where he and Jenny had attended Vic Hamilton's reception the night before, the Riggs Library once had been Georgetown's primary library. Now it served as a repository for the school's historical archives and book collections of historic significance.

For days Hoag had been troubled by the symbol with the star and the circle that he had seen on the cargo container in the surveillance video. The crest and star had been used as a symbol for thousands of years, but not quite like the one on the container. In traditional Islam, the two were juxtaposed in a manner that allowed each emblem to retain its distinct identity, never in a way that imposed one on the other. Images on the container had the crest, if that's what it was, all but encircling the star. And the star wasn't the usual five or eight-pointed versions common to Islam. The star on the cargo container had six points, similar to the one used by Israel—and that's what troubled him most.

Though the symbols formed an odd and unusual combination, something else about it was familiar. Not with the Star of David but with another star, a different star. Hoag was sure he had seen something like it somewhere, and though he spent the week thinking about it, he still couldn't remember where. To find the answer, he had decided to return to the beginning, to the text from which Western scholars of the modern era first became acquainted with Islamic life in the Middle East. He had decided to consult the writings of Marco Polo.

When he arrived at the Riggs, Hoag asked the curator for a copy of *The Book of Wonders*, a book purportedly written by Polo around the year 1300 as an account of his travels from Europe to China. Hoag had used the Riggs' collections many times and was a familiar face to the staff, but that morning the curator seemed particularly tense and responded to his request with nervous equivocation. He mumbled and whispered to himself about books and how precious and rare they were, then begrudgingly disappeared into the stacks. While he was gone Hoag took a seat at one of the long, smooth, oak tables in the library's central hall.

A few minutes later the curator returned with a large, crusty volume. He carried it in the crook of his arm like a baby, his free arm wrapped over the top. As he neared the table, Hoag reached up to take it from him.

"No," the curator snapped, and he twisted to one side to avoid Hoag's outstretched arms. Hoag sank back in his chair and rested his hands in his lap. The curator gently set the book on the table and reached into his pocket. "Use these," he said, and handed Hoag a pair of thin cotton gloves. "This is an ancient text and quite fragile. Oil from your fingers would ruin it." Hoag slipped on the gloves and reached for the cover to open it. "Be careful," the curator said curtly. "This is not some common novel."

Hoag glanced up at him. "I'll be careful."

The curator responded with a nervous twitter, as if suddenly aware of how overbearing he had been, then backed away. Hoag turned aside the cover from the book and let his eyes scan the first page. He had been exposed to Polo's account of his travels through a translation prepared by John Frampton during the reign of Queen Elizabeth. An accurate translation, it was, nonetheless, a translation. The version he read that morning in the Riggs was in the original French. In fact, it was a first edition copy.

As Hoag carefully turned the pages, he came to Polo's account of the destruction of a fortress called Alamut in 1256. The fortress, located on a mountaintop north of what was now Tehran, had been home to an Islamic sect known as the Hashshashin—the assassins. Hoag's heart seemed to skip a beat. He had heard of them but had forgotten their story.

The Hashshashin emerged in 1094 when Hassan-i Sabbah established the stronghold at Alamut. They were part of the Nizari, a group within Shi'a Islam more secular than most, who were devoted to science and the arts as a way of establishing an Islamic utopian society. The Fatimid Empire, which ushered in the golden age of Islam, was the result of their effort. The Hashshashin sought to ensure that empire's survival by the careful, strategic murder of those who opposed it.

Hoag was absorbed in study when Kinlaw appeared beside him. He pulled out a chair from the table and scooted up next to Hoag. "Visiting the Kublai Khan?"

"No," Hoag smiled. "Talking to Marco Polo."

"What's he telling you?"

"He's telling me about this."

Hoag lifted a page from his legal pad and slipped out a photo of the cargo container taken from the surveillance video he had seen with Jenny. He pushed it to one side for Kinlaw to see. Kinlaw frowned. "Marco Polo is telling you about containerized cargo?"

"He's telling me about that." Hoag pointed to the symbol on the container door.

Kinlaw's frown became a question. "Looks like a star with a circle around it. What is it?"

"They want you to think it's a circle. Actually, it's a star with a crescent." Hoag pointed to the photo again. "It's open right there. The circle. It doesn't quite close."

"Hmm," Kinlaw mused. "And the star is a Star of David."

"Exactly." Hoag leaned back in his chair. "Do you remember the Hashshashin?"

Kinlaw raised an eyebrow. "Have anything to do with hashish?"

"Not really."

"I didn't think so."

"The Hashshashin was a secret Islamic sect. Around the year 1200."

Kinlaw sat up straight. "Look, I'm sure this is fascinating stuff, but we've got a situation—"

Hoag ignored him and continued. "These guys were the original Fedayeen; sleepers who infiltrated their enemies, operated under deep cover, and struck when least expected."

"And you think they're still around?"

"They lived in a fortress on a mountaintop at Alamut. The ruins are north of Tehran."

"The Lords of Alamut?"

"Exactly," Hoag grinned. "You weren't sleeping in class after all."

"I remember bits and pieces." Kinlaw took a breath. "This is really interesting, but we need to get to the office."

"Why?"

"If you haven't noticed, everyone's a little nervous about the situation in LA, wondering what's coming next. They'd like us to help figure it out."

"Okay, but let me finish. The fortress at Alamut was eventually destroyed, but the Hashshashin lingered on. Several European kings employed their services during the Crusades."

"Sounds like an Islamic version of the Knights Templar."

"Man," Hoag grinned. "You are full of insight this morning."

"I'm good for a flash of brilliance once in a while."

"They eventually faded from public view and were thought to have simply died away, but rumors persisted into the twentieth century that descendants of the original Lords of Alamut remained in the Caucasus Mountains."

"And you think they've come back to finish the job?"

"Look at this." Hoag pushed the copy of Polo's book aside and picked up another book from the table. "This is a copy of a text from the collection at the Institute of Islamic Studies." Hoag opened the book. At the bottom right corner of the page was a picture of a star with a crescent. The points of the crescent were elongated and curved in a more dramatic fashion than normally seen, so much so that they wound around close to the star, almost encircling it.

Kinlaw pointed to the illustration. "That's an eight-pointed star." He pointed back to the photograph from the cargo container. "This one has six."

"Like the Star of David." Hoag paused for effect. "Encircled by a crescent moon."

Kinlaw ran his hand over his face. "Well," he sighed, "I see what you mean. You think this sect still exists?"

"I don't know," Hoag shrugged. "Maybe. Or maybe they just see themselves as the successors to the Hashshashin. Not actually their descendants physically but spiritually."

"And they morphed the symbol to suit their mission."

"Which I think is obvious when you look at the symbol."

"But would anyone be that obvious?"

"I thought about that." Hoag picked up the photograph and laid it in front of him. He pointed to it while he talked. "The message of this symbol is that Islam will devour Judaism, or that Islam will conquer Israel."

"They've been saying that for centuries," Kinlaw offered.

"Which means," Hoag continued, "the symbol is no more obvious than the rhetoric has always been. And, the symbol is ancient. Not many people would recognize it, especially the way they've made the crescent look like a circle."

Kinlaw tapped the photograph with his finger. "Wonder what's in that cargo box?"

"Good question."

"Where's it headed?"

"New York."

"Hmm." Kinlaw studied the photograph a moment. "Where'd you get this picture?"

"Jenny."

Kinlaw grinned. "Debby was glad to see you two together last night."

"That was nice, wasn't it?"

"Yes, it was."

"What did Debby have to say?"

"She's always liked Jenny."

"That was a good evening."

"Bring her to the house on Saturday." Kinlaw pushed his chair away from the table. "We'll cook out or watch a football game or something."

"Okay. I'll check with Jenny."

"I think Debby already talked to her." Kinlaw nudged Hoag on the back. "Hey. We need to get over to the office. They want us to give them something on the situation in California."

Hoag slid his chair back and stood. The curator stepped forward as if he had been waiting for an opportunity to retrieve the book. "You are finished?"

"Yes," Hoag nodded. "Would you like for me to put these away?"

"No," the curator said, shaking his head and waving his hands. "We'll take care of them. Thank you for being so careful."

Hoag followed Kinlaw to the door. As they stepped outside, Kinlaw glanced in his direction. "Still think what's been happening has nothing to do with ancient prophecy?"

"You mean ancient Christian prophecy?"

"Christian. Hebrew."

"Maybe," Hoag replied. "Tell me about it. Details, I mean. Not the belief part."

"I can't," Kinlaw said with a smile. "But I know someone who can."

"Who's that?"

"Vic Hamilton."

"Ah," Hoag smiled. "I should have thought of him myself."

Kinlaw glanced at his watch. "I'm sure he's home right now."

"But don't we have to get back to the office?"

"We could squeeze in a few minutes with him."

46

DENVER, COLORADO

THE MORNING WAS COLD and crisp as Mustafa Bandar arrived at the safe house in the Edgewater section of Denver. He parked out front and crossed the yard to the driveway. As he rounded the corner of the house, the garage came into view. Parked next to it was a blue Ford Explorer. Sedeh was standing at the rear bumper. He started toward Mustafa with a smile. "You are ready?"

"Yes," Mustafa nodded, nervously. "I think so."

Sedeh slipped an arm around Mustafa's shoulder as they continued toward the garage. "You said your prayers?"

"Yes."

"And you are wearing the beads I gave you?" Mustafa reached through the neck of his shirt and pulled them up for him to see. Sedeh smiled. "Good. They will keep you safe through your journey." He guided Mustafa toward the garage door. "Come. It is time for you to go."

As they walked up the driveway, the garage door opened. A black Chevrolet Suburban sat inside. Esfandak stood next to it. Mustafa came to a halt. "Why is he here?"

"To see you off." Sedeh tugged him forward. "Come. It is late."

Reluctantly, Mustafa stepped inside the garage. Esfandak opened the driver's door to the Suburban. Mustafa leaned forward and looked inside. A switch with a button on one end lay on the seat. Wires from it ran through the console. Mustafa pointed. "What is that?"

"We'll show you," Sedeh replied. "Time to get in."

As Mustafa stared at the switch, an uneasy feeling swept over him. "I don't know," he whispered.

"Come on," Sedeh nudged him. "Before it's too late."

Mustafa ducked his head and crawled inside the Suburban. When he was seated behind the steering wheel, Esfandak reached over and clipped the seatbelt in place.

Mustafa looked over at Sedeh. "Are you sure this will work?"

"Yes," Sedeh nodded. "It will work. Start the engine."

Mustafa turned the key. The engine sputtered at first, then it idled smoothly. Esfandak reached across to the console and picked up the switch. He placed it in Mustafa's left hand.

"Press this down," he said, pointing to a small button protruding from the end of the device. Mustafa pushed it down with his thumb. "Hold it there," Esfandak said, "and don't let go."

"Why?"

Esfandak pulled a pin from the bottom of the device. He leaned away and pointed to Mustafa's hand. "When you are ready to detonate, just slide your thumb from the button."

"You mean—"

"No," Esfandak snapped. "Not here. It will blow up." He stepped back from the driver's door.

Sedeh leaned close. "Allah will greet you. All of your brothers will salute your courage."

Mustafa's eyes darted toward Sedeh. "You are sure it will work?"

"I am certain. We will be watching to make sure." A frown wrinkled Mustafa's forehead. Sedeh pushed the door closed.

———— (((————

Twenty minutes later Mustafa steered the Suburban from the street into the driveway at Creekside Elementary School. A long line of cars filled the drive ahead of him. Children trudged up the sidewalk to the building, each with a backpack and a lunch box. The girls were all dressed in the same uniform, a blue jumper with a white shirt and saddle oxford shoes. The boys wore khaki pants and white shirts. Mustafa turned away and looked out the window. Across the street the blue Explorer was parked at the curb. Sedeh sat behind the steering wheel.

The cars in the driveway inched forward. Mustafa pressed the gas pedal and eased the Suburban up a few spaces. His heart raced. His palms were sweaty. The hand that gripped the trigger felt tired and cramped.

A few minutes later, he reached the drop-off point. A woman stepped up to open the passenger door. It was locked, and he watched her chuckle to herself as she tugged at it. With a curious look she tapped on the window then peered in to see the trigger in Mustafa's hand.

Mustafa turned the steering wheel hard to the left. The belt on the power steering unit squeaked. The Suburban jerked forward.

Just then, glass in the driver's window shattered. Pain knifed across Mustafa's head, passing from left to right. Blood spewed from his skull, filling the air with a warm, red mist. His right hand snapped back from the steering wheel. His left hand collapsed at his side. The trigger clanked against the bottom of the door as fire filled the passenger compartment. Mustafa felt his body hurdled upward toward the roof of the Suburban, then his world went dark.

47

GEORGETOWN, WASHINGTON, D.C.

KINLAW AND HOAG ARRIVED at Vic Hamilton's house a little before ten in the morning. They were greeted at the door by Hamilton's wife Shirley. She led them through the house to the kitchen, where they found Hamilton sitting at a table in the breakfast nook, dressed in pajamas and robe. He glanced up from a cup of hot tea as they entered.

"I hear you two have been busy lately."

"A little," Kinlaw replied. "Nice reception."

"Yes, it was." Hamilton took a sip of tea. He gestured with his cup. "Thank you. I appreciate your help in getting me on to the next phase of my life." His eyes were full. "And in making one of my dreams come true."

"Glad we could help." Kinlaw pointed with his thumb toward Hoag. "David did most of the work. I just recruited the president."

"Well, I thank you both." Hamilton gestured to the chairs that sat around the table. "Have a seat. Care for some tea?"

"I'd love a cup," Hoag nodded.

Shirley brought cups to the table and filled them with tea from a porcelain teapot. Conversation at the table turned to friends and colleagues they had seen the night before. While they talked, Shirley brought out a box of doughnuts and a plate of leftover coffee cake. When everything was set, she retreated from the room, leaving them alone to talk.

"So," Hamilton looked at Kinlaw. "I don't suppose you two came by to discuss my pending trip to Israel." A worried look came over him. "It's still on, isn't it?"

"Yes. It's still on."

"Then what did you want to talk about?"

Kinlaw cleared his throat. "Prophecy. We wanted to talk about prophecy."

"Prophecy?" Hamilton grimaced. "You want to talk about—" His eyebrows rose in a sudden look of realization. "Oh. You think these events we've been experiencing—Iran and the explosions in LA—you think they have some connection to prophecy?"

"The thought occurred to us."

"It occurred to them," Hoag said, pointing to Kinlaw. "He and Jenny Freed brought it up."

Hamilton smiled at Hoag. "Jenny looked rather elegant last night. I was glad to see her. You two make a nice couple."

"Yes," Hoag nodded. "She's..." He struggled to find the words. "She—"

"Relax," Hamilton laughed. "I'm not prying into your personal life. What did you want to know?"

"They kept pestering me with all this 'end of the world' talk, so I figured I ought to get some details."

"Details?"

"Yes."

"What details would you like to know? What are we talking about here? Hebrew prophets or New Testament?" Hamilton took a sip of tea. "Where would you like to begin?"

Hoag shrugged. "Pick a spot."

"Well, if you talk about prophecy, the first question one would raise is that of validity. Is it true? Did the prophets of old hear an accurate message? That's where they would have begun. Was it true? Their lives depended upon the answer to that question." He took another sip of tea. "Literally."

Hoag frowned. "What do you mean?"

"They didn't look at things like we do today. Today, if you say something's going to happen and it doesn't, everyone just laughs at you. Wasn't like that three thousand years ago. If the prophet said, 'Thus says the Lord,' and what he said didn't come to pass, he was a heretic and a blasphemer, which carried the death penalty."

"I assume the ones in the Bible weren't executed." Hoag took a bite of coffee cake.

"Not for prophesying falsely. Several of them faced the real possibility of death for being correct, but not for being wrong."

"So, what they said turned out to be true."

"Yes. Jeremiah prophesied about captivity. Israel was attacked and most of its citizens were carried away to Babylon. Daniel told about the fall of Babylon, the rise of the Syrians and then the Greeks and Romans, even the coming of Christ and the fall of Rome—and he was right on target. Zechariah talked about the return of Israel from exile, and they came back."

"Okay. Here's my problem. All of that looks backward. I mean, the prophets didn't look backward, but we look backward with the benefit of knowing what happened. But prophecies about the end of time look forward. They haven't happened yet. How can we know they are true if they haven't happened?"

Hamilton reached to a stack of books on the end of the table and took out a Bible. He opened it to the book of Revelation. "People who talk about this stuff in popular circles don't really think of it in big enough terms. They concentrate on the individual details of each thing. Each piece. And they try to parse out the imagery and say, 'This is an airplane,' or, 'This is an atomic bomb.' You can't do that. Ancient prophecy was too strategic for that."

"Strategic?"

"Yes, strategic. When Daniel spoke to Nebuchadnezzar about what God was saying, he didn't get all caught up in the details of the cloak the king was wearing or how long his hair would be or what kind of grass he would eat. He—"

"What kind of grass?" Hoag interrupted. "What are you talking about?"

"Daniel told Nebuchadnezzar that he would go crazy and wander around like a madman, eating grass like the cattle until he realized that 'God rules the kingdoms of man, and sets over them whomever he wills.' The point wasn't in the details. The details were just there to paint a picture. The picture was the point." Hamilton took a bite of doughnut.

"So, what does that have to do with Revelation?"

"Prophecy took a broad view of history and events." Hamilton turned to the beginning of Revelation. "Look at these first three chapters. These are arranged as letters to seven churches in the Roman province of Asia. That's Turkey now. Those letters issue a pending judgment. The language is figurative—lamps for the churches and swords for words of judgment, that sort of thing, but the message is clear. 'Do what I say, repent, return to me, or I'll take away your lamp.' He's saying, 'Do what I say or else I'll wipe you out.'"

"Okay," Hoag shrugged. "But how is that strategic?"

Hamilton leaned forward and lowered his voice. "None of those churches exist anymore. They're all gone."

"All of them?"

"Christians were deported from Turkey following World War I."

"Okay."

"Turkey is almost completely Islamic. They have a secular government… they try to have a secular government, but they are Islamic to the core. And when they reached the tipping point, when they gained the ability to move the Christians out, they did it. Look at a map. From Turkey, at the western edge of the Asian continent, all the way across, not a single country remains that is predominantly Christian. In spite of all the missionaries and all the years of work, the entire continent has gone over to non-Christian religions."

"Interesting."

"If you want to talk about details, how prophecy might coincide with events today, you have to begin with the fact that none of the seven churches in Revelation exists today." Hamilton leaned back. "They were removed by force in one of the biggest repatriations in the history of mankind. Greeks living in Turkey were sent back to Greece. Turks living in Greece were sent back to Turkey. And the way they decided if you were Greek or not was to determine whether you were Christian. If you were Christian, you were deported to Greece."

"You sure about this?"

Hamilton nodded. "Treaty of Lausanne. 1923. When they signed that treaty, human history moved beyond the third chapter of Revelation."

"I don't know." Hoag shoved his hands in his pockets. "That's a pretty bold statement."

Hamilton leaned forward. "You want some more?" Without waiting for an answer he turned a few pages and pointed to another spot in the text. "Here. The destruction of a third of the Earth—fresh water, plants, sea life, ships, and the darkening of one-third of the sun. It sounds like a cataclysmic event, doesn't it?"

"Yes," Hoag shrugged. "I suppose."

"What if it's already happened?"

"Already happened?" Hoag frowned. "How do you put out a third of the sun?"

"Think about this." Hamilton tapped his finger against the page. "Pollution, industrialization, and concentration of human waste have taken their toll on fresh water. Over a third of it's undrinkable. Potable water in Asia is a scarce commodity and getting scarcer. A third of the sea life is already gone." Hamilton paused to refill his tea cup. "I'm not making this stuff up. There are reports everywhere about the decline of sea life. And let me say this—no one in the Church is talking about prophecy this way."

"Why not?"

"They seem to prefer the sensational approach."

"What about the plant life, though? We haven't lost a third of the plant life."

"Right now, a third of the world is experiencing a drought. Areas that were once arable are no longer capable of supporting any vegetation at all. Smog blocks out a third of the sunlight for many of our cities. Light pollution takes out a third of the stars, or more."

Hoag had a curious look. "Okay, what about the Rapture? Has it already occurred?"

"You shouldn't get hung up on this." Hamilton shook his head. "Scripture doesn't use the word 'Rapture.'"

"But everyone talks about it."

Hamilton turned a few pages in the Bible. "Prophecy describes the end of time in terms of a horrible conflict, but there isn't any place in Scripture that explicitly says Christians won't be around to face that trouble. It's implied in a few places but not explicitly stated."

"So, no one knows for sure?"

"No one knows exactly when the end will come. But look here." He pointed to a place in Revelation. "In chapter seven John describes a large crowd gathered in Heaven. 'These are they who have come out of the great tribulation.' The tribulation he's talking about doesn't happen until two chapters later. So, if these people are already assembled in Heaven when the tribulation occurs, they must have been taken away earlier." Hamilton closed the book. "Hints like that are why people think there's going to be a Rapture, a time when believers are taken away."

"Hints." Hoag frowned. "All we have are hints?"

"These are prophecies, David. Ancient prophecies. An exact meaning, with scientific certainty, isn't always possible. It's like over-hearing a conversation from two thousand years ago. It's not like reading a self-help manual." Hamilton smiled. "But if you're here when it happens, you'll know it. Won't be any mistake about it."

"What do you mean?"

"Eighty percent of Americans claim to be Christian. If only half of them really are, that would be four out of ten people. Gone."

"Gone."

"Vanished. Taken in a moment. Driving a car. Flying a plane. Taking a shower. Gone."

"There'd be cars and trucks crashing everywhere."

Hamilton nodded. "Planes falling from the sky. A clerk hand-ing you change in a store, disappearing before the coins reach your hand."

"It would really happen like that?"

"I don't know," Hamilton shrugged. "But it could."

Hoag sighed. "What about the Four Horsemen of the Apocalypse?"

Hamilton reached for his Bible again.

48

WASHINGTON, D.C.

HOAG AND KINLAW LEFT Vic Hamilton's house and drove toward the Georgetown campus. Hoag sat quietly leaning against the passenger door, lost in thought. He recounted what Hamilton had told them, and for the first time in his life gave serious consideration to the notion that what he had heard just might be true. When they reached the office he sat at his desk, propped his feet on it, and rocked his chair back as far as it would go. He stared up at the ceiling, trying to assimilate what Hamilton had said.

A few minutes later Kinlaw entered. "Vic Hamilton is an interesting guy."

"I have never heard Bible prophecies discussed like that." Hoag glanced at Kinlaw. "Most of the time, it's a lot of cliché stuff about nothing. What he said actually made sense."

"Well," Kinlaw sighed, "we have to get back to work."

"I thought that was work."

"It was. But Winston wants to know if we have anything on Nasser Hamid." Kinlaw took a seat across from the desk. "I'd rather talk about the Hashshashin and ancient symbols and the deportation of Christians from Turkey, but I guess we better think some about Hamid."

"Nasser Hamid is also an intriguing guy," Hoag sighed. "He just doesn't have the heft of the Lords of Alamut or seven lampstands—or even Vic Hamilton."

Kinlaw slouched in the chair. "I'm wondering if Nasser Hamid is really a person."

"What do you mean?"

"I mean, is he real, or is he merely a carefully created figment of the Iranian government's imagination?"

"Interesting angle. But if he isn't real, then who is the guy in the photograph, and why is the FBI interested enough to have someone follow him?"

"I don't know," Kinlaw shrugged. "Just a thought." He looked up a moment later. "How do we know the photograph came from the FBI?"

"Jenny told us."

"No," Kinlaw corrected. "She told us what Winston told us—the FBI gave it to him. But how do we know it was actually taken by the FBI?"

"And your point is?"

"Maybe the photograph wasn't taken by the FBI."

"Who would have taken it?"

"I don't know."

"Is it possible Hamid is the missing link?"

"What missing link?"

"The logistics mastermind we could never find after the 9-11 attacks."

"I thought we found him." Kinlaw shifted positions in the chair. "Muhammad what's-his-name."

"Atta?"

"Yeah."

"Muhammad Atta wired some money to a couple of his buddies and picked out a couple of flight schools." Hoag rested his hands on this lap. "That attack wasn't a logistics problem. All he had to do was keep their credit cards working. What we didn't find was the person who kept the money flowing to Atta."

"I thought all of that came from the Saudis."

"So did everyone else. But what if it didn't? What if it came from the Iranians, only they made it look like it came from the Saudis?"

"Nah," Kinlaw said, dismissing the suggestion with a wave of the hand. "I don't think so. They're on opposite sides of the Muslim world. The Sunnis bomb Shi'a mosques. They don't even hit Christian churches, but they blow up Shi'a mosques. That's how much they hate each other."

"That's how much they want us to believe they hate each other."

Kinlaw sat up straight. "You're getting a little far out there, aren't you?"

"Maybe." Hoag raised an eyebrow. "But if I'm right, I'm really right."

"Back to Nasser Hamid. I think we should flag his passport."

"For entry into the U.S.? You think he's coming here?"

"No. Ask Interpol to flag it. Don't stop him, just let us know where he's been."

"Not a bad idea." Hoag moved his feet to the floor and rocked forward toward his desk. He pressed a key on the keyboard and entered a command. A new screen appeared. Within minutes the request to Interpol was on its way. "This should have been done before." He looked at Kinlaw with a new realization. "What if the FBI already flagged him with Interpol?"

"I don't think Interpol will tell them. They already know we're asking about him. They knew that when Winston sent the request for those files."

"We should have heard from them on that by now."

Beverly, their assistant, entered the room. "You guys need to turn on the TV." She took a remote from the corner of Hoag's desk, pointed it toward a television on the opposite wall, and pressed a button. An image of a burning building flashed on the screen.

Kinlaw turned to look at the screen. "What is that? Is that in LA?"

"Denver," Beverly replied. "Truck bomb went off at a school."

"A school?"

"Yes." Beverly placed her hands on her hips. "Actually, it was a Chevy Suburban. Blew up in the morning drop-off line."

"Drop-off line?"

"Kids," Beverly snapped. "Where they drop off the kids."

"Why?"

"No one knows."

"What's the FBI saying?"

"Nothing, yet." Beverly shook her head. "But word is, the guy behind the wheel of the Suburban was already dead."

"Already dead?"

Beverly nodded. "Shot in the head."

Kinlaw ran his hands over his face. "So much for Nasser Hamid."

"Why?" Hoag frowned. "What are you talking about?"

"Nobody's gonna be interested in the Iranian angle now. Winston will call in a few minutes and want us to get into this." Kinlaw pointed toward the television. "White House will be all over him for an answer."

Hoag looked up at Beverly. "Did they recover a body from the Suburban?"

"Somewhat," she scowled. "Why?"

"Would be helpful to confirm how he died."

Kinlaw glanced at Hoag, "Still think Al-Qa'ida isn't behind this?"

"They're bad, but this is a diversion."

"Pretty serious diversion."

While Hoag and Kinlaw watched the television, a courier arrived. Beverly met him in the outer office and returned with a manila envelope. "Something from New York." She offered the envelope to Kinlaw. "Looks like it's from the FBI." Kinlaw took the envelope and opened it.

Hoag glanced over at him. "Anything interesting?"

"FBI response to our request."

"What do they have?"

"Everything."

"Good." Hoag's face brightened. "Where is it?"

"They won't say." Kinlaw tossed the memo on the desk.

Hoag read it quickly. "This says they don't have anything. I know they have information on two of those guys. I checked our own database. They provided it last year on a DCI investigation. They sent it to us without question."

"Yeah," Kinlaw nodded. "I know." He pointed. "Look who wrote the memo."

Hoag glanced back at the top line. "Russell Cooper." He leaned back in the chair. "Why did Cooper send the reply to you?"

Kinlaw grinned. "Because he knew if he sent it to you, you'd just throw it in the trash." He reached across the desk and picked up the memo. "But if he sent it to me, I'd come to New York so he could tell me what they have." Kinlaw stuck the memo in his legal pad. "You never really got along with him, did you?"

"Ahh… I don't know." Hoag glanced away. "I think that went both ways."

They fell silent for a moment, then Kinlaw tossed his pen on the desk. "Somebody on that list was a hit with the FBI."

"Yeah." Hoag leaned back in his chair and placed his hands behind his head. "But which one?"

"We need to go to New York. Maybe Russell will tell us."

"Both of us?"

"Yes. Both of us. Why wouldn't you go?"

"I don't know," Hoag shrugged. "He's your friend."

"If we're gonna get into this, we both need to be there."

"I guess."

"We can go up in the morning and come back the same day."

"That quick?"

"Yeah."

"Then you could go by yourself."

"If I go by myself, you'll have one more question that you want answered that I didn't think to ask." Kinlaw stood. "We'll go in the morning."

"Where are you going now?"

"To get something to drink. Keep an eye on the television. We'll probably get a call from somebody on it." Kinlaw stepped through the doorway.

Hoag shouted after him. "That's the FBI's problem."

"I think it's going to be everyone's problem before it's over. I'm gonna get us something for lunch."

49

CHICAGO

SHAIR KASHAN LEANED to the left and gazed from the back seat through the front windshield of the Chevy sedan. Across the road a tanker truck sat at a loading dock. Atop the tank the driver disconnected the transfer pipe and raised it away from the truck.

"Is that the one?"

"Yes." Sabzevar was seated behind the steering wheel. He glanced over his shoulder and nodded. "That's the one."

"He is finished?"

Sabzevar nodded once more. "I think so."

Seated beside Kashan was Farah Shinad. They had been roommates since first arriving in Chicago. Kashan nudged Shinad. "Are you still with me?"

"I am with you," Shinad replied.

The tanker truck pulled away from the loading dock and rolled toward the gate, where it turned onto Algonquin Road. As it drove east, toward town, Sabzevar put the car in gear and followed at an inconspicuous distance. At Elmhurst Road the truck pulled into the parking lot at Jiffy Stop, a convenience store with an overhead canopy and pumps on either side of the building. Sabzevar brought the car to a stop at the traffic light. Kashan and Shinad watched out the side window.

"You sure he's making a delivery?"

"Yes," Sabzevar answered. "He does this every three days. He goes here and to the station on Echo Road and to the one on Fifth Street."

"And then back to the terminal?"

"Yes."

The traffic light was green. Sabzevar turned the car to the right. Kashan craned his head around to see out the back. "How long does it take for him to finish here?"

"About twenty minutes. Not more than half an hour."

A little way from the corner, Sabzevar turned into the parking lot at a shopping center behind the Jiffy Stop. He steered the car into a space that gave them a clear view of the truck and waited. Kashan leaned back against the seat. Shinad propped his head against the window and closed his eyes.

"Tell me again why we need him to empty some of his tank?"

"Vapors," Kashan replied. "We need vapors in the tank. The more vapors, the bigger the explosion."

"Okay," Shinad shrugged. "Whatever you say." He folded his arms across his chest and seemed to relax.

Twenty minutes later Sabzevar spoke up. "He's finished." Kashan and Shinad sat up straight. Sabzevar glanced at them in the rearview mirror. "Ready?"

"Yeah," Kashan sighed. He ran his hands over his face. "We're ready."

Shinad picked up a canvas backpack from the floor and drew a wooden club from it. About two feet in length, the club was fashioned from a baseball bat. He checked his grip around it, then stuffed it back in the bag and zipped it closed. As the car swung around toward the street, Shinad slipped the backpack over his left shoulder.

Sabzevar drove to the Jiffy Stop, sped past the gas pumps, and screeched to a stop near the tanker truck. Kashan and Shinad jumped from the car and ran toward the truck. Before the driver could react, they climbed aboard the cab and jerked open the doors. Kashan pummeled the driver with his fists while Shinad tugged him over to the passenger seat. Kashan pushed him over the center console, climbed in behind the steering wheel, and moved the truck forward.

As Kashan wrestled with the truck, Shinad wrestled the driver to the floor of the cab. Holding him with one hand, he struck him hard in the back of the head with the wooden club. The driver was knocked unconscious.

A woman darted from a car near the gas pumps and ran toward the store. Kashan steered the truck across the parking lot and swung the trailer wide to make a right turn.

Shinad glanced up and watched her through the mirror. "That lady saw us."

"Sabzavar will take care of it."

"What's he gonna do?"

"I don't know, but that's his job." Kashan shifted gears. The truck picked up speed.

They continued down Algonquin Road, moving east. Thirty minutes later they reached the on-ramp to the Eisenhower Expressway. Kashan pulled the truck to the side of the road and brought it to a stop. Shinad stepped from the cab with the backpack. Standing near the midpoint of the trailer, he took a one-pound package of C-4 explosive and pressed it into the space between the top of the valve rack and the side of the tank. With the explosive securely in place, he inserted a detonator and wired it to a timer. He set the timer for twenty-five minutes and pressed a button. Numbers on a display began to slowly tick past as he hurried back to the cab.

"It's ready." Shinad looked grim. "But we only have twenty-five minutes, so let's get rolling."

"Don't want to get there too early," Kashan grinned as he put the truck in gear.

The engine whined as the truck climbed up the on-ramp and onto the expressway. Kashan checked the rearview mirrors. No one seemed to be following. Fifteen minutes later they reached downtown near the lake. Kashan eased the truck to the right and started down the off-ramp toward the loop. As they neared street level, Kashan moved the truck to the left lane.

At State Street, they made a left. Kashan downshifted and kept rolling. Three blocks later, they turned left again, this time onto Adams Street. Narrower and more crowded, maneuvering the truck brought confused stares and puzzled looks from pedestrians on the sidewalk.

"We should have thought about this," Kashan growled. "These streets are narrow."

"Keep going," Shinad shouted. "We're almost out of time."

The truck jerked forward. Kashan moved the shift lever to the left and found a lower gear. The truck idled slowly down the street. At La Salle Street he swung the trailer wide and cut across two lanes of traffic to make the final left turn.

"Police," Shinad shouted.

Kashan glanced in the mirror to see a police car behind them, blue lights flashing, siren squawking. He downshifted once more and pressed the gas pedal. Smoke poured from the exhaust stacks. The engine whined. The truck picked up speed. In the middle of the block Kashan shifted gears then shifted again. The speedometer reached forty miles per hour. He shifted once more. The speedometer read fifty.

"Allah will be pleased!" Kashan shouted. He steered the truck into the left lane around a slower car and shifted one last time. The speedometer reached sixty. Street signs for Jackson Avenue flashed past. The Chicago Board of Trade loomed straight ahead.

"It is time!" Shinad shouted. "It should have blown by now!"

"We can't stop now!"

The front wheels of the cab jumped the curb. The force of the collision jerked Kashan's hands free of the steering wheel. His head banged against the rear wall of the cab. Still, his foot pressed the accelerator pedal to the floor. Glass and metal flew through the air as the truck plowed into the building, the chrome bumper shoving desks and chairs ahead of it. A woman screamed. Another went sailing to the right into the wall as the truck ground to a halt. Dust filled the air. The smell of diesel fumes hung thick around them. Steam boiled from the front of the truck.

Groggy and stunned, Kashan looked over at Shinad. "We have failed the Mahdi," he gasped.

Shinad, blood streaming from a cut to his face, struggled to open the door. "We will never fail," he grinned. "I told you it would work, even if I had to light the match myself."

Behind them sirens wailed as police cars filled the street. A fire truck rumbled to a stop. Policemen scrambled in every direction, yelling and shouting for people to stay back. The smell of gasoline filled the air. Kashan smiled.

"The tank has ruptured," he whispered. "Allah will—"

Suddenly, scorching heat burst through the cab. Kashan felt himself launched from the seat. Pain shot through the top of his head as he collided with the roof of the truck. He felt it bend and rip apart, slicing through his skull. Then he was surrounded by flame and heat and...

50

WASHINGTON, D.C.

WHEN KINLAW RETURNED WITH LUNCH, the television in Hoag's office showed images from Chicago. They both stared at the screen and watched as the smoke and fire poured from the Chicago Board of Trade building. A graphic box in the lower right corner of the screen showed the New York stock market was in a free fall.

"It doesn't look too bad," Kinlaw said. "Have they halted trading?"

"CBOT did. Market's down 1500 points."

"Which market? New York?"

"Yeah," Hoag pointed. "Look at the bottom of the screen."

The telephone rang. Hoag answered. The caller was Winston Smith.

"You watching this?"

"Yes, sir."

"Kinlaw with you?"

"Yes."

"Good. I want one of you to go to Chicago. The other to LA. Leave immediately. I'll get a plane for you."

Winston ended the call without waiting for a response. Kinlaw looked over at Hoag. "Who was that?"

"Winston."

"I told you he'd be calling. Surprised it took him this long. What did he want?"

Hoag had a mischievous smile. "Wants you to go to LA."

"Not me." Kinlaw shook his head. "I hate that town." He caught the look in Hoag's eye. "What are you grinning about? I thought we were going to New York."

"Plans change."

Kinlaw frowned. "He wants somebody to hang out with the FBI while they conduct their investigation?"

"Yeah," Hoag shrugged. "I guess."

"Don't we already have people in LA and Chicago?"

"Yes," Hoag nodded. "Plenty of them."

"Good. Let them handle it."

"What do we tell Winston?"

"He'll think of it in a minute and call us back."

"He's getting us a plane," Hoag smiled.

"Think we can get them to take us to New York first?"

"I don't think they'll listen to us. They usually get their flight plan from—"

The telephone rang, interrupting him. Winston Smith began talking as soon as Hoag picked up. "Kittrell's asking about Nasser Hamid. Thinks it has something to do with all this. You two got anything on him?"

"How does he know about Hamid?"

"FBI probably told him just to burn him as a lead for us," Winston growled. "You got anything?"

"We're working on it," Hoag said.

"Work faster. I need a briefing paper tonight."

"I thought we were going to LA and Chicago."

"Not now," Winston snapped. "We have people in LA and Chicago. I'll give it to them. Get me something on Hamid."

The call ended as abruptly as before. Hoag hung up the phone and smiled over at Kinlaw. "You were right."

"Winston?"

Hoag nodded. "Scratch that trip to LA."

"Good. I wasn't going there anyway. You were."

"And where were you going?"

"Chicago. What's he want now?"

"A briefing paper on Nasser Hamid."

Kinlaw scowled. "We don't have anything on him."

"Good reason to go to New York."

"We could leave now, but we'd have to spend the night."

"Think we could get a hotel room this late?"

"Have Beverly get to work on it while we travel." Kinlaw glanced at his watch. "We can catch a shuttle flight if we hurry."

51

NEW YORK CITY

LATE THAT AFTERNOON Kinlaw stepped from the 86th Street cross-town bus and rounded the corner onto Central Park West in New York City. Up the block a little way, he came to a bench. He took a seat and waited.

In a few minutes Russell Cooper appeared, loping up the sidewalk. He nonchalantly sat next to Kinlaw. "I see you found the place," he began.

"I've been here before."

"Yeah. How well I know. Where's Hoag?"

"Starlight Diner."

"You guys staying on that side of town tonight?"

"No," Kinlaw replied. "David just likes the food."

"How long are you staying?"

"We were hoping we could see you and get back tonight."

"I don't think that will work."

Kinlaw propped his elbow on the bench. "What's this all about, Russell?"

"I'm not really sure. I don't even know why Lansing told me to respond to your request."

"Lansing?"

"David Lansing. In charge of the office now."

"You still doing the same thing you were before? All that forensic computer stuff you were talking about?"

"Yeah."

"But he gave you the job of responding to our request."

"Yeah. Not really my job to respond to memos. I mean, I don't mind sending you a memo, but I spend all my time data mining computer files not pushing paper."

Kinlaw wasn't sure he was supposed to admit knowing Lansing. He decided to play ignorant. "When did this Lansing guy arrive?"

"He's been around a year or two. Don't you know him?"

"Maybe."

"He's head of COINTEL now. Nice enough guy. But this thing about responding to the memo and all that... I don't know why he did that."

Kinlaw looked up as a bus passed on the street a few feet away. "I know you have information on some of those guys. You sent it to me last year on that Libya thing. So I figure one or two of the people on that list hit a nerve with someone." Kinlaw looked over at Cooper. "You want to tell me about them, or would you rather I guess?"

A hotdog vendor was located near the next corner. Russell pointed in that direction. "You want a hot dog?"

"Sure," Kinlaw nodded. "A hot dog would be great."

They bought a hot dog at the corner and wandered into the park.

"Okay," Cooper said as he took the last bite. "It's true. We have files on the people you're interested in."

"So, what's the problem?"

"We have a major operation going on with one of them."

"Which one?"

"Nabhi Osmani."

"So, why not give us what you have on everyone else?"

"I knew you'd come up here."

"Something else going on?"

"I don't know," Cooper sighed. "The whole thing just struck me as odd. Lansing hasn't been here that long, but he knows what I do, and it doesn't involve this kind of thing. I don't have my own cases. I do a particular thing, and it doesn't involve responding to requests from other agencies." He looked over at Kinlaw. "Struck me as odd."

"Odd like interesting, or odd like there's more to it?"

"Odd like out of place, and made me wonder why."

A jogger passed. Then a woman with a dog. When they were gone, Kinlaw continued. "So what about Osmani?"

"Interesting guy. Born in Iran. Left home to join bin Laden in Afghanistan. Bin Laden sent him to school. Set him up in the shipping business. Pakistan Shipping. Started with one leased ship. Now he's a player in the containerized cargo business."

"Intermodal," Kinlaw offered. "Dry cargo."

"Yeah," Cooper nodded. "Inter-whatever. I don't know much about it, but whatever it is, Osmani is successful. Has an office in Karachi. Ten or fifteen of his own ships."

"Container ships."

"Right."

Kinlaw shoved his hands in his pockets. "I know all this from the business reports. What's the FBI's interest in him?"

"He made contact with one of our operatives while on a trip to India. They've continued to work him and think he's about to tell them something big."

"Aren't contacts like that always about to tell us something big?"

"Yes. But this guy is too good to walk away from. He's just one step from Osama bin Laden."

"We don't want you to walk away from him. Why not let us in on the operation?"

Cooper gave him a sarcastic grin. "Dennis, you and I both know that once you guys get involved, everybody stops talking. What you did in Iraq, the water-boarding and Abu Ghraib, rendition and the freelancing that went on in other places, that stuff did you no good. They don't like it that your guys turned their friends over to some sick, third-world interrogator, then watched to see what happened."

"Water-boarding was way overblown."

"Maybe so. But in the Islamic world 'creative interrogation' cost us whatever limited credibility we had. If Osmani finds out the CIA is involved, he'll run."

"Where are his ships?"

"All over."

"You've been watching this guy for how long, and you don't know where his ships are?"

"*Panama Clipper* sailed from Bremerhaven about a week ago, I think. The *Amazon Cloud* sailed from Yemen about ten days ago, passed through the Suez Canal, and cleared Gibraltar last week. The *Santiago* is in China. I'm not sure about the others. We have them all plotted and tracked at the office." Cooper stopped and turned to face Kinlaw. "Like I said, I don't really have cases. This is not my case. What I know about it I know from researching enough to write that memo to you. This response should have been given to someone actually assigned to the case. I can get it for you, but I don't work on this stuff regularly."

"Who's working with Osmani?"

"Our office in Mumbai is handling it. They have the lead. Lansing knows about it because he's in charge of COINTEL. We have a guy in the office who works as sort of a liaison on the deal, but he doesn't know much more than I do."

"Interesting."

Cooper glanced over at him. "That's what I've been telling you."

"These attacks, the ones in LA, Denver, Chicago, they're all related?"

"Looks like it."

"Any kind of connection to Iran's nuclear test?"

"Maybe. But Iran is Shi'a. Everyone else is Sunni. Most of what they've found about these attacks indicates the people behind them are connected with Al-Qa'ida. Them cooperating with Iran would be like Catholics and Baptists getting together for Holy Communion. It just ain't gonna happen."

"I don't think there's such a great divide between them. Especially when it comes to us."

"Maybe not." Cooper sat on a bench. "How's Hoag?"

"He's all right," Kinlaw sat beside him.

"That guy always found a way to get on my nerves."

"I know," Kinlaw chuckled.

"How can you work with him?"

"I like him. I don't know what it was between you two, but he's great to work with. Does his job. Complains, but then he gets busy." Kinlaw turned sideways, facing Cooper. "What do you have on Nasser Hamid?"

Cooper looked away. "I'm not familiar with him."

Kinlaw reached inside his jacket and took out the photograph of Hamid. He laid it on the bench between them. "Ever seen this?"

Cooper glanced at it, then looked quickly away. "Put that back in your pocket," he snapped.

Kinlaw grinned. "I thought you didn't know about him."

"Put it in your pocket."

"Tell me about him."

Cooper grabbed the photograph and shoved it against Kinlaw's chest. "Put it away, Dennis. I'm not kidding."

Kinlaw stuck the photo in his pocket. "We know the FBI's been following him. And we know that photograph was taken by one of your guys outside Nabhi Osmani's building in Karachi."

"How'd you get it?"

"Ahh…" Kinlaw shrugged. "You know. We have our sources."

"You're spying on us too?"

"Why was the FBI following Hamid?"

"I don't know."

"How long are you going to keep up this façade of ignorance?" Kinlaw chuckled. "You know everything that comes through the New York office. And nothing goes anywhere without coming through New York."

Cooper smiled. "You make a good point."

52

ATLANTA AIRPORT

WHILE KINLAW AND COOPER talked in New York, Don Naman sat in the air traffic control tower in Atlanta, watching a radar screen. Blips and dots scattered across the screen identified hundreds of aircraft as they entered and departed the airspace around Atlanta's Hartsfield International Airport. A new blip flashed as a Boeing 747 backed away from the gate on Concourse C.

The 747 lumbered across the apron near the concourse and rolled toward the runway. At the taxiway marker, it came to a stop. "Atlanta Control, this is Delta 4520 heavy. Requesting clearance for takeoff."

Naman pressed a button on the console. "Delta 4520 heavy, hold at the taxiway for inbound traffic."

"Delta heavy, roger tower."

Off to the east a small, single-engine Beechcraft Bonanza banked to the left at the far end of the runway. Naman pressed a button on the console. "Beechcraft 527, this is Atlanta Control. You are clear to land on runway 6-0."

Naman glanced over the screen for his next inbound airplane, a Boeing 737 identified as Continental flight 2341. Seconds later he realized the Beechcraft had not acknowledged his last instruction.

"Beechcraft 527, this is Atlanta Control. You are cleared to land on runway 6-0. Acknowledge."

Still, there was no response. Naman stood to look out the large windows that ringed the control room. From high atop the tower, he had a clear view of the entire airport. A 757 rose in the air above a runway on the opposite side of the terminal. Another descended to land on that same runway. Then he saw it, a tiny speck in the distance. He pressed the button for his microphone.

"Beechcraft N527Y, this is Atlanta Control. Acknowledge."

Jake Greenlee, a supervisor, glanced up, "You got a problem?"

"He won't respond."

"Who?"

Naman pointed to the screen. "That Beechcraft on final approach."

Greenlee scanned the horizon, pointing. "That's him? Coming in on 6-0?"

Naman glanced up, "Yeah." He turned back to the screen. "We need to recycle that runway." He pressed a button on the console. "Continental 2341, this is Atlanta Control."

"Atlanta Control, Continental 2341."

"Wave off your approach. Turn right, heading 180. Maintain ten thousand feet."

"Continental 2341, roger. Turn right, heading 180."

Greenlee leaned over Naman's shoulder. "That Beechcraft is still coming. What's his altitude?"

"He just passed two thousand feet."

"Try him again."

"Beechcraft, 527. This is Atlanta Control. Acknowledge."

There was no response. Greenlee stared out the window. "Looks like he's going to land. Maybe he has radio trouble."

The Beechcraft continued its descent to five hundred feet. Naman stood again to watch. "We need to declare an emergency."

"Nah." Greenlee shook his head. "I think he's gonna land. Where's he going?"

"Air Taxi."

"I'll have someone question him when he gets over there."

Naman and Greenlee watched as the airplane flew straight down the runway. Then, just past midpoint, the left wing pitched up. The plane veered sharply to the right and slammed into the 747 waiting at the taxiway, striking the fuselage at the wing.

A fireball rolled into the sky, followed by thick, black smoke. Windows in the waiting room at the end of Concourse C shattered, sending shards of glass and debris in every direction.

Someone shouted from across the control room. "We got two more. Inbound from the west. Failed to acknowledge!"

Greenlee turned to look. "Where?"

"There," Naman pointed. "Coming toward 2-4-0."

One plane was already over the field, near the end of the runway. The other was a mile behind. The first banked to the right and dove into the airport's main terminal building. The second plane approached just above the tree line, wagged to the right, then made a hard left turn and struck a 737 as it rolled along a taxiway near the highway.

Naman collapsed in his chair. Greenlee looked back at him. "Hey," he barked. "Get busy." He pointed to the radar console. "You got a hundred other planes up there."

"What do I do with them?"

"I don't know. Send them to Birmingham. Savannah. Down to Montgomery. Send them somewhere. You can't leave them stacked up here."

Naman glanced out the window. Smoke covered the airport. Flames rose from the wreckage of the 747. He wanted to go home. Instead, he scooted his chair up to the console and pressed a button. "Continental 2341, this is Atlanta control. We have an emergency. Repeat, we are declaring an emergency. Divert to Birmingham. Turn right, heading 280. Contact Atlanta Departure." Before the pilot could respond, Naman was on to the next one. "Delta 8921, this is Atlanta Control…"

53

BERLIN, GERMANY

JOSEF MUELLER HEARD A KNOCK on his bedroom door. "Yes," he called. A voice spoke to him from the hall outside, "Sir, there has been a development in America." Mueller recognized it as the voice of Franz Heinrich.

Mueller threw back the covers and rolled out of bed. As he slipped on a robe he glanced at his wife. "Perhaps you should go in the next room."

"Is that necessary?"

"Yes," Mueller said, sternly. "I think it best."

Anika laid aside the book she was reading and threw back the comforter. "Franz should learn to respect our privacy."

Mueller waited while she left the bedroom, then he opened the door for Franz. Heinrich stepped into the room. "Three airplanes crashed at the airport in Atlanta."

Mueller pushed the door closed. "This was a terrorist attack?"

"Most definitely. The White House notified us that they will close U.S. airspace."

"All their planes are on the ground?"

"They will be shortly."

"Shortly? Hedges has not made the decision?"

"The decision has been made. He will make the announcement within minutes. They were giving us the courtesy of advance notification."

"Unlike before."

"Yes."

"Is there any indication of threats against us?"

"None, sir."

"Any threats against other EU members?"

"No, sir."

Mueller thought for a moment then looked over at Heinrich. "I suppose we should prepare a statement."

"The writers are working on one now, sir."

"Make certain they indicate our sympathy, the sympathy of Germany, for those who have lost their lives, but couch our response carefully. We must speak in terms of our willingness to fulfill our commitment to NATO."

Heinrich looked puzzled. "Sir?"

"We cannot appear to be bowing to the Americans. We cannot appear to be joining the American team. This is not 2001. Things have changed." Mueller focused his gaze on Heinrich's eyes. "You understand?"

"Yes, sir."

Heinrich turned to leave. When he was gone Mueller crossed the room to a night stand near the bed and picked up a phone. An operator came on the line immediately. "Get me the Chinese foreign minister." Mueller's voice was clipped and curt. "Wake him if you must."

While Mueller waited for the call to go through, a door opened and Anika returned. "Was it really so urgent it could not wait just a few hours?"

Mueller, still waiting with the phone to his ear, held is finger to his lips in a gesture for silence. Anika gave him an angry scowl.

54

THE WHITE HOUSE
WASHINGTON, D.C.

PRESIDENT HEDGES ENTERED THE WHITE HOUSE press room and stepped to the podium. Members of the press corps filled every seat in the room. Others lined the walls on either side. Television cameras were packed into the far end of the room. Hedges glanced down at his prepared remarks and began.

"Today, following attacks on the airport in Atlanta using small, privately owned aircraft, I ordered the FAA to immediately halt all air traffic in the continental United States. At this moment military aircraft patrol the skies over our major cities with orders to shoot down all unidentified airplanes. Though highly disruptive, these measures were necessary to prevent further attacks. We will restore air travel as quickly as possible. However, those of you who are now stranded in airports across the nation should seek to make other transportation arrangements. I have ordered FEMA to provide all available assistance. FEMA director Bernie Fogarty assures me aide to travelers will begin within hours. In the meantime, I have asked our mayors and county officials to take extraordinary steps to provide additional public transportation to assist travelers in moving from the airports to hotels and other accommodations."

Hedges looked up. Hands shot in the air. He pointed to Barbara Allen. "Yes, Mrs. Allen."

"Will these recent attacks deter you from meeting with Iranian

President Kermani?"

"No." Hedges pointed to the man seated next to her.

"Do you have any reason to believe the bombings in Los Angles, Denver, and Chicago were related to the attack in Atlanta?"

"The investigation into each of those is ongoing. I don't have an official report on that yet, but it seems highly likely to me."

"Highly likely they are related?"

"Yes."

Hedges pointed again. Another reporter spoke up. "Who do we think is behind these attacks?"

"General Delmas will have a briefing at the Pentagon when we finish here. I think he has details that pertain to your question."

"Do you plan to retaliate?"

"Yes."

"Against whom will you retaliate?"

"Against whoever is behind these attacks. The biggest task right now is making sure no further attacks are successful."

A reporter leaped to his feet. "Do you think there are other groups out there preparing to attack?"

"Yes," Hedges replied. He looked directly into the television cameras. "And I remind the American people that they are our first and best line of defense. We don't have enough military personnel to monitor every block of every town or every inch of rural soil. Nor would we want to try. No one in America wants to live under the kind of restrictions the military would require to make us absolutely invulnerable. We can, however, attain that same level of security by guarding our own homeland. Be alert. Pay attention. Report any suspicious activity to the nearest authorities."

Hedges looked out at the press corps then stepped away from the podium. As he walked from the room, reporters continued to pepper him with questions.

55

WASHINGTON, D.C.

MOSHE DINITZ SAT AT HIS DESK in the Israeli Embassy and waited. Located off Connecticut Avenue in northwestern Washington, D.C., his office was a twenty-minute ride from the State Department. Half an hour earlier he had dispatched his assistant, Daniel Meridor, with a message for Secretary Lehman, asking for a private meeting in order to share sensitive information. With tensions running high between the United States and Iran, he had not wanted to risk public disclosure of Israel's concerns. The last thing either country needed was a public rift.

Dinitz checked his watch. By now Meridor should have reached the State Department. If he followed instructions, he entered through the Navy's Bureau of Surgery across the street and took the underground tunnel. That would get him inside the State Department's offices without being seen by reporters or others watching from the street.

Dinitz glanced at his watch once more then turned in his chair to face the window. As he stared at the lawn of the embassy compound, he remembered a day standing on the lawn of Hebrew University in Jerusalem. That afternoon he had been perplexed, much as he was now.

As a young college student he had made friends with Gamal Elmasry, a student from Egypt. That afternoon Gamal had been in an odd mood, and as they walked across campus, Dinitz finally coaxed him into talking.

"My father has demanded I return home," Gamal said, solemnly.

"Why? It is the middle of the term." Dinitz knew Gamal had wanted to study and become a writer. He had come there for that purpose. Already he had published several short stories. "Has something happened?"

"No. But it is about to."

"What?"

Gamal took him aside and whispered in his ear. "War is coming."

"War?" Dinitz frowned.

"Yes. War."

"Where?"

"Here." Gamal glanced around as if to make certain no one was watching. "Syria will attack from the north. Jordan will attack from the east. Egypt will attack from the south."

"That does not seem possible. We are at peace with them."

"They only want you to think that."

"This does not seem possible," Dinitz repeated, shaking his head slowly.

"My father has very good connections," Gamal assured. "What he says is true."

Gamal had gone home, and less than a year later the Six Day War broke out. Dinitz never told anyone about that conversation, not then and not now, but he had always thought less of himself for not speaking out. Perhaps others knew, but whether they did or not, he had an obligation to pass that information on to someone who could make use of it, and he had failed. Now he had information that was of great importance to the Americans. He would not shrink back from speaking this time.

Two hours later Meridor returned. Dinitz looked up from his desk. "What did they say? What time shall I expect her call?"

"She would not see me."

"She will call me later to arrange a meeting. This is how these things work. I send you. She calls me. We meet somewhere in private."

"No," Meridor said, shaking his head. "They would not even listen. I left no message."

"What?" Dinitz was stricken. "They would not accept my message?"

"When they saw me enter the office, one of her assistants took me by the arm and put me in a conference room. I waited there thirty minutes before someone came and escorted me from the building. They said she could not see me. I tried to leave a message, but they wouldn't accept it. They said under no circumstance could they do so."

Dinitz felt as if he had been kicked in the stomach. He leaned back in his chair and folded his hands in his lap. "Very well, then," he said finally. "We must go this alone. I will cable Jerusalem."

56

NEW YORK CITY

KINLAW AND COOPER LEFT the park and started back towards 86th Street. As they walked along, Cooper's cell phone rang. He took it from his pocket and answered the call. Kinlaw tried not to listen.

A moment later, Cooper returned the phone to his pocket and sighed. "You should have made a hotel reservation."

"Why?"

"They've closed the airport," Cooper replied.

Kinlaw gave him a puzzled look. "Which one?"

"All of them."

"All of them? We flew in to LaGuardia. They closed it?"

"The entire country."

Kinlaw was startled. "What?"

"Terrorists attacked the Atlanta Airport," Cooper began grimly. "Flew three private planes into the terminal. Hit a couple of jets on the runway. FAA put everything on the ground. Nothing is flying." He took a key from his pocket and handed it to Kinlaw. "Get Hoag and go over to my apartment. You remember where it is?"

"Yeah." Kinlaw took the key and slipped it into his pocket. "I think I can find it."

"I have an extra room and a sofa." Cooper shoved his hands in his pockets. "I gotta go to the office. I'll be back later."

Kinlaw watched as Cooper trotted across the street and climbed aboard a bus.

—— (((——

Late that evening Cooper arrived at his apartment. Kinlaw and Hoag were sprawled on the sofa, watching the news. Hoag stood as he entered.

"Russell." The two shook hands. "Appreciate you taking us in for the night."

"No problem," Cooper replied. "Glad to help out. Sorry I'm so late getting back."

"We got a pizza," Kinlaw said. He pointed toward the kitchen. "There's some left on the stove."

Cooper grabbed a slice of pizza and came back to the living room. Hoag looked serious. "What's the latest?"

"They don't expect air travel to resume any time soon. Might be a week before they get anything flying again."

Hoag looked over at Kinlaw. "We should think about getting a rental car."

"Probably too late for that." Cooper took a bite of pizza. "I imagine they're all rented by now."

"What about the train?"

"Might work."

Kinlaw sat up straight. "Any idea who did this?"

"Looks like all of the people involved had connections to Al-Qa'ida."

Hoag frowned. "Who says so?"

"We have people on the ground in every location. Your people are there, too. They've recovered bodies from all the attacks except the one in Chicago. All of them were members of cell groups that had definite ties to Al-Qa'ida." Cooper took a drink of Coca-Cola. "Where did the stock market end?" Cooper took another bite of pizza.

"Down 1200 points," Kinlaw replied.

Cooper swallowed. "Better than I expected. Good thing they closed before those planes hit in Atlanta. No telling how far it would have dropped with something like that."

Hoag took a seat in an overstuffed chair across the room. "I think this whole thing is just a diversion. LA, Denver, Chicago, now Atlanta—it's all just a diversion."

Cooper sat on the sofa. "A diversion from what?"

"Something bigger."

"Like?"

"A nuclear attack."

"They only did their first test a few days ago." Cooper had a sarcastic tone. "They can't have something ready that quick. A test is one thing. A deliverable weapon is something different."

"Assuming that was their first test."

"You think they could have tested before now without someone knowing?" Cooper had an arrogant look. "Don't we have monitors in Colorado that can detect an overloaded truck going over the Brooklyn Bridge?"

"That's just it. Make the test small enough, and our monitoring equipment will think it's just background noise."

Cooper took another sip of Coke. "I'm sure they'd love to hit us with a nuclear bomb, but even if they have one, they don't have a way to get it here."

"Did you notice they exploded that bomb the other day on the anniversary of the day they seized our embassy?"

Cooper scowled. "Seized our embassy?"

"In the 1970s. In Tehran."

A thoughtful expression came over Cooper's face. "I guess it was." He took another sip of Coke. "I hadn't thought about it."

"Same date. Same time."

"Six-thirty in the morning. November 4th. You're right. And you think that's significant?"

"I know it is," Hoag smiled.

"Well, they still have the problem of delivering it. They don't have a missile that can get it here."

"Don't need one," Hoag quipped.

"How else are they going to get it from Iran to America?"

"A ship."

"Just load one on a ship and send it over? They don't have a navy." Cooper finished the slice of pizza and wiped his hands on a paper towel.

"But they have commercial ships," Hoag countered. "Container ships, to be exact."

Cooper looked at Kinlaw. "Is that what this is all about?"

"It's a pretty good theory," Kinlaw replied.

"The Iranians aren't going to attack us," Cooper said, dismissing their concern. "This is just a bigger version of 9-11. Nearly brought us down then. Trying to do it better now. They might attack Israel but not us."

"The only way they can attack Israel is by attacking us," Hoag argued.

"How so?"

"If they attack Israel first, we would know it before their missiles cleared the launchers. What would our response be?"

"Counterstrike, probably," Cooper answered.

"Right. A counterstrike from any one of two-dozen ballistic missile submarines. Tehran and every known military installation in the country would be obliterated. So, if you're Iran, how do you prevent that counterstrike from happening?"

"I don't know," Cooper shrugged. "Suppose you tell us."

"You strike the U.S. first."

"But then we'd know it was them, and they still wouldn't get off their strike against Israel or anybody else."

"They would if they took out our communications ability. Create a window of opportunity, a moment between the attack and the time we could recover enough to respond."

Cooper rolled his eyes. "Here we go with all that EMP stuff."

"Yes," Hoag nodded. "An electromagnetic pulse. Shuts down everything electronic in the blast area. Do the blast high enough and you could shut down every electronic device on the East Coast. Computers, cell phones, right down to the chips in the sewer lift station pumps. Everything electrical." He gestured with both hands. "Knock it out with a single shot." He leaned back in the chair.

"You've been listening to too much talk radio," Cooper chuckled. "Get yourself a subscription to Air America. Watch some CNN. Do something to balance it all out."

"You two need to lighten up," Kinlaw interjected. "This is gonna be a long visit if we keep going like this."

Hoag ignored Kinlaw. His eyes bore in on Cooper. "You know about Osmani?"

"Yeah." Cooper's gaze dropped to the left. "We know about him."

"And you know about Hamid."

"I don't think I can answer that."

Hoag glanced over at Kinlaw. Kinlaw shook his head. Hoag took a deep breath. "Think we could come down to your office tomorrow and see what you have?"

Cooper took another sip of Coca-Cola. "Sure. I'm not sure what I can give you, but you're welcome to come have a look."

57

ISTANBUL, TURKEY

LAUREN LEHMAN RODE IN A LIMOUSINE from her office at the State Department to a hanger on the far side of Dulles Airport, where she boarded a specially equipped 757. Though commercial air travel was at a standstill, Lehman's plane took off without incident. Just to make sure, two F-18 fighter jets accompanied it.

Ten hours later the plane landed in Istanbul, Turkey. Lehman was met by Devlet Baykal, Turkey's prime minister. He escorted her to the Eresin Crown Hotel. After a moment to gather her thoughts, she met Iranian Foreign Minister Abadeh Ardakan in a conference room downstairs.

"Sorry to hear about the trouble," Ardakan began.

"Yes," Lehman replied. "I'm getting updates every hour. It isn't good."

"These things happen every day in Jerusalem, Baghdad, Mumbai."

"They don't happen in America."

Ardakan's face was expressionless. "They should not happen anywhere."

"Well," Lehman nodded, "that is why we're here." She took a seat at the conference table. When he was seated she began. "Dubai has agreed to host a meeting between our presidents."

"That is good. Dubai is a lovely place, and they will maintain excellent security."

"Our own Secret Service is already coordinating details for President Hedges. I assume your security people are working out their details as well."

"Yes," Ardakan nodded.

"We could do this the week of December 12. I know our assistants have discussed dates, but does their agreement still hold? President Kermani is in agreement with that date?"

"Yes. We are already making plans." Ardakan cleared his throat. "I assumed all of this was already in place. Is there some problem?"

"No. There is no problem. I just wanted to make sure we were both discussing the same thing."

"But this is not why you wanted to meet me."

"No." Lehman shook her head. "It isn't."

Ardakan gave her a tight-lipped smile, "What did you really want to discuss?"

"Al-Qa'ida." Lehman moved her hands from the table and rested them in her lap. "I wanted to discuss Iran's relationship with Al-Qa'ida and other similar organizations."

Ardakan smiled once more. "I assumed as much."

"We are very concerned that Iran not supply nuclear weapons to Al-Qa'ida and other asymmetrical organizations."

"Asymmetrical. That is much better than calling them terrorists."

"I am not trying to be any more difficult than necessary, but this is a big point for President Hedges and for the United States government."

"I understand. But what do you mean by 'other' organizations?"

"Hamas. Hezbollah." Lehman opened her briefcase. "I have a list." She took out a document and passed it across the table.

Ardakan glanced at it and laid it aside. "In the first place, Secretary Lehman, Al-Qa'ida, as you well know, is composed of Sunni Muslims. They have little sentiment for Shi'a Iranians."

"As between the two groups, that is true. But I also know that, 'The enemy of my enemy is my ally.'"

"And you think that because Iran and Al-Qa'ida both oppose American expansion in the region, Al-Qa'ida is somehow our ally?"

"That is our concern."

"We are not interested in handing out nuclear bombs." Ardakan gestured with his hands in the air. "What good would that do us? Iran wants only to be master of its own destiny. If we hand such a weapon to another group, we give them the power we have worked so hard to attain, with no assurance they would not one day use it against us." He gestured toward the list. "Personally, I would have no problem with this, except for the inclusion of Hezbollah. But my government cannot agree."

Lehman looked puzzled. "Why Hezbollah?"

"You must understand the nature of Hezbollah." Ardakan propped his elbows on the table and laced his fingers together. "They are not some band of radicals, roaming the streets, killing women and children. They are a major political organization in Lebanon. They provide 90 percent of the medical care in all but Beirut. They feed the hungry and care for the poor."

"They are a paramilitary group, bent on the destruction of Israel."

Ardakan's eyes flashed. "When have they attacked Israel?"

"You know their position."

"Last time I checked, it was Israel who attacked Hezbollah. And Hezbollah defeated them, with the support of the Lebanese people."

"They have sworn to push Israel into the sea."

Ardakan dismissed the comment with a wave of the hand. "Mere political rhetoric, as when your former president described us as part of the Axis of Evil."

"This could be a problem."

"What?" Ardakan blurted. "That we will not openly disassociate ourselves from Hezbollah? Your president would refuse to meet, at such a critical time, over our... theoretical refusal to denounce Hezbollah?" He threw his hands in the air. "Such a thing would be madness. And after he openly invited us to meet on international television. We did not seek this meeting. He sought us."

Lehman ignored his bluster. "We are not interested in dictating your internal political position, but any communiqué from the summit must include a clear agreement not to disseminate nuclear weapons to non-state organizations."

Ardakan's eyes brightened. "We can agree to that language and commit to the principle." He gestured toward the document on the table. "But we cannot agree to the inclusion of a list of particular organizations."

"Very well." Lehman took a deep breath then slowly let it escape. "I think that will be sufficient on that issue." She ran her finger over her chin as she thought for a moment. "We can make that work."

"Good," Ardakan smiled. "What else?"

"The Nuclear Nonproliferation Treaty."

"Which are you asking? For Iran to agree to the principles expressed in the treaty, or to become signatory to the treaty itself?"

"Signatory to the treaty." Lehman gave him a stern look. "Full ratification."

Ardakan rested his hands on the arm of the chair and scooted back from the table. "That is a very difficult thing."

For the next three hours Ardakan and Lehman held a wide-range discussion of Middle Eastern history, American foreign policy, and nuclear diplomacy. In the end they reached no agreement on the status of the treaty but agreed to discuss it further at a subsequent meeting the following week in Marseilles, France.

58

FBI OFFICE, NEW YORK CITY

COOPER, KINLAW, AND HOAG awakened early. They dressed quickly and left the apartment before seven. Already, the streets were crowded with traffic.

Hoag looked around. "Is it always this crowded this early?"

"No," Cooper replied.

"Where's everyone going?"

"Getting out of town. It started last night. I noticed it on my way home."

"Why are they leaving?"

"They know what a terrorist attack is like. If there's any possibility one might come here, they don't want to be around when it happens. Many of them were here when the September 11 attacks occurred."

Kinlaw glanced up and down the street. In every direction, as far as he could see, traffic was bumper-to-bumper.

"Come on," Cooper said. "Let's take the subway."

They arrived at the FBI office in lower Manhattan a little before eight. The office was crowded with people and the sound of constantly ringing telephones. People hurried up and down the halls, chattering excitedly.

"You'll have to look past the confusion this morning," Cooper explained. "We have extra people in from all over, working on our end of the attacks, trying to figure out who's responsible and whether more attacks are planned. As you saw on the way in, people in New York are a little touchy. We're trying to make sure their angst is unwarranted."

Cooper led Kinlaw and Hoag down the hall to a vacant office. A desk sat opposite the door. Behind it was a window that looked out on the city. There were two chairs parked against the wall to the left. A telephone rested on the desktop with a cord that dangled to the floor.

"You can work in here," Cooper directed.

Kinlaw frowned. "With all these people, why is this one empty?"

"I told them you were coming." Cooper glanced around. "A little small and a bit Spartan, but if you need anything, just ask. Someone will get it for you." He looked over at Hoag. "In spite of our reputation, we really don't hate you guys."

Hoag pulled a chair in front of the desk. Kinlaw moved to the opposite side and pulled the other chair around. "I'm sure we'll be fine. How do we get the files?"

"I'll bring you the one on Osmani. You can start with that."

"I thought you weren't going to give us Osmani?"

"I wasn't. But I asked Lansing, and he thinks you should at least see the stuff on him now. These attacks have changed the landscape."

Cooper disappeared. Kinlaw took a seat as Hoag leaned forward. "Did you check in with anyone this morning?"

"No. Did you?"

"No." Hoag took out his cell phone and scrolled down the screen. "No one called me either."

Cooper appeared with two file folders. Both were stuffed with papers.

"Okay." He laid the files on the table. "You can make copies of anything in here. I'll spare you the details about whose information it is. We're a little too busy to worry with that today. If you want to make copies, see Lois. She's down at the end of the hall, next to the copier."

"Okay," Kinlaw nodded. "Looks like there's plenty to read."

Cooper flipped through one of the files. "This is the non-redacted version. So, remember to treat it accordingly."

"Right," Hoag smiled.

Cooper moved to the doorway. "Read up on Osmani. I'll be back in a little bit to brief you on some other things." He stepped out to the hallway and disappeared.

Hoag looked at Kinlaw, "Other things?"

"I don't know," Kinlaw shrugged. "Maybe he'll surprise us."

Hoag took one file and opened it. Kinlaw took the other and began reading.

In a little while an older man with dark hair, a sharp nose, and deep-set eyes entered the room. He was dressed in gray work pants and a gray work shirt and had a name embroidered on the pocket of his shirt that identified him as Sarmad. He crossed the room, checked the trashcan, and retreated to the hallway.

An hour later Kinlaw left the room with a stack of documents and headed toward the copier. Hoag took a break and went to the restroom. When he returned, Sarmad was in the office, dusting.

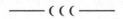

Shortly before noon Cooper returned. He pulled the door closed behind him. "You guys read that file?"

"Most of it."

"I only have a few minutes, and I'm not sure where I'll be this afternoon, so I wanted to tell you a few things now. One of our agents working counterintelligence in Guangzhou, China, was murdered a few days ago."

"Murdered?" Kinlaw frowned. "What happened?"

"We don't know. Someone found him in his apartment."

"In Guangzhou?"

"Yeah."

Hoag leaned back from the desk. "Any idea what happened?"

"They're still working on it, but with everything else that's going on, people are a little nervous right now."

Kinlaw folded his hands in his lap. "They think his death is related to the attacks here?"

"No one knows," Cooper replied. "When this stuff happens, everyone tries to connect everything." He paused and took a breath. "You were asking about Nasser Hamid." He took the photograph from the file showing Hamid in front of Pakistan Shipping's offices in Karachi. "You've seen this." Cooper tapped on the photograph with his index finger. "The day this picture was taken, Nasser Hamid was coming from a meeting with Osmani. As I'm sure you've seen from the file, Osmani has given our people verifiable information. This guy isn't just talking, he's talking about things that we've checked out. Most of what he's said is accurate." He tapped the photo again. "This is the reason no one wanted to show you Osmani's file."

"You think Osmani can get you to Hamid?"

Cooper leaned against the wall with his hands in his pockets. "Two weeks ago Osmani told our agents about a secret Iranian organization rumored to be working to create conditions that will usher in the Mahdi."

"The final prophet," Hoag nodded. "Some call him the Last Mahdi."

Cooper smiled, "The Last Mahdi. That's what Osmani called him."

Hoag scooted his chair back from the desk and crossed his legs. "Ushering in an era when all people acknowledge the truth of Islam, the enlightenment of Mohammed, and the singular deity of Allah."

"An Islamic apocalypse." Kinlaw rolled his eyes. "They borrowed it from the Bible."

Hoag continued. "He will arrive seven, nine, or nineteen years before the end—depending on which interpretation you follow."

Cooper nodded, "They don't know—"

"And, if I may," Hoag interrupted. "This is one prophecy on which Sunni and Shi'a agree. They may hate each other bitterly over which Caliph to follow, destroy each other's mosques, and shoot each other on sight over other issues; but they are in total agreement on the Mahdi."

"And before he comes," Cooper pressed, "there will be the red death."

"Yes," Hoag chimed in. "The red death and the white death. Red is death by the sword. White is death by the plague. A final apocalyptic war."

Kinlaw looked over at Hoag. "You gonna write any of this up for Winston?"

"This is what they believe, especially the Shi'a. Winston probably knows all about it by now. It's the kind of trivia those fresh-outs in his section would really dig."

"Nah," Kinlaw said, dismissing the comment. "It would be a little too mystical for them."

"What's more troubling," Hoag started again, "among an even smaller sect of Shi'a, they believe it is their obligation to bring about that cataclysmic end so that the Mahdi can arrive and bring peace."

He paused a moment and opened his legal pad. "Since we're sharing information." He took out the photograph of the container made from the security camera video. "This is a picture of a container that was loaded onto the *Panama Clipper*." He put the photograph on the desk so they all could see. "We got it from a security camera in Bremerhaven." He pointed to the photograph. "There's a symbol on this door. A star with a crest."

Cooper leaned over. "Looks like a circle."

"Almost. But it doesn't quite close on the left side."

"What does it mean?"

"I'm not totally sure, but the star isn't a traditional Islamic star. This one has six points."

"The Star of David," Cooper said.

"Yes. The traditional Islamic star typically has eight points."

"And you think this has something to do with the secret society Osmani was talking about." Cooper tapped his finger on the logo in the photo.

Hoag cut his eyes at Cooper. "How much do you know about the Hashshashin?"

"Not much." Cooper glanced at his watch. "Listen, I have to run. I have a dozen things going on right now." He stood. "I'll check in with you later, and we can talk about this some more."

When Cooper was gone, Hoag turned to Kinlaw. "Was it just me, or did he want to get out of the room?"

"He wanted out."

"Wonder why?"

"I don't know," Kinlaw shrugged. He pointed across the desk. "Any part of that file you haven't seen?"

"No."

"Good. Swap with me."

"Do what?"

"Swap with me." Kinlaw shoved the file he had been reading toward Hoag. "I've read all there is in that one. Give me yours. You read mine."

59

JERUSALEM, ISRAEL

EFRAIM HOFI STEPPED FROM A CAR and started up the steps of the Israeli prime minister's residence in Jerusalem. The tip of his cane clattered against the stone steps as he labored to reach the top. A guard held the door open as he moved inside, then an aide ushered him to a parlor. Hofi took a seat in a chair near the corner of the room and waited. A few minutes later the door to the parlor opened and David Oren entered.

Hofi braced himself with his cane and stood, "Mr. Prime Minister."

"Please," Oren gestured to the chair. "Keep your seat." The two men shook hands. Oren took a seat next to Hofi. "So," he began, "what have you learned?"

"Secretary Lehman has just concluded her meeting with Ardakan. Our operatives inside the hotel have confirmed the meeting is set for the middle of next month. They have not consulted with us on any of this. Apparently they have chosen to lead with the Iranians."

"Are they aware of the dangers they face?"

"Ambassador Dinitz has attempted to warn them, but his attempts were rebuffed."

"But they are not aware of Hamid's trip to Mingora?"

"No, they are not."

"And they are not aware of the other issues we have uncovered?"

"No, Mr. Prime Minister. They do not appear to be aware of any of these developments."

Oren crossed his legs. "Can we wait until they meet and examine the results then?"

"Certainly we should not conduct a preemptive strike. That would clearly set us against the Americans. They have not yet issued any public statement that would signal a break with us."

"But you are certain their sentiments have shifted."

"Yes, Mr. Prime Minister. I am certain."

"Then we must prepare for the inevitable." Oren sighed. "How long will it take to target our missiles?"

"They are already programmed for the Samson Option."

"Samson." Oren gave a wry chuckle. "I doubt he ever imagined we would follow his lead in pulling down this house of cards."

"Samson would be proud of our bravery," Hofi said, confidently. "And he would welcome our determination to vindicate the cause of God against our enemies."

"Samson never thought of the nuclear option." Oren ran his hand over his cheek. "You are certain we can render their military ineffective?"

"They will be unable to respond militarily or in any other manner."

"How long will that take?"

"From launch to impact, less than ten minutes."

"Very well," Oren nodded. "Keep me informed." Both men stood. Oren extended his hand to Hofi. "Thank you for coming on such short notice."

Hofi shook his hand firmly and nodded. "It is an honor to serve you in such a trying time, Mr. Prime Minister."

60

FBI COINTEL OFFICE
NEW YORK CITY

RUSSELL COOPER STEPPED into the office he shared with Lansing. "You got a minute?"

Lansing was seated at his desk, scribbling notes on a yellow legal pad. "Only a minute," he replied without looking up. He had a distracted frown on his face. "What do you need?"

"Hoag and Kinlaw are here from D.C."

Lansing looked puzzled. "Who?"

"David Hoag. Dennis Kinlaw. The guys from the CIA who sent that request for information on Nabhi Osmani. You had me draft a response."

"Oh yeah, yeah," Lansing nodded. He looked back at the legal pad then stopped short and glanced up. "I thought that request came from Winston Smith."

"It did. These guys work for him. They were the ones who wanted the information."

"Oh," Lansing nodded again. "They're here?" He turned back to a file on his desk and continued making notes from it while Cooper talked.

"Parked in an office down the hall reading files."

A frown wrinkled Lansing's forehead. "I didn't know they were coming."

Cooper ignored him and kept talking. "They have a picture of a container that has a symbol on it."

"A container? What kind of container?"

"A cargo container," Cooper continued. "Like you put on ships. Trains. You know."

"Oh. Okay. What's that got to do with us?"

"There's a symbol on the door of the container. It looks just like the one our guys found on the envelope in Sisson's apartment."

A guilty pang stabbed Lansing in his chest. It was happening. Winston had taken the bait and passed along the photograph. Now the CIA would come to the rescue. They would find out about Sisson and connect the dots. The whole thing would collapse and, perhaps, he could lay it all at Sisson's feet. If not, he would take his chances, but at least he would be free of Tajik al Shahan once and for all.

Lansing tossed his pen on the desk and laid aside the legal pad. "You sure it's the same?" He pushed his chair back and turned to face Cooper.

"Star of David with a crescent. Crescent almost surrounds the star."

"In blue?"

"Yes."

"Why'd they show it to you?"

"I told them about Osmani and that the reason we didn't want to tell them about him was because of Nasser Hamid."

Lansing feigned a disapproving tone. "You told them about Osmani and Hamid?"

"Yes."

"I told you not to tell them about Osmani." Lansing purposefully made himself appear angry. "I certainly didn't want you telling them about Hamid."

"Calm down," Cooper said. He gestured with both hands. "They had a copy of the photograph our guys took of Hamid coming out of Osmani's office."

Lansing looked surprised. "Where'd they get that?"

"I don't know." Cooper had a know-it-all look. "I thought maybe you could explain that."

The look on Cooper's face caught Lansing off-guard. "I don't know anything about how they got it." He glanced away and shuffled papers from the file on his desk. "Where are they now?"

"Still down there looking at files."

"Good." Lansing pushed the file to the corner of his desk and stood. "Come on. Let's go talk to them."

Cooper held the door closed and looked Lansing in the eye. "We need to tell them about Sisson and the envelope we found."

Lansing had a questioning look. "Is that really necessary?"

"Why wouldn't we?"

"Sisson was a career man. He has a family. We'd be implying he was doing something illegal."

"I don't think we'd be implying anything," Cooper responded. "But I think Kinlaw and Hoag need to know. This is the kind of thing we get hammered on after the fact, when someone finds out we had critical information and an opportunity to share it, and we didn't."

"Yeah. I suppose you're right." Lansing was glad for the cover. He had wanted to talk about Sisson but wasn't sure how to do it without appearing obvious. "Whatever it was, it is what it was."

Cooper smiled. "Let the facts speak for themselves?"

"That, too."

CIA HEADQUARTERS LANGLEY, VIRGINIA

WHILE HOAG AND KINLAW were busy in New York, Jenny Freed sat at her desk in the basement of the CIA building. Using a computer monitor on her desk, she reviewed images from a surveillance camera located on the frame of an overhead crane at the container port in Guangzhou, China.

As part of the CIA's investigation into David Lansing and the FBI's COINTEL office in New York, Jenny had been asked to review information regarding the death of Bill Sisson. When they learned Sisson had been at the Guangzhou container port just a few days before he died, the deputy director authorized her to hack into the port's security system in hopes of capturing a picture of Sisson there.

Images from cameras along the Guangzhou waterfront were transmitted by a microwave link to a central system located in port authority offices a mile away. Using computers aboard a Navy EF-18G "Growler" aircraft patrolling off the Chinese coast, Jenny was able to intercept the microwave transmission without disrupting it. With a stable link to the source, the computer onboard the aircraft accessed the Guangzhou port's main computer and downloaded two weeks' worth of surveillance images. She had spent the last three days culling through those images, hoping to find a picture of Sisson.

Jenny stared at the monitor and watched as yet one more container ship came into view. As with the other ships she had seen, she tightened the image on the point of the bow to read the name. There she saw the word *Santiago*. Something about that name seemed familiar. She checked her notes but found no mention of it. Then she remembered the list Hoag had given her. She took it from the drawer and glanced over the page. "*Santiago*," she whispered. "There it is."

Slowly and meticulously, Jenny shifted the image on the screen, carefully working her way down the side of the ship, checking each cargo container as it was lifted into place. When she saw nothing out of the ordinary, she pressed a button to fast-forward. Within seconds the container stack on the ship's deck grew as the video sped past. Part-way through the process, a blip caused the image on the monitor to jump. She clicked an icon to stop the video and backed it up, then started again, this time running it at normal speed.

A group of people appeared between the end of the container stack and the ship's superstructure. She tightened the picture on the group and continued to watch. A few minutes later the group moved near the containers. Someone stepped to the door with a tool in his hand and then the door swung open. Jenny stopped the image, backed up, and ran it more slowly. Seeing it at a slower speed, she caught sight of the numbers and markings on the container door.

"There," she said to herself, tapping the screen with her finger. "Right above that guy's head. The star and the circle. Just like the one we saw on the ship at Bremerhaven." She pressed a button to print the screen.

A quick search produced records for the *Santiago*, showing it was owned by Pakistan Shipping, just as Hoag and Kinlaw had suggested. Ten minutes later she had a list of all six container ships owned by the company. For the next three hours she combed through ships logs and dock reports from around the world in an effort to locate each of the ships. As the afternoon faded she located them all.

Panama Clipper sailed from Bremerhaven almost a week ago. A day later *Amazon Cloud* departed Aden, Yemen, bound for Newport, Virginia. *Santiago* left Guangzhou, China, headed to Long Beach, California. The company's three other container ships—*Central Gold, Ocho Del Rio*, and *Costa Del Sol* were in port at various locations around the Indian Ocean basin.

A chill ran up Jenny's spine as she stared at the information on her computer. "Three ships, each with oversized cargo containers bearing a suspicious symbol, bound for the United States." She drummed her fingers nervously on the desktop. "New York and Long Beach are busy ports. That makes sense that they would go there, but why Newport? Nothing there but the Navy." She leaned back in her chair. "And why was Hoag so interested in those containers and that symbol? What was he looking for?"

For almost an hour Jenny scribbled notes on a legal pad in an effort to make sense of what she had learned. Finally, she picked up her cell phone and punched in Hoag's number. The phone rang four times, then rolled over to his voice mail. She left a message and hung up.

62

FBI COINTEL OFFICE
NEW YORK CITY

KINLAW AND HOAG WERE SEATED around the desk reading the files on Osmani. Hoag spoke without looking up. "I'm still wondering why Cooper cut out of here so fast."

"Don't worry about it," Kinlaw said. His face was buried behind the file. "I'm sure if there was anything to it he'd tell us."

"You think so?"

Kinlaw peered around from behind the file. "Yes. He would. If you had information you thought was critical, you'd tell him wouldn't you?"

"I think I already did."

"Okay, then."

Just then the office door swung open. Hoag turned around to see Russell Cooper coming through the doorway. Behind him was a tall man with square shoulders and a narrow waist. He wore a white shirt, muted dark tie, and gray wool pants held in place by leather suspenders. Cooper gestured to him as they entered.

"Guys, this is David Lansing. He runs the office here."

Hoag and Kinlaw stood. The three of them shook hands.

"Glad we could help you out," Lansing said. He reached behind him and pushed the door closed. Cooper moved to one side and leaned against the wall. Lansing stood near the desk, "Russell tells me you have a photograph of Nasser Hamid."

"Yes," Hoag nodded. He took the photograph from his legal pad and handed it to Lansing. "You guys have been following him a while."

Lansing glanced at the photograph and handed it back to Hoag. "Yes. We have." He looked over at Cooper. "Russell, get some chairs so we can all sit." Cooper opened the door and stepped outside. He returned a moment later with two chairs. Lansing took a seat at the desk. Cooper closed the door and joined them.

"We've been working the Osmani-Hamid connection for some time. Osmani recently told our agents about a secret group working from Iran, an Islamic sect of some kind. When he told our agents about it, he showed them an envelope." Lansing reached inside his pocket. "This is that envelope." He laid a small linen envelope on the desk. "You'll notice the symbol stenciled on the back."

Hoag took the photograph of the container from his legal pad and pushed it in front of Lansing. "Looks just like that." He tapped the photograph with his finger.

"Yes," Lansing said. "It does." He smiled at Hoag. "Which is why I'm in here." Lansing leaned back and folded his arms across his chest. "We had an agent working in Guangzhou, China. A man named Bill Sisson. Career man. Been with the Bureau a long time. Two days ago Sisson was found dead in his apartment. In the course of their investigation, our agents conducted a thorough search of his apartment." He tapped the linen envelope with his finger. "They found one of those in a drawer in the bedroom. Filled with cash."

Hoag felt his cell phone vibrating in his pocket. He ignored it and continued talking to Lansing. "You think he was involved in something illegal?"

"That's what we'd like to know." Lansing stood. "I've got to run. A thousand things happening at once today. Russell can fill you in on any other details about Sisson. I don't think we know much more." He looked at Cooper. "You can show them the file on Sisson's case," then turned to Kinlaw and Hoag. "Can't give you Sisson's personnel file, but you can see what we've developed on his murder."

Kinlaw raised an eyebrow. "He was murdered?"

"Yes," Lansing replied. "Shot once." He indicated with his finger. "Right between the eyes."

Lansing opened the door and disappeared up the hallway.

63

CHICAGO

JAKE DELAMONT AND HIS PARTNER, Bobby Thompson, stood outside the coroner's office and waited. Through the doorway Jake watched while Brian Ladnier sorted through the papers on his desk.

"It's around here somewhere," Ladnier said. "It just came in this morning."

Jake felt the muscles in the back of his neck grow tense. After twenty years on the Chicago police force, he still hated coming to the coroner's office. It was always like this. Papers everywhere. Nothing in the file. Finding anything was always a chore. And the place smelled awful.

"I sent this over to the FBI," Ladnier continued. "They didn't give you a copy?"

"I don't know," Jake grumbled. "I guess they didn't think about it. This is the driver, right?"

"That's what the file says." Ladnier glanced at an open file lying on the desk. "Driver from the truck that rammed the Board of Trade downtown." He looked over at Jake. "Bet that sent the price of cows up."

"You don't watch TV?"

"Jake, I don't have time for much of anything." Ladnier picked up a stack of papers from the corner of the desk and flipped through them. "Here it is." He scanned down the page. "Dead man's name is Shair Kashan."

"Does it give an address?"

"I don't know." Ladnier stood. "I'll get you a copy, and you can read the report for yourself." Ladnier came around his desk, stepped past Jake, and started toward the hall. As he moved through the doorway, he looked in Thompson's direction. "I don't recall seeing you here before."

"Just came over from records."

Ladnier glanced at Jake. "A new guy?"

"Yeah," Jake nodded. "Real new."

Ladnier continued across the hall toward the copier. He glanced over his shoulder at Thompson. "Didn't know they made detectives from the records department."

"It was part of my rotation," Thompson replied. "Everybody goes through there now."

"Right," Ladnier grinned as he took the copy from the machine.

───── (((─────

The report from the coroner's office had given an address for Kashan on South Rhodes Avenue. Jake checked the house numbers as they came down the street. "Should be up here."

Thompson pointed. "That brick duplex right there."

Jake steered the car to the curb. "You go up the side of the house and come around back. I'll knock on the door."

"I don't know," Thompson said as he shut his door. "Maybe we should call for backup."

"The guy's dead. I don't think he's gonna be waiting for us inside."

"How'd DMV know where he lived?"

"Went to truck driving school. Got a commercial license. They do a background check, of sorts. Had to give them an address."

"And they know this is correct?"

"They test for all kinds of stuff when you do that. Somebody had his DNA. Matched it to the records." Jake gave him a needling look. "You ought to know about all that."

Thompson took his pistol from the waistband of his trousers. "You guys ought to lighten up on me about that. It ain't like before, when a guy got sent to records 'cause he couldn't cut it on the street. Everybody goes through there now."

"Relax," Jake scowled. "Guys give you a hard time 'cause you're new. Part of the deal." He nodded toward the driveway. "Get going. If anybody's in there, they'll see us and run."

Jake drew his pistol and started up the sidewalk. Thompson moved around the corner toward the back of the house. Jake waited a moment to give Thompson time to get in place then banged on the front door with his fist. When no one answered, he grabbed the doorknob and gave it a twist. When that didn't work, he rammed it with his shoulder and forced it open.

"Police!" Jake called out. "This is the police." There was no response. He called out again. "Chicago police. Anybody in here?"

The door opened to a living room. A sofa and chair sat along the wall to the left. A fireplace filled the wall to the right. Beyond the living room was a dining table. Pistol ready, Jake moved quietly across the room. As he came past the sofa, he heard the sound of footsteps coming from the kitchen. He froze and listened. The steps drew nearer. Then a face peered from around the corner. Jake jumped to the right and pointed his pistol in that direction, ready to shoot, only to see Thompson standing in the doorway.

"Back door was unlocked," Thompson grinned. "I didn't see anybody."

Jake's shoulders slumped. "Don't ever do that again." He slipped his pistol in its holster. "If you start into a room like that, say something. Holler out. Let everyone know where you are."

"I scared you?"

"Anybody else would have shot you first and then checked to see who you were." Jake took a cell phone from his pocket. "Don't touch anything. I'm gonna let them know we found the place. We need somebody down here to go through it."

"Why are we chasing this stuff down? I thought the FBI had this case."

"The FBI is assisting. It's still our case." Jake pressed a button on the phone to call the dispatcher. While he talked to them, Thompson wandered through the apartment.

When Jake finished the call, he slid the phone back in his pocket. "Hey, Thompson. Where are you?"

"Back here."

Jake followed the sound of his voice to a bedroom. "Find something?"

Thompson pointed to a table that stood next to the bed. On it was a small notebook and a CD. "Want to see what's on the CD?"

"No," Jake replied. "Not right now. Did you touch anything in here?"

"You think I just graduated from the academy?"

"That's how you act." Jake slipped a pen from his jacket and used it to lift open the notebook. Inside he found notes written in Arabic. "They'll need a translator."

Beneath the tabletop were two drawers. Jake pulled open the first. An envelope lay inside. The flap was tucked inside the opening. On the back of it was a small blue star with a circle around it.

Thompson pointed. "I'm guessing that means something?"

"I'm guessing you're right."

Using the pen, Jake pushed open the flap to find a stack of twenty dollar bills.

"I'm supposing that means something, too."

"Probably right on both—"

"FBI!" Jake wheeled around as two men entered the room. Dressed in gray suits and white shirts, they looked almost identical. "FBI," the first one repeated. "Keep your hands where we can see them."

"Relax guys," Jake scowled. "We're on your side." He pulled his jacket back and pointed to a badge hanging from his belt. "Chicago PD. Who are you?"

The first man lowered his pistol and drew a badge from his jacket. "Steve Morgan." He nodded to the second man. "This is Jerry Miller."

Morgan slipped his badge into his pocket and came closer. "Find anything?"

"Just got here. Waiting for a crime scene unit."

"Good."

Morgan leaned past Jake and looked in the drawer. "What's in here?"

"Money."

"Anything else?"

"I don't know."

"We'll take it from here." Morgan stepped back. "Let you know if we need anything."

Jake hesitated. Morgan smiled. "Really. We've got it."

A car door slammed outside. Jake glanced through the window to see a van parked out front. Two men wearing dark blue blazers approached. On their jackets were the letters FBI in bright yellow. Jake nudged Thompson. "Come on."

Thompson frowned. "I thought this was our case."

"Come on," Jake growled and started toward the door.

64

NEW YORK CITY

THAT EVENING SARMAD AHMAD placed his cleanup cart in a utility closet across from Russell Cooper's office and walked down the hall to a service elevator. From there he rode to the basement and clocked out. The November air was cool and crisp as he stepped from the building. He slipped on a jacket and walked across the parking lot to the street. Three blocks later he came to the subway station at Park Row and boarded the train for Brooklyn. Twenty minutes later he arrived at Atlantic Avenue in Brooklyn. He stepped from the train and climbed the stairs to the street. Down the street to the left, he entered a coffee shop across from the Al-Farooq Mosque. He took a seat at a table in back and waited. Ten minutes later Abdullah Annon entered.

Originally admitted to the United States as a student, Annon had attended New York University but dropped out after the first year. Undetected by immigration officials, he had lived the past fifteen years in the Bedford Stuyvesant section of New York. During that time he obtained three wives with whom he fathered a dozen children. He owned two businesses and lived with his wives and children in a four-story brownstone. Everyone in the neighborhood knew him, though few dared acknowledge that fact.

Annon took a seat next to Sarmad. "Assalamu 'alaykum."

"Wa'alaykum," Sarmad replied.

"You have something you wish to discuss?"

"Saifa told you where I work?"

"Yes."

"They had many extra people in the office today. People I've never seen before in all the time I have worked there. But two men were on my floor all day. They did not leave to eat. They did not attend meetings. They only met with two men. One is a man named Russell Cooper. I am not sure what he does, but he sits at his desk all day. The other was David Lansing. He is in charge of everyone."

"Where were these men from?"

"I am not sure. But I heard these two men discussing someone named Nabhi Osmani."

Annon's eyes grew dark. "What did they say about him?"

"I could not hear much. But I heard his name and I heard them discuss something called *Amazon Cloud*."

Annon sighed and leaned back from the table. "Did you hear anything else?"

"Bits and pieces. Then Russell Cooper came in and they closed the door. After they were gone, I found a note in the trash."

"You have this note?"

Sarmad took a crumpled piece of paper from his pocket and handed it to Annon. Sarmad smoothed out the wrinkles. On the paper was the name Nasser Hamid. Next to it was a star with a circle around it. Annon pointed to the symbol. "Did they discuss this?"

Sarmad glanced at the note and shrugged. "I do not know. The door was closed most of the time when David Lansing and Russell Cooper were in there. I did not hear them discuss that name. I found that in the trash. I thought someone might find it useful."

Annon nodded and slipped the note into his pocket. "But you heard them mention *Amazon Cloud*?"

"Yes."

"You do not know these men?"

"I know David Lansing and Russell Cooper. I do not know the others. They came from somewhere else. They were stuck here when the airports closed."

"You could recognize them if you saw them again?"

"Yes," Sarmad nodded. "I would know them."

Annon took something from his other pocket and pressed it into Sarmad's hand. Sarmad glanced down and saw it was a wad of twenty dollar bills. He shook his head. "You do not have to pay me. I do it as a service to Allah and to his servant, the Mahdi."

"I am rewarding your faithfulness," Annon smiled. "Allah is pleased."

Annon stood and crossed the room to the door. He stepped outside and disappeared up the street to the right.

65

THE EGYPTIAN BORDER NEAR GAZA

ABDUL AL-JAWAD STARED OUT THE WINDSHIELD of the Volvo truck into a moonless night. Around him was a darkness only the desert could bring. The sky was ablaze with stars, more stars than one could imagine, but there on the highway the beam of the headlights cut like a knife through blackness that seemed thick and solid.

Across the seat, on the far side of the cab, Al-Jawad's son Abdulla leaned against the door. Eyes closed, jaw slack, he was fast asleep. Al-Jawad glanced at him and smiled with pride. He was a good son. Always respectful, did as he was told, never caused any trouble. Soon he would take his place with the men and assume the mantle of responsibility that fell to those aspiring to positions of leadership, but right now he was a boy of ten, having his first taste of the business in which men of their position must engage.

As the truck rolled across the desert, Al-Jawad grew tired. The drive from Alexandria had been long and hot but uneventful. There was little to do but hold the steering wheel and let the truck do the work. He pressed the accelerator to the floor and propped his elbow on the ledge of the open window. Cool night air blew against his face as his mind wandered to the mountains and home.

An image of his uncle, Abdul Rahman, drifted through his mind. Rahman, his childhood hero, left the mountains for America when Al-Jawad was a young boy. He lived first in New York then eventually settled in Chicago. He steadily progressed through the ranks of leadership, rising to the level of Sheikh in a mosque on the Southside. Using his position, he had coordinated attacks on the World Trade Center, providing funds and logistics for a first attempt that was unsuccessful and a second that finally brought the buildings down. That success had come at the loss of life and with the loss of Rahman's freedom. He had spent the last twenty years in federal prison. "It is no heavy burden," Rahman had said. "It is only the price of leadership, and a price Allah will repay."

Leadership. The thought of it made Al-Jawad smile. Leadership was the mark of their family. Even now two of his brothers lived in the mountains near Chitral, not far from the Afghanistan border, training the next generation.

Al-Jawad reached into the pocket of his shirt for a cigarette and stuck it in his mouth. He took a match from the same pocket and struck it against the steering wheel. The flame burned brightly as he touched it to the end of the cigarette. He took a long draw and let smoke slowly escape his nostrils. Satisfied for the moment, he shook out the flame of the match and tossed it out the window.

From memories of home, Al-Jawad's mind moved on to recall the many events that had transpired during his lifetime. He had seen the Shah of Iran removed from office, an Islamic revolution rise from the streets of Tehran to spread throughout the world, and then the fall of the Soviet Union. *Israel and America are next*, he mused. *Soon they shall be no more. And when they resist, we shall see the age of the Mahdi.* He took a long drag on the cigarette. *And I am preparing the way.*

Just then a light flickered up ahead. Al-Jawad lifted his foot from the accelerator. The engine rumbled as the truck slowed. He moved the shifter to a lower gear and pressed his foot against the brake pedal.

Abdulla opened his eyes and sat up in the seat. "Where are we?" He rubbed his hands over his face. "Why are we slowing down?"

"We are here," Al-Jawad grinned. "We have reached our destination."

Abdulla glanced at his wrist watch. "So soon?"

"It has been hours," Al-Jawad laughed. "You have slept the entire way."

A look of disappointment swept over Abdulla's face. "I wanted to see the desert."

"There it is." Al-Jawad gestured with a broad, sweeping motion. "This is all you would have seen. Darkness in every direction."

Abdulla smiled. "I like it out here."

"It is a very lovely place. Both in the day and the night."

Up ahead the truck's headlights fell on a man standing in the road. He was dressed in a flowing white thawb that came to his ankles. On his feet, he wore leather sandals, and on his head was a white keffiyeh, held in place by an agal of camel hair pulled tight against his forehead and tied in back. He looked convincingly like a Bedouin, but Al-Jawad recognized him immediately as Nasser Hamid. He eased the truck off the road and brought it to a stop.

Abdulla reached for the door handle. Al-Jawad tapped him on the shoulder. "Wait here. Let us see what will happen." Abdulla let go of the handle and slumped against the seat.

Al-Jawad took the cigarette from his mouth, flipped it out the window, and opened the driver's door. As he rounded the front of the truck, Hamid met him with a traditional greeting—left hand on the right shoulder and a kiss on each cheek. Over Hamid's shoulder, Al-Jawad saw lights from a cluster of Bedouin tents a hundred yards from the highway. Hamid gripped Al-Jawad's shoulder and gently guided him in that direction.

"Come," he smiled. "You must be tired."

Al-Jawad hesitated. "What about the truck?"

"We will take care of it," Hamid soothed. "Come." Two men brushed past them. "They will bring the truck."

Al-Jawad took a few steps then stopped and pulled free of Hamid's grasp. "My son is in there. I should get him. He's probably hungry."

As he turned back toward the truck, Al-Jawad heard a faint crackling sound. The door of the truck was open on the passenger side. A man stood on the running board and leaned over the front seat. Through the windshield Al-Jawad saw a hand rise in the air, then come down swiftly, passing out of sight beneath the window. As he watched, his eyes wide with fright, something spattered on the windshield.

"No!" Al-Jawad shouted. He jerked his head around to face Hamid. "What is happening?" He gestured with his hands in the air. "I did as you asked. I did everything." He lunged for Hamid's neck, arms outstretched, fingers like claws, his face contorted in anger. "Why did you do this to me?"

Hamid backed deftly away. "You did everything as instructed, and Allah is pleased for the service you have offered him. Now it is time for your reward."

Al-Jawad took another step toward Hamid, then froze as he felt the muzzle of a pistol pressed hard against the side of his head. There was a puzzled look on his face. "Why? Why would you do this?"

"It is best," Hamid said softly. "It is the only way." His eyes looked away, focusing on the man at Al-Jawad's side. He paused a moment then nodded.

Al-Jawad heard the faint sffzzzt of a silenced gunshot, then his legs crumpled beneath him and everything turned black.

66

BOUND BROOK, NEW JERSEY

LANSING ARRIVED HOME around nine o'clock that evening. He was exhausted from a long day and glad for a break. When he left that morning he wasn't sure he would be able to come home any time soon. Seeing his house with the autumn leaves and the front lights glowing made him feel warm and glad inside. Since talking to Hoag and Kinlaw, he had been worried about the plans he had made. Perhaps he didn't need to get out. Things weren't so bad. For a while, he had thought he had made a mistake sending that photograph to Winston and toyed with finding a way to stop what he was sure would become a far-reaching, internal investigation. But seeing the house again and thinking of his family, he was sure he had done the right thing. It wasn't like coming clean and confessing, but almost.

Lansing parked the car in the driveway and opened the door. As he stepped from his car, a black Mercedes stopped on the street behind him. The rear passenger window slowly lowered. Seated inside was Tajik al Shahan. A smile appeared on his face. "Let's go for a ride, David."

Lansing's heart sank. The relief he had felt just moments before suddenly evaporated. He placed his briefcase back in the car and locked the door, then turned aside and started toward the end of the driveway. He glanced back at the house as he came around the car. His wife stood on the front porch. "I'll be back in a minute," he called. When he reached the Mercedes, Tajik leaned over and pushed open the rear door. Lansing crawled onto the seat beside him.

"You look tired," Tajik said. "You've been working too hard. Haven't you made enough money to take a vacation?"

"We're a little overwhelmed right now."

"Yes," Tajik smiled. "I suppose you are."

The car turned the corner and started down Mountain Avenue. Tajik looked away and stared out the window. "I'm a little worried about your situation in China."

"What about it?"

Tajik turned back to face him. "Sisson."

"He's dead," Lansing replied.

"I know he's dead." There was a look of disdain on Tajik's face. "That isn't what worries me."

"What's the problem?"

"Two agents from the CIA showed up in your office today asking questions. Questions about signs and symbols and things they do not need to know about."

Lansing wondered how Tajik knew about Kinlaw and Hoag, and how he knew so quickly, but he thought it better not to ask. "I tried to tell you those symbols would be a problem."

"Yes," Tajik said slowly. "As well you did. But as I have told you many times, we had to make concessions in order to obtain cooperation." He gestured with a twist of his wrist, turning his palm up in a matter-of-fact way. "I agree, the Shi'a are stupid people, but our business requires cooperation."

Lansing shook his head. "This is way beyond what I agreed to."

"You knew what you were getting into. You did not know the details, but you knew the possibilities. You are not as naïve as you would like others to think."

"It's late. This has been a long day. Cut to the point." Lansing turned to look at Tajik with a disgusted frown. "What do you want?"

"Nothing." Tajik smiled over at Lansing. "I want nothing. I am giving you a gift."

"A gift? What kind of gift?"

"These men who visited you today have put you in a vulnerable position. Much is at risk. I have already taken care of it." Tajik patted Lansing on the thigh. "I have solved your problems for you."

A sinking feeling stabbed Lansing in the stomach. "What do you mean?"

Tajik tipped his head forward in a questioning look. "Do you really want to know?"

"No," Lansing sighed. "I suppose not."

"I should suppose not, indeed."

By then the car had returned to the front of Lansing's house. He pushed open the door to step out. Tajik touched his hand.

"Tell your daughter I hope she enjoys the gift."

"What gift?"

Tajik smiled. "The dress you sent her, of course."

Lansing frowned. "I didn't send her a dress." He stepped from the car.

Tajik leaned over to look at him. "Yes, you did. Her favorite color is pink. And it is the perfect size. You made a wise choice for her. She will enjoy wearing it to the school dance this Saturday."

Lansing froze. His hand gripped the door handle. The car started forward, snatching it from his hand and pulling the door closed at the same time. Lansing stared after the car, watching the red taillights as they moved up the street. He thought of a thousand things. His daughter on the day she was born. The afternoon of her first date. And now, she was a senior in high school. Sadness swept over him in waves. The meaning of what Tajik had said was not lost on him. He understood the message. But to think that he had endangered his daughter, his wife, and all they had worked so hard to attain. He took a deep breath and let the moment settle into his soul.

Sisson was dead. Two more men would be dead, perhaps by morning. That was no longer his concern. They knew the life they chose when they took the job. Perhaps it was a mistake to have involved Winston. He took another deep breath and let it slowly escape. Anyway, he told himself, there was nothing that could be done about it now.

67

NEW YORK CITY

KINLAW SAT ON THE SOFA at Russell Cooper's apartment and flipped through the front section of *The New York Times*. "I think I've read this section twice," he grumbled.

Hoag sat in a chair on the opposite side of the room and stared at the television. "There's nothing on worth watching. Not even a *Seinfeld* rerun." He tossed the TV remote on the sofa. "Was Russell coming back tonight?"

"Said he would if he could get away. He wasn't real sure what was going to happen."

Kinlaw folded the newspaper and laid it beside him on the sofa. "We've read all the files they have for the people on our list. We've seen all they have on Hamid."

"All the files they'll show us," Hoag groused.

"I don't think they have much more, at least not at this office. Might be something in the field that hasn't surfaced yet." Kinlaw sighed. "We should get out of here. Get back to D.C."

"Do you think Sisson's death has any connection to Hamid?"

"I think there's a lot about this we don't know."

"How could we connect the dots?"

"I don't know," Kinlaw sighed. "You and Russell weren't getting along too well last night. You okay with him now?"

"Yeah, I think so."

"I thought maybe we were going to be sleeping on the street."

"I like him fine. I just… I never understood what your sister saw in him."

"I knew it," Kinlaw laughed. "I knew there was more to it."

Hoag grinned. "I just never understood the two of them."

"You liked her, didn't you?"

"I don't—"

Kinlaw interrupted. "Ohhh, come on now. Tell the truth. I can see you're blushing." Hoag smiled. Kinlaw pressed him. "I won't say anything to her."

"We were…" Hoag felt his cheeks grow warm. "All right. Yeah. I liked her," he sighed. "But she wasn't interested in me."

"It's just as well. If you two had gotten together, there'd be little Hoags running around by now, calling me Uncle Dennis. Not sure I could take that."

"I'm glad things worked out well for her."

"Me, too." Kinlaw stood and stretched his arms out wide. "I'm going down to that store on the corner. Maybe get a soda or a candy bar or something." He stepped over Hoag's outstretched legs. "I gotta get out of here for a few minutes. You want to go?"

"Yeah." Hoag stood. "Great idea."

They rode the elevator to the lobby. The doorman greeted them as they started outside. "Better be careful. Police are really patrolling the streets tonight. I've seen four cars go by in the last hour. It's a crazy time."

"Thanks. We'll be careful," Hoag replied.

Kinlaw smiled. "Just going down to the corner for a soda."

On the sidewalk Hoag and Kinlaw turned right and walked slowly along. Lights glowed in the windows of the surrounding buildings, but the streets were empty.

"Think it's open?"

"Yeah." Kinlaw turned up the collar of his jacket. "This is New York. Something's open all the time. No matter what the emergency, somebody here's always trying to make a buck."

Hoag shoved his hands in the front pockets of his jeans. As he did, his left hand struck his cell phone. "Oh, man," he sighed. "I had a call this afternoon while we were with Lansing. I forgot to check it." He pulled the phone from his pocket and glanced at the screen, then shoved it back in his pocket.

"Who was it from?"

"Jenny."

"You aren't going to call her back?"

"Nah. Not now." Hoag sighed.

"Why not?"

"I don't want to get into it."

"Love?"

"We have some things to work out. If I call her it'll either be some deep conversation over the phone, which I don't want to have, or one of those long silent calls where you can't hang up so you just sit there listening to each other breathing."

"She might be worried about you."

"She might." Hoag tipped his head to the side and popped his neck. "Think we could take the train back to D.C.?"

"Let's talk to Russell about it, if he gets back tonight." Kinlaw gave Hoag a nudge. "Call Jenny."

"Right now?"

"Yeah."

"It's late."

"That'll give you an excuse not to talk so long."

Reluctantly, Hoag took the cell phone from his pocket and placed the call. Jenny answered on the first ring. "Oh, David," she blurted. "I've been worried about you. Didn't you get my message?"

"I was in a meeting when you called. Forgot to check the phone afterwards."

"You're okay?"

"Yes. We're fine. Everything okay there?"

"We need to talk."

Here it comes, he thought. Just what he had wanted to avoid. "I'm walking down the street to the store with Dennis."

"David," Jenny's voice was urgent, "I found more about those ships."

"More what?"

"Get to a place where you can talk and call me."

"If it's urgent you can tell Winston."

"Okay. But call me."

"Okay." Hoag pressed a button to end the call.

Kinlaw looked over at him. "Trouble?"

"I don't know." Hoag slid the phone into his pocket. "She found some more about the ships."

"We need to get home," Kinlaw replied. "I'll make some calls when we get back to the apartment."

At the corner store Hoag opened the door and held it as Kinlaw stepped inside. A counter ran from the door to the left along the front wall with a cash register in the middle. Behind it was a cigarette case. Along the top of the counter were racks for small merchandise. Two cramped aisles ran perpendicular to the front counter between rows of merchandise. Across the back wall was a cooler filled with drinks.

A slender man with an olive complexion and black hair stood behind the counter. Kinlaw acknowledged him with a nod as he walked past. He continued to the back of the store and took a can of ginger ale from the cooler. Hoag lingered near the chips.

Kinlaw called to him. "You want anything to drink?"

"Yeah," Hoag replied. "Get me a bottle of water."

"What are you looking for?"

"Platanos chips."

"Plata-what?"

"Plantains. Fried green bananas. They make them in packages like potato chips."

"Sounds good. Get me a bag."

"I will if I can—"

Just then, the door opened. Hoag glanced around in time to see three men enter, their faces covered with ski masks. The first one wore a black, hooded sweatshirt that was loose and baggy. Behind him was a man wearing a brown T-shirt and cotton twill pants. The last man wore a blue and orange jacket.

Hoag ducked low and hurried to the back of the store. Kinlaw was crouched at the end of the shelves near the cooler. Hoag dropped beside him and peeked out in time to see the man in the brown T-shirt coming down the aisle toward them. "He's headed this way," he whispered.

Kinlaw looked up. "There's a guy with a black hood in the next aisle."

"What do we do?"

"I don't know." Kinlaw craned his neck to see over the end of the counter once more. While he watched, the man wearing the blue and orange jacket spoke to the cashier at the counter. The cashier said something and stepped back, his hands raised high in the air. The drawer to the cash register was open. Then, without warning, a shot rang out. The man behind the counter fell backward, crashed against the cigarette case, and slid to the floor.

Kinlaw glanced over his shoulder to the left. There was a door at the far end of the cooler near the corner of the wall. "Come on." He tapped Hoag on the shoulder and started toward the door.

Suddenly, shots rang out and bullets whizzed overhead. Glass in the cooler doors shattered. Soda cans ripped by the bullets spewed liquid in the air. Kinlaw hit the door in the corner at a run. It flew open and banged against the wall. Hoag was close behind and caught the door with his shoulder as it rebounded from the wall.

Cases of soda were stacked behind the cooler, next to a rack of bread and three cases of milk. Kinlaw picked his way past them to a door on the opposite side. He grabbed the door knob and jerked to open it, but the door didn't budge. "It's locked," he whispered. "It's locked."

Suddenly the door behind them at the corner of the cooler burst open. The man in the black sweatshirt rushed through, gun drawn. Hoag snatched a bottle of Coca-Cola from a flat and hurled it in his direction. The man ducked. The bottle hit the wall and bounced off the side of his head. Hoag threw another and another, keeping up a steady barrage of bottles and cans. "Kick it!" he shouted. "Kick the door open!"

"It opens the other way!" Kinlaw yelled. He kicked it anyway and found the bottom panel was made of plywood. It cracked down the middle from the force of his foot. He kicked it again and broke it free of the door frame. "Come on!" he shouted as he ducked through the hole.

Hoag tossed two more bottles then followed Kinlaw through the door to an alley behind the store.

68

EGYPT, NEAR THE GAZA BORDER

THE BODY OF AL-JAWAD was placed on a carpet and carefully rolled inside it. His son was accorded the same treatment. When they were prepared, the bodies were hoisted onto the back of a camel and secured with a cotton rope. Two men dressed in Bedouin garb led the camel over the dunes.

Al-Jawad's truck was driven into the tent compound and parked in an area reserved for it beyond the last tent, out of sight to anyone passing on the road. Covered with brown mesh, it blended with the sand and became invisible from the air. Workmen swept away the tire tracks with brooms made of coarse straw. As the gray light of dawn slowly crept across the dunes, the sand looked as it always had—windblown and drifting.

Two hours later Hamid stood near the camouflaged truck and waited. In the distance two men approached from beyond the dunes. Riding atop a camel, they looked like something one would expect to see in the Egyptian desert. Slowly, the men crossed the sand and brought the camel to a stop at the tether line a hundred yards away. When the camel was tied to the line, they made their way to Hamid. He pulled them behind the truck and lowered his voice to little more than a whisper. "You disposed of the bodies?"

"Yes."

"You are certain no one will find them?"

"We are certain."

"No wild animals will dig them up?"

"We covered the bodies as you requested and buried them deep."

"Did you check them for identification?"

One of the men handed him a canvas sack. "This is everything that was on them. We checked their pockets. The waistband of his trousers. This is it."

Hamid glanced inside the bag to see a wallet, two U.S. twenty dollar bills, and a pocket knife.

"Okay," he said. "Have something to eat and rest. There will be much for you to do when you awaken."

The men backed away and disappeared among the tents. Hamid turned aside and entered a tent to his left. Technicians were huddled around a work table. On it were components from a conventional warhead. The men worked feverishly.

Hamid stepped closer. "You can do this?"

"Yes," one of the men nodded. "We can do it."

"And it will be ready on time?"

"Yes," they all nodded. "It will be ready on time."

Karim Atef, the senior physicist in the group, spoke up. "What we are doing is an exact duplication of the device exploded at Al-Akbar. That detonation was a test of this technology—of taking an Iranian-made, conventional warhead and using it to detonate a nuclear bomb. We've already proved it works."

Hamid smiled at the confident explanation and inwardly congratulated himself for having chosen Karim for this task. He had reviewed many potential candidates for the job, but there had never been much doubt about whom he would select. Karim was well educated and, as the father of Iran's indigenous missile program, an obvious choice. Beyond that, he had a reputation as an ardent follower of Shi'a Islam. Stories that he once brutally beat his own cousin for converting to Christianity were not exaggerated. He was also fifteen years older than anyone in the group. His calm demeanor and self-assured expertise went far to temper the youthful enthusiasm and tempestuous tendencies of the others.

"You can fit it in there and make it explode," Hamid continued, "but will it fit on top of the Shahab missile?"

"Yes," Karim nodded. "There is enough room inside the warhead to place the nuclear fuel. As I said, this was the reason for the test at Al-Akbar. It will work." He smiled. "Do not worry."

"I know it was the reason for the test," Hamid countered. "I'm asking if you are certain it will really work."

"There is no problem," Karim reassured him. "And there will be no problem. It will work as I have said."

"I do not have the luxury of not worrying," Hamid sighed. "If this missile and the others do not work, more than time will be lost. The Americans will see our failure and realize what we are doing. Such a mistake would prove fatal to hundreds of thousands in our country. Perhaps millions."

Karim stepped from the work table and came to Hamid's side. He placed his hand on Hamid's shoulder and guided him to the far side of the tent. "We did this before. At Al-Akbar. I was there. I designed it. I saw the test. I was standing right there when the earth shook."

"I know, but—"

"Last year, we placed a reconfigured warhead cone on the Shahab missile and launched it. The missile flew perfectly. There was not a single problem. Now we have designed a way to use that warhead cone to contain both the conventional device for which it was originally intended and as a detonator for a nuclear device of later configuration. We have tested that configuration and it worked flawlessly."

"We have no room for error."

"The margin is of no significance to us." Karim grinned. "There will be no error. Therefore, the margin of error is only something from a statistician's imagination." He smiled again and patted Hamid's shoulder. "Have some coffee, Nasser, and relax. We are ahead of schedule."

Hamid left and walked to a second, larger tent in the center of the compound. He pushed aside the flap and ducked inside. Two men, armed with AK-47s, jumped to their feet. Hamid held up his hand in a reassuring gesture.

"It is only me," he said quietly.

The men relaxed. Hamid stepped closer.

First produced in 1998, the Shahab-3 had been modified several times. The one on the launcher inside the tent had a range of 1,200 miles. Hamid placed his hand on a tail fin and ran his finger along its edge. He imagined the fire that would pour from the missile when it was launched into the air. In his mind he saw it soar into the sky then, as if riding on it, he looked back to see the ground receding far below. A smile slowly stretched across his face. "Fire from this rocket will take it aloft, and it will rain down fire from above," he whispered.

Hamid admired the confidence Karim had shown in the tent, but he knew what Karim had not said, and in his heart there was nagging doubt. The missile had been designed by an Iranian team and constructed entirely by Iranian production facilities, but not all the parts for the package could be produced in Iran on an acceptable timetable. Components were acquired from suppliers, some of which were in Russia. One of those components was a Russian-made mobile launcher. Using it meant the Shahab missile could be easily and quickly transported to any location. Buying it from Russia meant it was available immediately. Likewise, the most crucial components for the warhead to which Karim referred were actually Russian components. What Karim and his assistants were doing now was reconfiguring them to fit in a modified version of the missile's original cone. It was the most critical part of the entire operation—and the most unsettling.

Hamid moved to the opposite end. He gazed into the missile's open top, where the payload cone had been removed. As he ran his fingers over the exposed wires, he quietly whispered a prayer to Allah that it would work as planned.

69

NEW YORK CITY

HOAG AND KINLAW STUMBLED into the alley behind the store. Kinlaw leaned against the wall on the opposite side and gasped for breath. "I have never been so scared," he said.

Hoag propped his hands on his knees and bent over. "Neither have I."

Kinlaw glanced around. "Where's that guy?"

"Which one?"

"The one who was chasing us just now." Kinlaw jerked his head around, first this way then that. "Where'd he go?"

Suddenly, the man in the orange and blue jacket appeared from the left. Hoag charged toward him, grabbed him around the waist, and pinned the man's arms at his side. The man twisted and turned and kicked with his knees, but Hoag held on.

"Get the gun!" Hoag screamed. "Get the gun."

To the right a broken board lay on the ground near an overflowing dumpster. Kinlaw grabbed it and swung at the man's head. The board made a swishing sound as it sliced through the air and grazed the top of the man's head. Through the hole in the ski mask, Kinlaw could see he was grinning. Kinlaw smacked him on the head again. This time the edge of the board caught the man squarely on the head and knocked him out cold. The pistol slipped from his fingers and clanked to the ground near his feet. His torso flopped forward and draped over Hoag's shoulder. Blood trickled from his ears. Hoag staggered backward as the man's weight fell on him. He twisted to one side and released his grip. The man slumped to the ground.

Kinlaw stared at him. "What do we do now?"

"Run," Hoag blurted out. "Let's get out of here." He turned away and started up the alley.

"Wait," Kinlaw called. "Don't we need to call somebody?" He stepped forward and peeled back the ski mask from the man's face. "You ever see this guy before?"

Hoag had gone a few steps away. He stopped and turned back. "No. Let's go."

"I think we should call someone."

"Call them later," Hoag snapped. "Those other two guys can't be far behind."

Just then the man in the brown T-shirt came around the corner. Kinlaw, still with the board by his side, struck him in the knees. The gun flew from his hands and sailed in the air. Hoag and Kinlaw spun in the opposite direction and ran up the alley toward the street.

"We should have gotten the gun," Kinlaw shouted.

"No time for it," Hoag replied.

At the end of the alley, they turned right and ran down the street. Three blocks later, they came to a stop in the shadows outside an apartment building near Columbus Circle. Kinlaw bent double, trying to catch his breath.

Hoag panted nearby. As his heart rate slowed, he moved his hands to his hips. "Where are the police?"

"Good question," Kinlaw stood up straight and listened. "I don't hear them. They should have been at the store by now."

"Maybe no one called."

"I thought you didn't want to call."

"I didn't want to call when we were in the alley." Hoag glanced around. "No one's on the street. Might be hours before someone else goes in there."

"Not our problem now."

"But in the meantime, those guys could be doing who knows what." Hoag took out his cell phone. "I'm calling someone."

Kinlaw grabbed his hand. "No you're not."

"Why not?"

"Think about it."

Hoag's forehead wrinkled in a frown. "Think about what?"

"About where we really work." Kinlaw pressed a button on Hoag's phone to end the call. "They'll ask too many questions, and we don't have time for it. You can't help that guy behind the counter now, anyway."

"But I—"

Kinlaw cut him off. "David, let it go."

70

ABOARD PANAMA CLIPPER
OFF NEW YORK HARBOR

A BELL RANG IN THE NIGHT as engines aboard the *Panama Clipper* slowed to an idle. The ship's deck rumbled and shuddered. Far below, the propellers slowed to a halt. Hakim Murad, captain of the ship, turned to a mate standing beside him. "Maintain your heading." He stepped toward the door. "Inform me of any contacts. I will be back in a moment." The man acknowledged him with a nod. Murad opened the door and stepped from the bridge.

Outside he leaned over the rail and scanned the main deck. A lone man stood between the stack of cargo containers and the superstructure. By the pose he struck—hands in his pockets, feet spaced apart, elbows wide—Murad knew the man on the deck below was Ephraim Zaheden. At the sight of him, Murad felt a pang of guilt.

Two years ago this moment had seemed a lifetime away. Now it was as though he had been instantaneously transported from that moment in the past to this moment in the present. His mind raced back to the day Nasser Hamid first approached him. He had been sitting in a café in Greece, waiting for clearance to unload the ship, the first stop on *Panama Clipper's* maiden voyage. Hamid took him for a ride along the waterfront and outlined the barest details of what he called a "special plan."

"You have been selected," Hamid had said, "by Adnan Karroubi."

Even now Murad felt something inside him leap at the thought of it. Karroubi was a member of the Assembly of Experts. One word from him could make or break a career, even a life. That a man like him knew Murad's name was an honor in itself. Later, on a visit to Tehran, Hamid arranged a meeting between Murad and Karroubi. It was one of the most special days of Murad's life.

For the following year Hamid had slowly revealed more and more of the plan. It had all seemed so innocent at first, but as the true nature of the endeavor became known, Murad had grown reluctant to participate. Life, even the life of an infidel, had been much too precious to treat with contempt. Then his cousin had appeared in photographs taken at a secret detention facility in Honduras, a facility operated by the CIA. His cousin, captured during a raid in the Philippines, depicted in the most... Murad pushed the image from his mind and thought of something else. Those photographs had driven him over the edge. Anyone who treated people with such disrespect must be opposed. Allah required it.

Still, the thought of what was about to happen—the enormity of it, the irreversible finality of it—struck a hollow place deep inside. He had done many things in life, some of them good, some of them bad; but this was one he could never undo.

Murad made his way down the steps. When he reached the deck, Zaheden glanced in his direction. Murad gestured for him to follow. Together, the two of them stepped around the corner of the container stack and walked toward the bow of the ship.

"We are twenty-three miles off the New York farewell buoy," Murad said. "We cannot lie outside the buoy long, or we will raise suspicions."

Zaheden smiled. "We are ready."

"Good," Murad sighed. "I can give you a few hours, but that is all. After that, someone will come to see why we have not called for a harbor pilot."

Zaheden turned away, walked past the container stack, and disappeared around the corner. When he was gone, Murad stepped to the railing and stared out at the dark, black sea. Wind from the east blew through his hair. Overhead, the sky was bright with stars. He took a cigarette from his pocket, stuck it between his lips, and lit it. A long, slow draw filled his lungs with smoke. He let it slowly escape as he leaned forward and propped his forearms on the railing.

These things must be done, he thought. Men of courage and valor were always called upon to take their place in history. They were not cowards, as the Americans often said, but men of dignity and commitment, men who could see beyond themselves. The Americans had once been like that, but not anymore.

"They are dogs," he mumbled to himself. "Eat like gluttons and lie in their own vomit."

Allah had chosen him not Hamid nor Osmani nor Karroubi. Allah had chosen him. Evil must be opposed, and he had been singled out as worthy to participate in that great cause. Waves of confidence and pride swept over Murad. He had been given a role in historic events, a destiny decreed by Allah. All that remained was for him to step into that moment.

A clanking sound interrupted Murad's thoughts. He turned to the left and caught a glimpse of Zaheden at the far end of the container stack. Murad took one more drag from the cigarette, then he flipped it over the railing and walked back toward the superstructure. As he turned the corner of the container stack, he saw Zaheden standing with two men at the door of an oversized container. Taller than the standard size, it had required special attention to fit it and a second one of the same size into the stack, placing them end-to-end.

One of the men, Sajjad Hadi, held a pair of snips in his hand. Of all the men on the crew, Sajjad made Murad the most nervous. His dark, deep-set eyes and hollow cheeks gave him the appearance of a madman. Murad had not wanted him onboard, but Zaheden had insisted. Murad watched as he clipped the wire seal from the door latch.

With the seal removed, the second man, Abu Hezaan, swung open the door. Hezaan was Murad's favorite. He had been on the crew since the ship first set sail. Murad had hired him from a list provided by Osmani, picking him at random from more than a hundred names. Even then, he had known Hezaan was someone special.

Through the open doorway, light from the upper deck reflected off the windshield of a truck parked inside the container. Murad studied it a moment then glanced away. Zaheden and the men with him stepped inside and pulled the door closed. When they were out of sight, he turned to find a crane operator.

71

NEW YORK CITY

KINLAW AND HOAG STARTED from the shadows by the building and walked up the street. At the corner, they hurried across the intersection, glancing in every direction, making sure they weren't followed.

As they reached the curb on the opposite side, Kinlaw grabbed Hoag's arm. "That's them," he whispered.

"Where?" Hoag looked around. "I don't see anyone."

"Up there," Kinlaw said, nodding to the left.

From the trees by Lincoln Square, three men hurried toward them. Kinlaw and Hoag turned to the right and ran in the opposite direction.

As the three men reached the corner, a police car rolled slowly past. The three men melted into the shadows. Hoag and Kinlaw ran up the street to the next corner then hurried downstairs into a subway station.

"What if it's not open?"

"It's open."

"We'll be trapped."

Kinlaw scanned his Metro card and pushed through the turnstile. Hoag followed him.

Moments later a train arrived. Kinlaw and Hoag got on and took a seat. They anxiously waited and watched through the windows for any sign of the three men. The platform outside was empty when the doors closed and the train started forward. They took a deep breath and tried to relax.

"What train is this?"

"I don't know," Kinlaw said, shaking his head, "and I don't care."

"We need to know." Hoag got up and checked a map near the door. "This is the A train."

"Good," Kinlaw replied. "Let's take it to the end of the line. That'll give us some time to think."

"Think Russell's back yet?"

"We better call him. If those guys are after us, they know where we've been staying."

"They'll be waiting for us when we get there."

Kinlaw took his cell phone from his pocket and glanced at the screen. "Never mind," he grumbled. "No service in this tunnel."

"So, what do we do?"

"We can't go back to the apartment."

"We can't let Russell walk into a trap, either."

72

ABOARD PANAMA CLIPPER

INSIDE THE CONTAINER, Zaheden switched on a portable light. The sudden, brilliant glare made his eyes squint. He blinked and focused on the floor to give his eyes a moment to adjust then handed the light to Sajjad. "Hold this and point it away from us."

Sajjad set the light on the front bumper of the truck and turned it to face the doors. Sitting in the container was a Russian-made tractor truck. Designed to tow a mobile missile launcher, it was built with the cab over the engine. Though the container was larger than the standard box, it was barely large enough to hold the truck.

Zaheden steadied himself with one hand against the fender of the truck and made his way along the side. There was just enough room for him to scoot between the tires and the wall of the container. When he reached the driver's door, he pulled it open and leaned inside. A tool belt lay on the floor beneath the steering wheel. He grabbed one end and pulled it out.

Two hammers hung from the belt, along with a large screwdriver and a heavy steel chisel. Zaheden strapped the belt around his waist, closed the door, and continued toward the opposite end of the container. Hezaan followed and Sajjad brought the light.

Unlike other containers, the back wall of this one was held in place by four pins, one at the top and bottom on each side. "Here."

Zaheden handed Hezaan a hammer then took a screwdriver from the tool belt. "Use this to get it started." He handed Hezaan the screwdriver. "Take out the pin at the bottom first."

While Hezaan worked on the left side, Zaheden placed the chisel against the head of the bottom pin on the right side and struck it with the hammer. The ringing sound echoed through the box. He struck it again and again. Finally, it moved upward. Hezaan did the same. With the bottom pins free, they stepped onto the rear frame rails of the truck. Reaching overhead, they repeated the process. Minutes later the top pins came free and fell to the floor. The back wall was now loose.

Hezaan and Zaheden jumped from the truck to the floor of the container. Working together, the three men moved the rear wall to the left and leaned it against the wall inside the box next to the truck. The glow from the light revealed the doors on the end of the next box.

Sajjad and Hezaan crawled beneath the truck and retrieved two bottles of gas and a long hose with a nozzle fitted at one end. Hezaan connected the hose to the regulator on the bottles and handed the nozzle to Sajjad. Moments later the torch produced a bright blue flame. Sparks flew as Sajjad cut the hinges from the doors on the next box.

With the hinges gone, Zaheden cut the seal from the door latch and unhooked it. The doors fell forward against the frame of the first box. Hezaan and Zaheden muscled them out of the way against the wall inside the second box.

Sajjad lifted the light from the truck and let it shine into the second box. They stood in awe as they gazed at the Shahab-3 missile resting on the launcher.

"Wow," Hezaan said. "That is big."

Sweat dripped from Zaheden's body. He wiped his face on the sleeve of his shirt. "Yes, it is very big. And wait 'til you see what happens when it blows up."

Sajjad moved the light to one side to see farther into the box. "Do you think we should be in here with this? Is it safe?"

Hezaan and Zaheden burst into laughter.

"Come on," Zaheden said. "Let's finish this."

They made their way back alongside the truck to the front of the first box and pushed open the door. The cool night air felt good against Zaheden's sweaty skin. He took a deep breath and glanced up to see the crane lift a box from the stack.

Working quickly, the crane operator and crew lifted the boxes from the stack above the second container. One by one, the crane swung them from the deck and dropped them into the sea. The containers bobbed on the water, then slowly sank out of sight.

When the crew removed the stack down to the box with the launch trailer, Zaheden stepped inside the container where the tractor truck was parked and climbed into the cab. He turned the switch and listened as the engine started. Hezaan carefully guided him back to the tongue of the launch trailer. Sajjad slipped the pin in place on the hitch. Coughing and gagging from the fumes, he and Sajjad hurried along either side of the truck to the cab and ran from the container.

Zaheden slipped the truck in gear and started forward slowly. When the trailer was clear of its container, the crane operator picked up the now-empty cargo container and dropped it over the side. Zaheden put the truck in reverse and eased the trailer backward into the open spot in the stack where the container had been. He left the engine idling and climbed from the cab.

73

RUSSELL COOPER'S APARTMENT
NEW YORK CITY

KINLAW AND HOAG EMERGED from the subway several hours later and slowly worked their way to Russell's apartment building. They hid in the shadows across the street and watched the front entrance.

"I don't see anyone." Hoag looked to the right. "Nothing down here. You see anything your way?"

"No."

"No vans." Hoag looked down the block once more. "Nothing out of the ordinary."

"It's been too long since we did this for real. We need to get out of here."

"Come on."

Kinlaw grabbed his arm. "We can't just walk in the front door."

"We can't stand out here all night, either."

Hoag led the way into the building. "Stairwell or elevator?"

"Elevator's a trap."

"Somebody might be in the stairwell." Hoag pressed a button for the elevator. "I'm riding." He and Kinlaw got on.

As they rode up, Kinlaw looked over at Hoag. "What do we do when the doors open?"

"Pray," Hoag replied.

"I've been doing that already."

Moments later, they reached the floor and the doors slid apart. Hoag and Kinlaw waited near the back of the elevator, but nothing happened. As the doors started to close, Hoag reached out and stopped them with his hand. He stood there, listening. When he heard nothing but the sound of his own breathing, he stepped quickly into the hallway to find it was empty. "Come on," he motioned. Kinlaw came from the elevator and followed him toward Russell's apartment. As they drew near, they saw the door was ajar. Hoag took Kinlaw by the arm to stop him. "This isn't good."

Light from the apartment streamed through an opening between the door and the doorframe. Kinlaw backed away. "I'm getting out of here."

Hoag grabbed his arm again. "We can't. Russell might be in there."

"And there's nothing we can do for him, just like that clerk in the store."

Hoag crept forward and gently pushed open the door with his foot. Kinlaw leaned over Hoag's shoulder. "Well, if we're going in, let's go." He gave the door a shove. It flew open and bounced off the wall with a loud bang. Startled, Hoag jumped to one side. Kinlaw stepped past him into the apartment.

"Hey Russell," he called. "Hoag is worried about you." He reached the doorway to the kitchen and stopped.

Hoag collided with him then leaned around to see. "What's the—"

Across the living room, Russell Cooper lay sprawled on the sofa, arms flung wide, feet dangling above the floor. Blood trickled from a single gunshot wound to his forehead, leaving a dark red line over the bridge of his nose, down through the corner of his right eye, and across his cheek. His eyes were open but set. His body was motionless.

The room was a mess. Papers, books, and magazines were strewn about the floor. The table that sat in front of the sofa was turned on its side. The overstuffed chair was upside down, its cushions ripped and torn. The television was smashed. Glass from the picture tube littered the floor in front of it.

Kinlaw started toward the sofa. Once again Hoag grabbed his arm. "Dennis, let's go."

"I need to check—"

"Let's go," Hoag repeated, his voice stern and commanding. "We gotta get out of here."

"I risked my life to come up here," Kinlaw retorted. "I'm getting my stuff." He jerked his arm free and walked to the bedroom where they had been sleeping. Like the living room, the bedroom was in shambles. The mattress had been shoved off the box springs and lay at a precarious angle against the window on the far wall. Drawers from the chest had been pulled out and tossed aside, the contents dumped in a pile near the foot of the bed. Kinlaw kicked his way across the room and pulled a leather satchel from the rubble.

Hoag watched from the door. "What's so important about that?" He tossed his hands in the air in a gesture of frustration. "Let's go."

"It has my notes." Kinlaw opened it and looked inside to make certain, then closed the flap and hung the strap of the satchel over his left shoulder. Using his foot as a rake, he pushed aside clothes and magazines. Underneath it all, he found a notepad. He stooped over, picked it up from the floor.

Hoag stalked across the room and grabbed him. "Let's go," he demanded.

"Where's the photograph of Hamid?"

"What photograph?"

"The one Winston gave us."

"I don't know," Hoag replied. "You can get another one when we get back to the office. I'm sure that wasn't his only copy."

"They took the photograph," Kinlaw said. His mind lost in thought, his voice had a light and airy tone, almost wistful. "Why would they take that photograph?"

"They didn't take it," Hoag countered. "If they had wanted the photograph they would have taken the satchel."

Kinlaw turned to face Hoag. "That photograph was here, in this notepad. I was looking at it earlier. They took it."

"Okay." Hoag said, impatiently. "They took it. Let's go."

"Nasser Hamid is the key." Kinlaw glanced around the room then turned back to Hoag. "Whatever they're up to, he's the key to it."

Hoag pulled him toward the door. "We really need to go."

"Why?" Kinlaw jerked free. "Where's your stuff?"

"I don't know. I don't care." Hoag took Kinlaw by the shoulders. "Look, they're coming back to finish the job." He was all but shouting. "They're coming back for us."

Kinlaw shifted the satchel strap higher on his shoulder and started toward the hall. As they walked down the hall toward the elevator, the sound of footsteps echoed from the stairway. Hoag rushed forward and pressed the button. The elevator doors opened just as the door opened from the stairway. Hoag shoved Kinlaw inside and jabbed his finger on the button for the first floor. Footsteps drew nearer. The elevator doors moved to close. Just as they were about to shut, a hand shot through to stop them. Brown-skinned fingers gripped the edge of the door. Through the sliver of a crack Hoag caught a glimpse of an orange and blue jacket. He jammed his foot against the door and wedged it tight to keep it from opening. "It's him," Hoag said in a coarse whisper. "The guy with the jacket."

Suddenly, a feeling of rage swept over Kinlaw. Rage that someone had tried to kill them at the corner store and chased them through the streets. Rage that someone had murdered Russell Cooper. In an instant he moved away from the wall, opened his mouth wide, and bit down hard on the fingers that gripped the door. He clamped tighter and tighter until he tasted blood on his lips.

In the hallway outside the man howled and struggled to pull back his fingers. Kinlaw slackened his grip. The man wrenched his hand from the opening, and the doors closed. The elevator bell dinged and the car started down.

74

ABOARD PANAMA CLIPPER

MURAD STOOD AT THE RAILING on the top deck outside the bridge and took a drag from yet another cigarette. Smoke escaped from his nostrils, wafted across his face, and drifted away with the wind. He paid it no attention. His eyes were fixed on Zaheden and the men below as they backed the missile launcher into place.

As the launch trailer came to a stop, the door to the bridge opened and a seaman leaned out. "Captain, we have received a coded message."

Murad stubbed out his cigarette in a receptacle near where he stood and turned away from the railing. The seaman held the door while Murad stepped onto the bridge and started toward the control panel. The first mate met him with a transcription of the message.

"We received this just now," he said. "The computer cannot decipher it. It does not appear to follow the company program."

"Very well." Murad took the message, glanced at it, then turned away. "I'll take care of it." He stepped from the bridge, moved downstairs to the deck below, and made his way to his stateroom. Inside, he took a key from his pocket and opened the closet. Three uniforms, cleaned and neatly pressed, hung there. Next to them were six white shirts, starched and pressed with creases down the sleeves. For the last five years they had been cleaned and prepared

329

by a woman who operated a laundry in Karachi. Twenty years his junior, she had never married and lived alone in an apartment above the shop. Each time he came to pick up the uniforms and shirts, she smiled at him in a way that always made him feel as though she wanted him to stay. She made him feel as though he wanted to as well. He thought of her every time he opened the closet. Now he wondered what she would think when she learned of his involvement in what was about to happen.

To the left of the uniforms was a single, smooth shelf. On it was a small, wooden box that held his uniform brass. Next to the box was a black leather notebook. He took the notebook from the shelf and turned away.

Across the room three portholes lined the wall. Beneath them was a desk. Book in hand, Murad made his way to the desk and took a seat in the chair behind it. He laid the coded message on the desk and looked at the first line. Numbers there told him which page to use in the notebook and which line to begin with on that page. He found the correct page and ran his finger down the line to the starting point. Using that as a key, he began to decipher the message, writing it on a pad as he translated it letter for letter and symbol for symbol.

Embedded in the translated message was yet another set of numbers. Using them, Murad turned to a different page and found another line from which to start. He worked through the message, deciphering it one more time. At a meeting in Oman, they had explained the process to him many times. They drilled him over and over on how to use the notebook, which numbers were critical, and how he would know he had deciphered the true message. It had been confusing at first, with numbers and lines and pages swirling around in his head, but they had assured him it was necessary and, when done right, provided a code that would defy all attempts to break it. He still remembered them saying, "No American computer, regardless of its power, can untangle the puzzle we have created."

Twenty minutes later Murad had completed the note. He placed the original message in the desk drawer, folded the deciphered version, and put it in his pocket. He returned the notebook to the closet and locked it away. Then he stepped from his room and started back to the main deck, where he located Zaheden. "We received this a few minutes ago." He handed Zaheden the note. "I think you will know what to do with it."

Zaheden gazed at the paper. On it was the numeric code necessary to launch the missile and the coordinates for the strike. Without a word he turned aside and made his way around the container stack to the launch trailer.

Murad climbed the stairs to the bridge deck and took his place once again along the railing. He folded his arms across his chest and watched as the cradle on the launcher began to rise from the trailer frame, bringing with it the precious cargo. Slowly, the missile lifted into an upright position.

The ship's crew, now fully aware of what was taking place, came to the main deck. Sajjad shooed them away and forced them back beyond the container stack, but they were curious and would retreat no further.

When the missile was in a vertical position, the cradle locked in place. Hezaan secured it there with two large steel pins then tipped his head back and gazed admiringly up at the missile. Almost four feet wide, it stood fifty-two feet tall. Stabilizer fins at the bottom protruded another two feet from the body. It was sleek and powerful and looked to him like one of the minarets at the mosque in Ashgabat, where he had lived as a child. His cousins lived on a street near there, and when he visited them he would sometimes stand at the window and listen to the mournful sound of adhan blaring over the loud speaker, calling the men to prayer. Soon the missile would rise above everything and rain down a warning to the Great Satan, calling them to prayer and to Allah.

75

NEW YORK CITY

HOAG WATCHED THE NUMBERS above the elevator door, which indicated the passing floors. Kinlaw spit to the side of the elevator and wiped his mouth in disgust.

"They'll be waiting for us at the bottom," Hoag said, quietly.

"It'll be sunup before long," Kinlaw sighed. "People will be out. It'll be tougher for them to do anything then."

"Yeah. And someone will find Russell lying on the couch and think we did it."

"They have no way to connect us to the murder."

"Two murders."

"Two?"

"The guy at the store and Russell."

"Boost me up." Kinlaw pointed to the ceiling. "Maybe there's an escape door."

"I thought you said they'd be gone by now."

"Boost me up anyway."

Hoag laced his fingers together to form a stirrup and held his hands near his knees. Kinlaw placed his foot on Hoag's hands and stepped up. Reaching over his head, he felt along the ceiling for an opening. As he pushed against the ceiling tile, one of them moved.

"Hey," he exclaimed. "I've found something."

Just then, a bell dinged. The elevator stopped. Hoag let go of Kinlaw's foot, and he dropped to the floor with a thud. Both men jumped to either side of the door and pressed their backs against the wall. The numbers showed they were at the second floor.

As the door opened, a middle-aged woman stepped inside. Yawning and unaware, she turned to the right to press a button. She saw Hoag and jumped.

Kinlaw spoke up. "Thought you were going to be someone we know."

The sound of his voice caught her off guard and she jumped again. She let out a breath then turned with her hand on her chest to face Kinlaw.

"Didn't mean to scare you," Kinlaw said, smiling.

She gave them a suspicious look. "What are you two doing in here?"

"We thought you were someone else."

"Yeah, right," she said. A frown pursed her lips. "Do I need to tell the doorman? You know, they have cameras in here."

Hoag's eyes brightened. "Where?"

She pointed to the back corner. "Right up there."

Hoag looked up at the camera, then over at Kinlaw. The woman moved to the back of the car. "You two are being weird." She pointed at the panel on the wall by the door. "Push the button for the lobby, and stand over there where you can't touch me." Hoag pressed the button and moved next to Kinlaw.

76

ABOARD PANAMA CLIPPER

MURAD STOOD AT THE RAILING outside the bridge and scanned the horizon. Sunlight reflected off the water with a brilliant glare. The sky was clear and blue. To the east white, puffy clouds drifted slowly toward the west. *Perhaps there will be rain tomorrow*, Murad thought to himself, *but not today*. He raised his hand to his brow and shielded his eyes as he checked the water around the ship. Only hours before it had been littered with cargo containers, bobbing on the waves. Now there was nothing but blue water and gently rolling waves.

Satisfied there were no other ships in the area, Murad turned his attention to the main deck below. From his vantage point high above, he watched Sajjad retrieve a laptop from the cab of the truck. A few moments later he emerged from the opposite end of the container. He squeezed around the rear tires of the cab and made his way alongside the launch trailer.

A seaman came from the bridge and tapped Murad on the shoulder. "They need you inside, sir."

Murad turned away and disappeared through the door.

At the back of the launch trailer, Sajjad handed the laptop to Zaheden and took a cable from his pocket. Zaheden pressed one end of the cable into the USB port on the computer and connected the other end to a cable jack on a panel at the base of the mobile launcher. He rested the laptop on his knee and pressed a switch. The screen flickered. Zaheden shifted positions and adjusted the angle of the screen to shield it from the early morning sunlight.

On the screen was a login page. Zaheden checked the decoded message from Murad and entered the numbers for the access code. A programming screen appeared. He moved the cursor to the proper box and entered coordinates for the guidance system. A second screen appeared. He checked his watch and entered a launch time in the box on the screen. A message appeared, indicating the computer was processing the information. Zaheden's fingers twitched while he waited. Less than a minute later, the screen changed. A new message appeared, indicating the code was authentic and the information had been accepted.

Zaheden disconnected the laptop, removed the cable from the panel on the mobile launcher, and handed them to Sajjad.

"Okay," he shouted. "We need to clear the area. Five minutes to launch."

The ship's crew retreated inside the superstructure. Sajjad and Hezaan climbed the steps to the top deck by the bridge. Zaheden checked one last time to make sure the wheels on the launch trailer were chocked and secured, then he ran to join them. Murad came from the bridge and stood at the railing next to Zaheden.

"It is ready?"

"Yes," Zaheden smiled. "It is ready."

"Think it will work?"

"Yes. This missile has been tested many times."

"No one has ever launched one from a ship before."

"No," Zaheden shook his head. "I do not think it has ever been done before. We are the first." He grinned at Murad. "The Americans will be surprised. The world will be surprised."

Murad nodded thoughtfully, "Will it set the ship on fire?"

Zaheden's countenance fell. "I…" he stammered. "I don't think so. Isn't the deck made of steel?"

"Yes." Murad pointed. "But that missile will give off quite a flame."

Zaheden glanced at his watch. "It is time. I set the program for six-thirty. It should have gone by now." A worried look swept over his face.

"What are you saying?"

"The missile should be going by now."

Murad's eyes darkened. "What do we do if it does not work?"

"Reprogram it," Zaheden shrugged. "I guess."

"You would go down there to do that?"

Zaheden leaned away from the rail. "Yes," he replied. "I will do that if necessary."

Suddenly, smoke boiled from the bottom of the missile and billowed like a cloud, rising up the missile, engulfing all but the very tip of the point. Flames burst in every direction, rumbling from the nozzles of the engine with a dull roar and then an earsplitting shriek. Zaheden shouted something at Murad, but he could not hear a word.

Finally, the missile broke free of the launch trailer, shot from the deck of the ship, and lifted into the sky.

77

FORT MEADE, MARYLAND

TWO HUNDRED MILES above the earth, transmissions sensors on a Northstar KH-12 surveillance satellite detected a signal from the guidance system on the Shahab missile as the missile communicated with a computer on the launch trailer aboard the *Panama Clipper*. The satellite's sensors alerted its onboard computer to the detection. Within seconds, telemetry transmitted from the missile was read, analyzed, and interpreted.

At the same time, tracking sensors mounted just above the satellite's solar panels locked onto the missile's position. The onboard tracking system triggered micro-bursts from retrorockets located at either end of the satellite to slow the speed of its normal orbit around the earth, causing it to maintain its position directly over the launch site.

While all that happened, the satellite's cameras focused on the launch point, collecting images of the *Panama Clipper*. Within seconds the satellite began transmitting digital pictures to a computer at the National Security Agency (NSA) on the grounds of Fort Meade, a U.S. Army installation outside Baltimore, Maryland.

Clear, sharp images in the pictures showed the missile as it cleared the launcher, Zaheden's wide grin as he looked up from his place along the railing, and Murad's name on a small nameplate pinned in place above the pocket of his uniform jacket.

At NSA's Threat Assessment Section, those images fed automatically into a predetermined database. Activity in that database sent an alert message to a monitor in an office down the hall. The alert message triggered a warning signal that beeped from a speaker embedded in the lower right corner of the monitor frame.

Evan Runyon, the duty information clerk, sat at the monitor, feet propped on the edge of the desk, head back, and his eyes closed. In each ear were ear-buds attached by thin, white wires to an iPod player. Music blared from the player loud enough to be heard down the hall. The warning tone ceased before Runyon could realize anything was amiss.

78

CHEYENNE MOUNTAIN, COLORADO

WHEN THE COMPUTER AT NSA processed images from the satellite, it simultaneously transmitted them over a fiber optic cable to a computer in the North American Aerospace Defense Command (NORAD) operations control center at Cheyenne Mountain, Colorado. Seconds after the launch from the *Panama Clipper*, alarm bells sounded there.

A tightly arranged room, the control center was organized around a central console located in the middle of the room. A large main screen covered the wall directly opposite the console. Smaller screens filled the spaces on either side and on the two perpendicular walls. Additional work stations filled the area around the center console, each with a keyboard and an array of flat-screen monitors, telephone panels, and indicator lights, each one designated for a particular officer and a particular purpose.

When the alarm sounded, the missile's launch point in the Atlantic Ocean flashed in red on the main screen. Seconds later, computers buried deeper in the mountain calculated the trajectory and impact point. That information was plotted with a red line superimposed on the map. A digital clock in a small textbox inserted at the projected strike point counted down the time to impact. Similar information appeared on the monitors at the work stations around the room. By the computer's calculations, impact would occur near DuPont Circle in Washington, D.C., not far from the White House, three minutes, forty-nine seconds from launch.

Across the center, personnel swung into action. As operations officers and analysts struggled to cope with the situation, Air Force Brigadier General Tom Simpson, NORAD's deputy commander, burst into the control room. Tall, with broad shoulders and a slender waist, he had a commanding presence and looked like a character from a Hollywood movie. He talked fast, loud, and rough, always with a cigar shoved in the corner of his mouth.

"All right, people," Simpson shouted. "As you can see, this is not a drill." He looked to the right. "Threat Assessment, what is this Alert Warning flashing on my screen?"

"An Iranian Shahab-3 missile, sir. Inbound from fifty miles off the tip of Long Island."

"Conventional?"

"Negative, sir. It's carrying a single nuclear device. Armed when it left the launch rack."

"Scramble whatever we have on the East Coast and get it in the air. Alert the Navy and find out where that thing came from."

"Sir, we have the location plotted already."

"I don't mean the location," Simpson shouted. "Your launch point is in the Atlantic Ocean. Unless that missile can swim, it came from a boat of some kind. Tell the Navy to find it. Now!"

Simpson snatched a phone receiver from its cradle. "Get me Admiral Keating," he barked.

A moment later Keating, NORAD's commanding officer, was on the phone. Simpson pulled the cigar from his mouth and held it in his hand while he talked. "Admiral, we've detected the launch of an Iranian Shahab-3 missile, apparently launched from onboard a ship lying fifty miles off New York City. The missile's headed for Washington, D.C. Impact will occur in approximately three minutes."

"That's good, Tom," Keating chuckled. "I suppose this is another one of your unscheduled drills. They've lost their novelty, you know, but I'll go along with it." He paused to take a breath. "Authenticate this message."

"No, sir," Simpson snapped. "This is not a drill."

"Authenticate, Tom. This is a covered line. Follow the procedure. It always saves paperwork when you follow procedure. After all, isn't that the purpose of these drills?"

Simpson snatched a card from his pocket and read the authentication code. "Simpson, Tom. Brigadier General. Authentication code X3Y2874." There was no response. "Sir, are you there? We have an actual casualty, sir."

Keating's voice was barely audible. "They're going to hit the White House?"

"Very close, sir. About fifteen blocks."

"Then stop talking to me and call somebody!" Keating shouted. "Call the White House! Get the Pentagon!"

Without waiting for further instructions, Simpson pressed a button to end the call. He extended his hand to the right to press a red button on the console, then hesitated. Unlike most communications panels, the red button on this one wouldn't connect him to an operator or a switchboard. Pressing that button gave him instant access to the White House and set in motion predetermined procedures that would be followed to the letter, no matter what, even at the cost of human life. Simpson drew back his finger and glanced up at the screen. The line tracking the trajectory indicated the missile already was a quarter of the way to its destination. Simpson jabbed the button. Immediately, the duty officer in the White House situation room was on the line.

"This is Simpson at NORAD. We're tracking an inbound missile with a nuclear warhead. Impact in three minutes on your position. Get the president in the bunker. Now!"

Simpson pushed a button to end the call then pressed the green button next to it. Before he could shove the cigar back in his mouth, the duty officer at the Pentagon picked up.

"This is Simpson at NORAD. We have a Code Red alert on your position. I repeat. We have a Code Red on your position."

79

ASHDOD, ISRAEL

AT THE MOSSAD OPERATIONS CENTER in Ashdod, Israel, a technician stared at the screen on the wall, mouth open, eyes wide in disbelief. Finally, he shouted, "We have a launch. Alert! Alert! Alert!" A buzzer sounded. The room came alive with activity. The doors to the room opened and Efraim Hofi entered.

"What happened?" Everyone pointed toward the screen. Hofi turned in that direction. A thin blue line rose from a point in the Atlantic Ocean, off the coast of New York. Hofi ran his fingers through his hair as he stared at the image. "We are certain this is correct?"

"Yes," the technician replied. "Launch was detected less than a minute ago."

"Did the Americans see it?"

"Yes. Telemetry was transmitted to NSA and to NORAD."

Hofi looked down at a monitor on a desk a few feet away. "Are we still in their system?"

"Yes," someone responded. "They have not requested that we disconnect."

"Is this from our satellite or theirs?"

"This is ours."

"The missile is armed?"

"Yes. Carrying a single nuclear warhead. Armed at launch."

"Very well," Hofi replied. "Notify our troops. Place all forces on Alert One status."

An operator at the central console pressed a button on the panel in front of him and spoke into a microphone that hung from his headset. "This is a forces status emergency update. Alert One. Alert One. This is not a drill."

Hofi leaned against a desk and folded his arms across his chest. "Point of impact?"

"Washington, D.C."

Hofi's eyes were wide. "You are certain?"

"Impact in approximately three minutes."

"Exact location of the strike?"

"A little north of the White House. DuPont Circle."

"Any activity in our region?"

"None detected."

Hofi picked up a phone. "Get me the prime minister." Moments later David Oren was on the line. Hofi spoke in an even, calm voice. "Mr. Prime Minister, we have detected a missile launch from the Atlantic Ocean. Point of impact is Washington, D.C."

"There is no doubt?"

"No sir," Hofi replied. "Impact will occur in less than three minutes." The phone was silent. A frown wrinkled Hofi's forehead. "Sir?"

"Have you notified our troops?"

"Yes sir."

"Any activity in the region?"

"No, sir. None that we have detected."

"This is happening quicker than we thought."

"Yes, Mr. Prime Minister. They were further along than we realized."

"Very well. I shall convene the cabinet at once. No point in holding anything back from them now. We must be ready for the inevitable."

80

WHITE HOUSE, WASHINGTON, D.C.

BRAXTON KITTRELL SLAMMED THE PHONE DOWN on his office desk and sprinted up the staircase to the second floor of the White House. As he came from the stairs the door to the residence flew open. Brett Davis, head of the president's Secret Service detail, burst into the hall. Behind him came six agents with Hedges and his wife, Mary, in tow.

"Brax. I was hoping you'd join us," Hedges quipped. "They tell me we're going to the bunker."

Kittrell looked him in the eye. "Jack, this isn't a drill. It's the real thing."

"What?" The smile vanished from Hedges' face.

By then they'd reached the stairs. Kittrell joined them as they hurried down the steps. "NORAD detected a missile launch from somewhere east of Long Island."

"The ocean?"

"Yes sir. A ship."

"Whose ship?"

"We don't know yet."

At the bottom of the steps, Davis guided Hedges into the hall- way. Agents formed a wedge and hurried forward, knocking White

House staff aside in a rush toward yet another stairway at the far end. Kittrell worked to keep up.

Hedges shouted over his shoulder. "Where's the vice president?"

"We'll get him, sir," Davis replied. "Agents are with him now."

"Brax, are you still back there?"

"Yes sir, Mr. President," Kittrell shouted. "I'm here."

81

CHEYENNE MOUNTAIN, COLORADO

OFFICERS MANNING THE OPERATIONS CONTROL CENTER at NORAD's Cheyenne Mountain facility watched the screen on the main wall as a thin, red line plotted the track of the Shahab-3 missile. For three minutes they saw it rise in the air and curve in a long, dreadful arc toward its destination in the center of Washington, D.C.

At desks and computer terminals throughout the center, calculations were being made in a desperate attempt to determine the consequences of the missile's impact. The number of projected human deaths rose to millions. Estimates of the physical destruction and misery seemed incalculable, the cost and financial impact beyond comprehension.

All too quickly the line on the screen reached the city. Everyone braced for news of the impact, of buildings leveled in an instant, houses obliterated, and lives evaporated in a moment of intense heat and unspeakable devastation. Instead there was only stunned silence as the missile reached an altitude of nearly 120 miles above Washington then abruptly disappeared.

Simpson stared at the screen, his eyes wide and his jaw slack, waiting any moment for what everyone knew would happen. Slowly, as if all the energy had been drained from his body, he brought his hand to his lips and took the cigar from his mouth. "What's going on?"

"We're checking, sir."

"Checking?" he shouted, the energy suddenly returning. "We don't have time for checking. We gotta know what's happened."

"Sir," someone shouted, "there's been a detonation!"

"A detonation? Where?"

"At one hundred twenty miles, sir."

Simpson shoved the cigar back in his mouth. "Damage reports," he barked.

"Nothing yet, sir, but a blast like that will take out all communications," someone suggested. "The East Coast will be in the dark."

Simpson ran his fingers through his hair. "How far does the zone reach?"

"We've calculated it at five hundred miles, sir."

"Put it on the map. I need to see it."

An officer seated to the right pressed keys on a keyboard. A red circle appeared on the map. "This is it, sir. North to Boston, south to Atlanta, west to Louisville, Kentucky."

"All right." Simpson's voice was unusually calm. "Anything domestic going to survive?"

Guy McCook, a civilian analyst, came to his side. "I doubt it. Gamma rays generated by the explosion will cause almost every piece of electronic equipment within the zone to stop working."

"I know about the science."

"Anything plugged into the power grid will be ruined."

"So the answer is, nothing commercial will survive."

"Not much."

"Any damage to our satellites?"

"We don't think so. All our links are still functioning. And, we have no reports of structural damage within the blast zone. Most people won't even realize a nuclear explosion has occurred."

Simpson sighed. "Until their cell phones stop working."

"They noticed that immediately, but they won't know it was a nuclear explosion."

"News media will be all over it," Simpson groused. "They'll know about it within the hour. There'll be panic in the—" He cut himself off. "They won't know that because they don't have power."

"Right," McCook replied. "Might be an issue in the West, but not in the East. At least, not immediately."

Simpson had a stricken look. "Airplanes," he mumbled.

McCook looked puzzled. "Sir?"

Simpson glanced around the room. "Those planes I scrambled on the East Coast," he barked. "Did any of them get off the ground?"

"One made it in the air before the blast," someone called from across the room. "Two were at the end of the runway. The rest were still in the hangars."

"Is it still flying?"

"Sir?"

"The one that made it up. Is it still in the air?"

"We don't have a report on that yet, sir."

"Get me a report."

"Yes, sir."

Simpson picked up the telephone receiver. "Get me the White House."

"The White House switchboard is down, sir," an operator replied.

"Then get me the Situation Room." His voice sounded irritated.

"They're out too, sir."

"Well then, get me the bunker." His frustration had reached the boiling point.

"We're working on it."

He slammed the phone down and shouted, "We're supposed to be able to survive this!"

82

NEW YORK CITY

KINLAW AND HOAG SAT AT A TABLE near the windows in the Corner Bagel Market on Lexington Avenue. Bright morning sun reflected through the glass. It felt warm on Hoag's shoulder as he took a bite of bagel. "I still think we should go back to that store first."

"Would you quit with the store?" Kinlaw took a sip of coffee. "We aren't going back there."

"Think they found him yet?"

"I'm sure they did. But I'm not going back there. You can keep bringing it up, but I'm not going back there." Kinlaw sighed. "We need to get back to Langley. Talk to Winston."

"Good." Hoag swallowed the bite of bagel. "How do we do that?"

"Go to the train station," Kinlaw grinned. "Get a train out of here. If there's not a train running, we'll take a bus. If there's no bus, I'll call Debby and she can come get us."

"You should have thought about that yesterday," Hoag needled.

"We were still reading FBI files yesterday." Kinlaw tipped his cup and drank the last of the coffee. He set the empty cup on the table, wadded the bagel wrapper, and looked at Hoag. "You about ready to go?"

Hoag took one more bite of bagel and nodded. "Yeah," he said with his mouth full. "I'm ready."

From the bagel store they started down Lexington Avenue, heading south. Kinlaw walked with a purpose, taking long strides. Hoag had to adjust his gait to keep up.

"Don't you think it's pretty clear we've found what we were looking for?"

"I think it's obvious we've asked the right questions," Kinlaw replied. They reached the corner. Kinlaw paused to check for traffic on the cross street then stepped from the curb. "But now we have new ones."

"Like?"

"Like why that FBI agent in China was murdered and what his connection is to all this."

"You think Winston can answer that question?"

"Maybe. Right now, I can't think very clearly, though."

"Being shot at has a way of befuddling the mind."

Kinlaw glanced at Hoag. "Befuddling the mind?"

Before Hoag could respond, his cell phone rang. He took it from his pocket and glanced at the screen. The call was from Jenny. She sounded irritated.

"You didn't call me back."

"Sorry. I've been kind' a busy."

"Busy?"

"I'll tell you about it in a little while. We should be back today."

"This can't wait. I found—" The call ended abruptly. Hoag moved the phone from his ear and glanced at the screen to find it was blank. He pressed a button, but nothing happened. "This thing is dead." He looked over at Kinlaw. "You got any charge left on yours?"

"I think so." Kinlaw took his phone from his pocket and pressed a button. The screen on the phone was blank. "Hmm," he mused. "Mine's blank, too."

Hoag tapped him on the shoulder. Kinlaw looked up. Hoag pointed toward the street. "Look," he said. "Nothin's moving."

Kinlaw glanced around, suddenly aware of how quiet the city had become. "Listen."

"To what?"

"The silence."

Hoag and Kinlaw stared in awe as they surveyed the scene around them. In every direction the streets were jammed with cars and trucks, all silent on the pavement. No engine noise. No car horns blaring. Not even the rumble of subway trains beneath the sidewalk.

"Nothing's working."

"No lights. No cars. No trains."

"A blackout."

"But why?"

Slowly, their eyes met. Mouths agape, they stared at the city around them. Every traffic light was out. Every car was stopped.

"Winston was right," Hoag whispered.

"What?"

"Winston was right. Nothing is working."

"What are you talking about?"

"The other day, when we were in the Operations Center, he was talking about how a nuclear explosion would make everything stop working."

"An electronic pulse."

"Yeah," Hoag nodded.

"But there hasn't been a nuclear explosion."

"Wouldn't have to be here. Could have been anywhere within four or five hundred miles, even farther if they did it at a higher altitude."

"They did it?"

Hoag looked at Kinlaw, his eyes wide with realization. "They did it."

"I didn't mean they would actually do it," Kinlaw mumbled. "I was just throwing it out as an idea."

"Well, you were right."

"You think it really was a ship?"

"How else could they do it?"

"But could it be that simple?"

"Yes. It could be that simple."

Kinlaw grabbed Hoag by the shoulder. "Come on, we have to tell someone."

"How are we going to do that?"

"I don't know. But we can't stand around here gawking like tourists."

83

CIA HEADQUARTERS
LANGLEY, VIRGINIA

AFTER A RESTLESS NIGHT wondering why Hoag hadn't called her back, Jenny had driven to work early. She parked in the deck across from the headquarters building and placed the call to Hoag's cell phone from the car. When the phone went dead she moved it from her ear to find the screen was dark. "Did he hang up on me?" She pressed a button to illuminate the screen, but nothing happened. "What's wrong with this thing? I charged it last night." Then she noticed the lights in the parking deck were off. She opened the car door and got out.

As she walked away from the car, she pressed the remote to lock it. Nothing happened, so she pressed it again, and again, but still nothing happened. "This is too weird."

Jenny walked across the drive and entered the headquarters building. She passed through building security and started toward the elevators. A guard stepped out to stop her. "We're having a problem with the elevators this morning, ma'am."

"A problem?"

"Yes ma'am."

"Can I get to the basement?"

"Only if you walk."

"Okay."

"Not sure you want to do that."

"Why not?"

"It's dark down there. No light at all."

"I'll be okay." She turned away and started toward the stairs. As she opened the door to the stairwell, the lights flickered then came on.

Expanded and renovated in the 1990s, the CIA building had been designed and engineered to withstand all conceivable catastrophes, both manmade and natural. Every system in the building—electrical power, telephone, heating, air conditioning—all had redundant alternatives. Though wired to the utility power grid, the facility used two generation units located on the grounds as its primary source of electricity. If the building was without electrical power, it meant both the commercial grid and the on-site generators were not functioning. Jenny ticked off a list of reasons why they might not be operable—none of them were good.

The computer screen on Jenny's desk glowed green. She switched it off and then turned it back on. It made a sizzling sound and showed only black and white images. "This thing is fried," she grumbled. The door to her office was open. She called with a loud voice to no one in particular. "Anybody know what happened?"

The sound of footsteps came from the hallway, then Winston Smith appeared in the doorway. He had a grim look on his face. "We have a problem."

"Somebody forget to pay the electric bill?"

"I wish it was that simple." Winston closed the door, pulled a chair near her desk, and sat down.

Jenny turned to face him. "What's the matter, Winston?" She thought of David, the phone call that ended abruptly, and the way he sounded that morning. Her heart beat faster. "Has something happened?"

Winston nodded. "There's been an explosion."

"What kind of explosion?"

Winston lowered his voice to a whisper. "A high-altitude nuclear explosion."

Deep furrows wrinkled Jenny's brow. "Where?"

"NORAD says detonation occurred at one hundred twenty miles. And almost exactly above DuPont Circle."

"High altitude? A missile?"

"Yes."

"Where did it come from?"

"A ship off the New York coast."

"A warship?"

"No. Looks like it was launched from a commercial freighter."

Jenny had a sinking feeling in her stomach. "What ship was it?"

"Nobody's saying yet. Electrical impulse hit the grid pretty hard. Blackouts are spreading up and down the coast. Telephone service is spotty, at best. Not a lot of information available right now."

"Let me show you something." Jenny scooted her chair back from her desk and opened the top drawer. "I came in early to bring you this." She took out prints she had made of the ships owned by Pakistan Shipping. "David asked me to help him locate surveillance video for several container ships."

"He showed me that list. What did you find?"

She spread the prints across the desktop. "This is the *Santiago*. It was loaded in Guangzhou, China. Sailed for Long Beach five days ago." She pointed to the next print. "This is the *Amazon Cloud*. It sailed from Aden, Yemen, bound for Newport, Virginia. It ought to be close by now." Then she pointed to the third print. "This is the

Panama Clipper. Left Bremerhaven about ten days ago." She looked over at Winston. "The *Panama Clipper* was sailing for New York."

Winston closed his eyes and shook his head. "They were right."

"All three ships are owned by Pakistan Shipping, a company controlled by Nabhi Osmani. David was interested in the *Panama Clipper* because of this." She took another print from the drawer and laid it in front of Winston. "Two oversized cargo containers. Both with the same symbol on their doors." She laid an image of the symbol next to the print.

"A star with a circle."

"A Star of David," Jenny explained, "with a crescent moon shaped in a way that surrounds the star."

"This doesn't look good."

"It gets worse. We have video of all three of these ships at their last known port. All three of them took on oversized cargo containers just like the two loaded in Bremerhaven."

"Hoag and Kinlaw talked to me the other day about using ships to launch missiles."

"If they're right, there are two more ships out there."

Winston pointed to the prints on the desk. "Have you written any of this up?"

"It's a rough draft."

"Get your stuff." He scooted back the chair and stood. "You're coming with me."

"Where are we going?"

"Way above your pay grade."

84

PRESIDENTIAL EMERGENCY OPERATIONS CENTER EAST WING OF THE WHITE HOUSE

MARY HEDGES SAT AT THE conference table and watched as her husband paced back and forth across the room. On the opposite side of the table, Braxton Kittrell sat with his fingers laced behind his head, eyes closed, legs stretched out in front. "Mr. President, why don't you have a seat and try to relax," Kittrell suggested.

"Relax?" Hedges fumed. "A missile with a nuclear warhead is coming straight for us, and you think I should relax? Forget it." He turned toward the door. "I'm getting out of here." He strode across the room.

Brett Davis moved to block his path. "Mr. President, I can't let you do that."

"Why not?"

"We don't know what conditions are like up there."

"That's right," Hedges retorted. "And for all we know, there could be nothing left. This could be part of a coup, a plot to take over the government." There was a hint of irony in his voice. "Don't kill the president, just lock him in the White House bunker and let him starve to death."

"Mr. President, we have people who can work the situation, no matter what has happened. They're trained well. They'll do what they've been trained to do." Davis took a deep breath. "Besides, you can't get out anyway."

"Why not?"

"The blast doors weigh twenty tons. They're locked in place and won't open without the proper code."

"You have the code?"

"Yes, Mr. President. I do."

"And you aren't using it."

"No, Mr. President." Davis shook his head with the hint of a smile. "I can't. Not until someone notifies me that it's safe for you to get out."

"Well they can't do that, Brett." Hedges pointed in frustration over his shoulder. "The phones don't work."

Davis pointed toward the ceiling. "The lights are still on, Mr. President. The system is operating according to plan. They know we're down here. I assure you, someone will get the phones working soon enough."

"I'm not supposed to be down here." Hedges' voice took a sarcastic tone. "I'm supposed to be aboard the Doomsday plane, preparing for the destruction of the world." He looked around with disgust. "This place hasn't been used since Truman was president."

"Actually." Braxton paused to move his arms from behind his head. He brought his feet around to stand. "This room was used by Dick Cheney during the 9-11 attacks." He pointed. "Moved the phone to the table and sat right over there, about where Mary's sitting."

"Mr. President, the E-4B would be a much better place for us," Davis explained, "but there wasn't time to get there. According to NORAD, we only had a three-minute warning."

"NORAD," Hedges groused. "They're used to living under-ground. Nothing but a bunch of well-paid moles." He shook his head. "I feel so powerless!" he shouted. "I'm the leader of the most powerful nation on earth and I'm hiding in a hole under the White House!"

"We're doing the best we can," Davis assured him.

"Is this the best we can do, Braxton?" Hedges looked across the room at Kittrell. "Three minutes? That's all our billions of dollars gets us? Just three minutes?" Hedges paced back and forth. "Minutemen with binoculars looking out their bedroom window could get us three minutes."

Mary patted the back of the chair next to hers. "Calm down, Jack. Come over here and have a seat." Out of sight beneath the table, her left knee bounced uncontrollably. Her hands shook and her heart raced. Fear gripped her deep inside, but she summoned every ounce of strength in her body and forced her mind to maintain control. This was no time to give in to emotion. "Take a seat next to me," she cooed. "There's nothing you can do right now, anyway." Hedges stopped pacing and stared at her. "Come on," she smiled. "Sit with me. Maybe Braxton will find us something to drink."

Reluctantly, Hedges gave in. With four defiant strides he reached the chair and flopped down on it. He sat there a moment then looked over at her. "Mary," he sighed, "did you ever think it would come to this?"

"In all the years I've known you, I never once thought about being locked in the bunker with you. But, yes," the smile on her face spread to a grin, "I always knew you'd be president."

"That's way more than Braxton gave me." Hedges gestured across the table. "He thought we were done when I was governor and decided not to support the marriage bill."

"You were being a politician," Kittrell groaned. "I don't like it when you do that."

"I was being a Democrat," Hedges chided. "Which is something you ought to consider trying sometime."

Mary listened to their easy banter and let her mind wander back to memories of years gone by. She had known them both since their days at Dartmouth College. Braxton was her roommate's brother. He asked her to a football game during their junior year. Hedges played quarterback on the team. President of the student body, Mr. All-American, she had always admired him but had never found a way to meet him. After the game, she and Braxton attended a party at the Kappa Sigma fraternity house. Hedges was there with one of the cheerleaders. They met, of course, and even danced together but nothing more.

Two days later Hedges came to the dorm to ask her out. Braxton had already sent her a note telling her Hedges was interested and urging her to say yes. Just now, sitting in the bunker, listening to them and thinking about all that had happened between them, she realized that evening at the fraternity house had been part of an elaborate scheme, a way to get the two of them together. She smiled at the thought and felt warm inside. She reached over and ran her fingers along Hedges' arm.

Braxton was right, too, about Hedges' political career reaching an impasse over the marriage bill. Mary knew it and so did he. If he had been standing for reelection that year, he would have lost. But by the following year the issue was forgotten as everyone scrambled to find a way to balance the budget. When legislators tried to cut state social programs, Hedges used a veto to bring the government to a halt. That showdown was the turning point in his career. It had been a heady time, so important and critical to so many. Now it all seemed so long ago and utterly irrelevant.

Davis stepped forward. "Mr. President, we're going to be moving shortly."

"Where are we going?" At the opposite side of the room, the blast doors started to open. Hedges stood. "What's happening, Brett?"

"There's been a nuclear detonation."

"Where?"

"A hundred twenty miles above DuPont Circle."

"A hundred twenty miles?"

"It was a high-altitude detonation, sir. There's been no physical damage on the ground, but the power grid is out on the East Coast. We have to get you to a secure facility."

Hedges had a stern look. "I don't want to leave the White House. George Bush was away from the White House during 9-11 and it didn't look good. No one else can leave. It'll look bad if I do."

Kittrell spoke up, "Mr. President, you have to go. We can't run the risk of something happening to you. The country can't afford a succession of office right now. Not on top of this."

"Where would I go?" Hedges looked around at the others with a bewildered expression. "If they can drop a bomb on DuPont Circle, where can we go and be safe?"

Two agents hurried into the room. They took Hedges by either arm and hustled him toward the door. Davis followed behind them, explaining, "We have secure bases outside the affected area, Mr. President. We need to get you aboard the Airborne Command Center now."

85

BERLIN, GERMANY

JOSEF MUELLER SAT IN THE BACK SEAT of a Mercedes limousine and watched as Berlin's central city moved past. The car turned into the drive at the Chancery complex, came to a stop under the portico, and Mueller stepped from the car. As he crossed the pavement to the building entrance, a guard snapped to attention. A few feet from the door Franz Heinrich rushed to his side. "Mr. Chancellor, we have a crisis."

"What is it, Franz?"

"We need you in the Situation Room."

A six-member Chancery security detail fanned out ahead of Mueller and Heinrich as they walked briskly inside, turned right, and started downstairs. At the bottom of the steps they entered the Situation Room, a self-contained command center beneath the Chancery's first floor.

At the far end of the room was a large projection screen. Television monitors were mounted on either side. The main screen showed a map of the world. News from Berlin, New York, and London played on the monitors.

A conference table occupied the center of the room. Around it were seated Georg Scheel, the Foreign Office minister, and representatives from the German army, navy, air force and the Federal

Police. They all came to attention as Mueller entered. He acknowledged them with a nod and pulled a chair from the end of the table. "Good afternoon. Take a seat, please." Everyone sat. Mueller looked around the table. "I understand we have a situation. General Erhard, what do we know?"

Erhard, commander of the German air force, stood. "Mr. Chancellor, ten minutes ago our satellites detected the launch of a missile from a point in the Atlantic Ocean approximately forty kilometers off the coast of New York City. The missile carried a nuclear warhead. It was armed at launch. At an altitude of approximately one hundred ninety kilometers, the warhead detonated directly above Washington, D.C."

Mueller kept a calm external appearance, but inside his heart raced. It had happened, even better than he had planned. Someone had finally struck the United States a crippling blow. Now Germany could return to her rightful place as leader of the world. He had predicted a catastrophic event. Now that catastrophe had occurred. Nothing could stop him now. He cleared his throat and tried to act in a predictable manner. "Are there any casualties?"

"None, sir. However, the electromagnetic pulse of the blast has disabled most of the electrical grid for the eastern half of North America."

"The grid?"

"Yes, Chancellor. Electrical generation facilities have been rendered inoperable. Everything electronic no longer works."

"Wall Street financial markets?"

Erhard shook his head. "It is early still. They have not yet opened. Our estimate is they will not be trading for the foreseeable future."

Beneath the table Mueller rested his hand along the top of his thigh. His fingers ran lightly over the fabric of his trousers, tracing across the sun wheel medallion tucked safely inside his pocket. "And what has been the American response thus far?"

"Their military is on alert. Their navy has gone silent."

"Silent?"

"Yes, Chancellor. We have been unable to locate any of their submarines. Two of their carriers have disappeared."

"Should we anticipate an immediate military response from them?"

Someone down the table spoke up. "If they can figure out who to hit, I'm sure they'll blow up something in retaliation."

"Does anyone know who did this?"

Scheel nodded. "Initial sources point to Iran, but the Americans will no doubt link this to Al-Qa'ida."

"Why?"

Hermann Schroeder from the Federal Police stood. "As best we can determine, the ship from which the missile was launched was owned by Pakistan Shipping. That company has ties to Osama bin Laden."

Scheel continued, "And if they think it was Osama, they'll surely suspect he obtained the missile from Pakistan."

"A knee-jerk reaction," added Schroeder.

Mueller looked around the table. "Is there any indication of a threat against Germany?"

Schroeder shook his head. "None, sir."

Mueller rested his hands on the tabletop. "Very well. Establish a naval perimeter around our ports. Make certain nothing enters that does not already have clearance." He looked over at Erhard. "Can we re-task our satellites to concentrate on the German coast?"

"We already have three monitoring the region."

"Good. Place our navy and air force on alert. Come up with a plan to reinforce the Federal Police should we need extra security on the streets." Mueller paused and looked around the room. "Is there anything else?" When no one spoke, Mueller stood. The others did as well. "Keep me informed of developments, and let me know immediately of any American response."

Mueller glanced at Scheel and gestured toward the door. Together, they stepped outside to the hallway. When they were alone, Mueller leaned close to Scheel's side. "Arrange a meeting of the European ministers."

"You wish to convene a meeting of the Council?"

"Yes."

"Very well, Chancellor. I will issue the call immediately."

As Scheel stepped away, Heinrich came to Mueller's side. "I thought you wanted to avoid the Foreign Office."

"Not now." Mueller smiled at Heinrich. "This is better than I ever imagined."

"Better than you imagined?"

"Yes," Mueller said, gleefully. "You do not see the opportunity in this?"

Heinrich took Mueller by the arm and guided him to a vacant office. Once inside, he closed the door. "Josef, have you forgotten how this happened?"

Mueller looked puzzled. "What are you talking about?" He straightened his jacket with an indignant tug of the lapels, then brushed his hands down both sleeves. "I am the German chancellor. We are no longer schoolmates, Franz."

Heinrich ignored the snub. "The missile that struck Washington is the missile discovered by dock workers in Bremerhaven." He leaned close to Mueller. "You told them to let it pass."

"This is not a problem. We can deny it if it's ever discovered."

"The Americans have a way of finding out these things."

"The Americans have bigger things with which to be concerned."

Heinrich leaned away, a puzzled look on his face. "Sir?"

"Those good-as-gold U.S. Treasury bonds everyone was clamoring to buy are now worthless."

"Yes, I suppose so. And that is an opportunity?"

"China just lost its greatest trading partner, and the one trillion dollars in bonds they hold are now good for absolutely nothing. Russia will lose its largest petroleum customer. The world's economy will teeter on the brink of collapse. Only Germany will remain strong and powerful." He laid his hand on Heinrich's shoulder. "Are you coming with me in the things I must do?"

"Yes, Chancellor." Heinrich lowered his head. "I am with you."

"Good." Mueller patted Heinrich's shoulder. "I have a plan that will resolve these conflicts and bring peace to the world once and for all. But first, we must solidify our position of power. Then we can impose our will from a position of strength." A grin turned up the corners of his mouth. "When they are selling their gold to buy bread, they will beg us to act."

86

CHEYENNE MOUNTAIN, COLORADO

SIMPSON STARED AT THE MAP on the screen and worked the cigar to the opposite side of his mouth. "Put up a map of the electrical grid," he commanded. "Show it as an overlay on what we already have on the wall."

A map of the electrical grid appeared as thin lines forming a web that covered the United States. Lines from Massachusetts down the East Coast to northern Georgia and westward through Ohio were yellow.

Simpson ran his fingers through his hair once more. "Continental Command, what do we have?"

Colonel Bob Nelson, the Continental Force Command liaison, answered. "Yellow lines indicate areas where the lines are intact but the grid is down, sir."

Simpson stroked his chin and watched as the lines continued to turn yellow on the eastern side of the Mississippi River. Nelson left his desk and came to Simpson's side. A worried look clouded his face. "Sir, we have massive power outages from Washington, D.C., north almost to Maine, and as far south as Charleston."

"What about emergency backup?"

"None of it has come online, sir."

"Any estimate for when the grid will be operable?"

"No, sir. This is a massive, system-wide failure. A catastrophic failure. The generating plants in the Northeast aren't simply off-line. They've been physically damaged, many of them beyond repair."

Wrinkles creased Simpson's brow. "Fried."

"Yes, sir." He gestured toward the screen. "Some of what you see west of Ohio, north of Boston, and down along the Gulf Coast is the result of a cascading effect. That part might be restored in a matter of days, but the power generation facilities in that core Northeastern area may never be repaired. Most of it will have to be replaced."

"We are the command center for the nation."

"Yes, sir," Nelson shrugged. "It would seem so."

Simpson staggered under the emotional weight of what had happened—the enormity of it, the extent to which the country had been rendered inoperable, and the long struggle that lay ahead. Then, without conscious thought or effort, years of training and experience took over. He squared his shoulders and glanced around the room. "Alert our bases." His voice was firm and confident. "Notify them we have been attacked by a nuclear device. Washington is not able to communicate. Tell them to route all information through us." He called out to his left. "Johnny Lea."

Navy Captain John Lea turned to face him. "Yes, sir."

"Call PAC COM in Hawaii. Alert our submarines. Launch the Looking Glass. Until the president orders otherwise, we are at DEF-CON ONE."

Nelson spoke up. "Sir, the E-4B was at Andrews. It was designed to withstand this sort of thing, but we have no way of knowing whether it worked, or whether they can even get to it."

"We have another one at Barksdale," Simpson replied. "Get a status report on it and get it activated. The power grid there's still operational isn't it?"

"At Barksdale?"

"Yes. Northern Louisiana." Simpson pointed to the screen. "I don't see any yellow on that part of the map. Find that plane's crew and get it ready. We'll fly them to Dulles if we have to." Simpson took a deep breath and forced himself to relax, then rested his hand on Nelson's shoulder. "Bob, I'm not trying to be difficult, but we have to get ourselves in the most defensible position possible. Right now, you have command of all North American installations. Make it happen."

"Yes, sir."

Simpson let go of Nelson's shoulder. "And I need you to locate the installation nearest Washington, D.C., that is still functioning. Contact them and get units moving toward the White House. We need to find the president."

Nelson gave Simpson a questioning look. "Sir, do you have the authority to do this?"

Simpson pointed to the screen, "You see anyone else out there who can make the call?"

"But who attacked us? Who are we responding to?"

Simpson pointed his index finger toward Nelson and jabbed him in the chest. "I don't know all the answers, Bob." His voice grew louder. "All I know is we've been attacked, and if we don't move quickly, a follow-up strike will make us incapable of responding." He was shouting now. "We have procedures to follow! Anybody still alive on the East Coast—at the White House or the Pentagon or any other installation—is following standard procedure and hoping we are, too. So until someone with more brass than me says otherwise, we'll do the best we can and sort it out later."

"Yes, sir," Nelson replied.

Simpson snatched the cigar from his mouth. "Get me every-thing on the West Coast that can fly and spread it around. We need patrols over every major city." He glanced down at his desk. "And where are those status reports I asked for? I want to know what we have that still works!"

Just then the door opened and Admiral Keating entered. Simpson acknowledged him with a nod. "Admiral."

"General. Sounds like you're about to declare war."

"Just trying to mount an appropriate response, sir."

"Don't you think we better let the president do that?"

"We haven't been able to locate him, sir."

"Looks like we just found him." Keating pointed to the screen on the wall. "Isn't that the E-4B there on the map?"

A red and blue light flashed on the map. Simpson's shoulders sagged. "Yes, sir. It is."

John Lea spoke up. "Admiral, we were about to launch Looking Glass."

"What are you waiting for? Launch it. We need all the command and control we can get." Keating looked over at Simpson. "You've done a good job, Tom, but I'll take over now, if you don't mind."

87

NEW YORK CITY

A FEW BLOCKS DOWN THE STREET, Kinlaw saw a policeman standing on the opposite corner. He tapped Hoag on the chest and pointed. "Maybe he can help."

"You'll just walk up to him and say, 'Hey, I work for the CIA. Can I use your phone?'"

"Something like that." Kinlaw stepped from the curb. "Come on."

They threaded their way between stalled cars and around confused drivers and passengers. Kinlaw led the way. Hoag jogged to keep up. When they reached the opposite side, Kinlaw went straight to the policeman.

"Do you have a cell phone that works?"

"Yeah," the policeman said slowly. "But I can't let you use it."

"Officer, I work in Washington, D.C., and I need to get through to my office. It's very important."

The officer chuckled. "Mister, I got a couple thousand people right here on the two blocks I can see." He gestured to their surroundings. "They'd all like to use my phone to make a very important call."

"Okay." Kinlaw took his wallet from his hip pocket and slipped out his employee identification card. "Do they all have one of these?" He held it up for the officer to see.

"Is that thing for real?"

"It's the real thing."

The policeman took it in his hand for a closer look. "I don't know. Looks like it came from a bubblegum machine."

Kinlaw reached in his hip pocket and took out his building ID. "It goes with this."

The policeman handed Kinlaw the employee ID card. With a skeptical frown he unhooked the phone from his belt and handed it to him. "You got two minutes."

Kinlaw dialed a number for Winston Smith but received only a busy signal. He ended the call and dialed a number for his home but had the same result.

"If you're trying to get a call out of New York, nothing on the East Coast is working," the policeman offered.

Hoag looked up. "Nothing?"

"Last I heard, nothing from here to Boston, down to Richmond, and way out past Pennsylvania. No cell phones. No land lines. Not even television or radio."

Hoag reached for the phone. "Let me try." He took the phone from Kinlaw and entered Jenny's number. Almost instantly he heard a fast busy signal. "That's a system signal. The system is busy."

"Overloaded with everyone calling," Kinlaw said.

"Or completely down," the policeman smiled. "I'm telling you, nothing is working except our department system."

Hoag looked over at him. "You can call on this thing?"

"I've been calling the station with it." The policeman reached for the phone. "I need it back now."

Kinlaw took the phone from Hoag and turned away, avoiding the policeman's grasp. "Give me one more call. Let me try a guy in New Orleans." He pressed the buttons and listened. The call went through. He turned to the policeman. "It's ringing," he grinned.

Three rings later, Drew Powell answered. Kinlaw grinned at the sound of his voice. "Hey Drew. This is Dennis."

"Oh, man," Powell sighed. "You're alive."

"Yes, I'm alive." A frown formed on Kinlaw's forehead. "Why do you seem so surprised?"

"Where are you?"

"New York." Kinlaw looked around as he talked. "Nothing is working here. What's going on?"

"Dennis." Powell's voice was low and grim. "D.C. was hit."

"Hit? With what?"

"A five-kiloton, high-altitude burst. The electrical grid is down on the East Coast. We have power along the Gulf but everything else is blacked out."

"The White House?"

"I guess it's still there, but nothing in it works. They're supposed to be shielded but no one can call in, and no one's calling out."

"Who did it?"

"No one knows for sure," Powell replied. "Lots of speculation. Streets are crazy." He paused. "Hey look, Dennis, I got someone at the door. I gotta go."

There was a click on the line and the phone call ended. Kinlaw held the phone limply in his hand. The policeman took it from him and returned it to the clip on his belt. "Who'd you get through to?"

"A friend," Kinlaw mumbled as he thought about what Powell had said. "Lives in New Orleans."

"New Orleans? You got a call all the way down there?"

"Yeah," Kinlaw nodded

"What did he say?"

Kinlaw heard the policeman's voice, but his mind was far away. Even though he'd suggested this could happen and had realized just moments before that it had occurred, news of its actual effect was difficult to grasp. He felt someone grab his arm and turned to see Hoag staring at him. "Dennis, what's the matter? What happened?"

Kinlaw pushed aside the confusion. "There was a high-altitude detonation. Right over Washington."

"Washington? D.C.?"

"Yeah."

"How bad?"

Kinlaw forced his mind from the emotional fog. "Five kilotons."

The policeman looked surprised. "Kilotons? That's nuclear."

"Yeah," Kinlaw said. "Looks like nothing's working east of the Mississippi River."

"I told you that already," the policeman continued, his voice rambling. "I didn't know it went that far, but I told you nothing around here's working."

Now Hoag looked dazed. Kinlaw nudged his elbow. "Come on."

"Why?"

"We have to get moving."

"What for?"

"Because staying here isn't an option." Kinlaw took him by the arm. "Come on. We'll think of something while we walk." They set off down the street, heading south toward lower Manhattan.

88

CIA HEADQUARTERS
LANGLEY, VIRGINIA

JENNY FOLLOWED WINSTON SMITH out of her office to the hallway.
A few feet farther Winston stopped and jerked open the stairwell
door. Jenny paused. "Where are we going?"

"The director's office."

"Director's office? I can't go in there."

By then Winston was halfway up the first flight. "Come on."
He gestured with a wave of his hand. "Talking to Hoyt Moore's just
like talking to me."

"He may be Hoyt to you, but he's Mr. Director to me."

"Well, come on. We have to get this information out to someone, and right now he's the only one who can do it."

When Hedges became president, one of his first acts was the
appointment of Hoyt Moore as Director of the CIA. Though not as
powerful as the position once had been, the post still controlled the
agency's daily operations. Moore, who had been head of the Office
of Management and Budget, had come to the office amid skepticism
about his lack of experience in the intelligence community. So far
he had proved most of his detractors wrong.

As reluctant as Jenny was about sharing raw intelligence data
with the director, she was even more concerned that she had par-
ticipated in several meetings at which Moore was present, meetings

about the investigation of David Lansing and the New York FBI office. She was certain Moore would recognize her. She just didn't know if he would remember to keep their association quiet.

When Jenny and Winston arrived on the third floor, they found Moore's office swamped with people, most of whom she had never seen before. Staffers hurried in every direction, papers in hand, shouting and waving their arms. Others clustered in groups of three or four, alternately whispering in hushed, secretive tones and then shouting and yelling. Winston seemed to ignore them all. Without hesitating, he barged into Moore's office and threaded his way through the confusion.

To the right, windows looked out on a courtyard. The wall to the left was filled with bookcases. Moore sat at a dark mahogany desk at the far end of the room. Jacketless, he appeared calm and relaxed. He looked up as Winston approached. "You got something, Smith?"

"One of our analysts found some information about the container ships."

The room fell silent. Moore looked at Jenny. "You would be that analyst?"

"Yes, sir."

For an instant his eyes seemed to recognize her. Then, just as quickly, his expression changed. Winston gestured toward her with his left hand. "This is Jenny Freed. She works in the base—" Winston checked himself. "The Information Operations Center."

Moore kept his eyes on Jenny. "The basement."

"Yes, sir" Jenny replied. She was certain he had recognized her and was relieved he let it pass.

"What do you have?"

Jenny quickly recounted what she had told Winston about the ships then handed Moore the images she had printed. He glanced up at her. "You have this written up?" She handed him a memo.

Moore scanned the memo. "Missiles launched from container ships. Ingenious idea." He turned to Winston. "Did we work up this scenario?"

"I put two men on it last week, after the Iranian test," Winston explained.

"What did they find?"

"They found the first of those ships. The *Panama Clipper*." Winston pointed to the pages Moore was holding. "They asked Jenny to help them locate surveillance footage on the others."

Moore frowned. "Three ships owned by Pakistan Shipping." He looked at the memo. "*Panama Clipper* left Bremerhaven two weeks ago. *Amazon Cloud* left from Aden, Yemen. *Panama Clipper* was bound for New York. *Amazon Cloud* for Virginia. A third ship, the *Santiago*, sailed from Guangzhou, China, headed to the Port of Long Beach." He looked up at Winston again. "And what do we know of this Pakistan Shipping?"

"The company is controlled by Nabhi Osmani."

Someone from across the room spoke up. "He's an Al-Qa'ida contact."

"We don't know that for certain," Winston countered.

Another voice chimed in. "And if Al-Qa'ida is involved, then Pakistan must be in play. That explains where they got the missile."

"I think it was…" Jenny tried to interrupt, but her voice was drowned out as the room came alive once again.

Moore turned to a man standing nearby. "Get this to the president."

Jenny leaned close to Winston. "We can reach the president?"

"We have a secure line that's operational from the Command Center."

Moore stood and slipped on his jacket. "Thank you, Ms. Freed." He started across the room. "Winston, you better come with us."

Winston gestured for Jenny to stay put. She stood near the desk and watched as Moore made his way out the door and into the hallway. The room quickly emptied as everyone else swept through the doorway after him.

89

ABOARD THE E-4B AIRBORNE COMMAND CENTER SOMEWHERE ABOVE THE AMERICAN MIDWEST

PRESIDENT HEDGES SAT IN THE forward compartment of the Airborne Command Center and read through a written assessment of the country's situation. Across from him was his wife Mary and Braxton Kittrell.

Officially designated the E-4B, it was built on a Boeing 747 airframe and equipped with all the electronic hardware necessary to conduct a two-front war. Using its midair refueling capability, it could stay aloft until the galley ran out of food and water. Given its usual load of crew and passengers, that was about a week.

When Hedges finished reading the memo, he laid it on his lap. "Everything east of the Mississippi River is trashed." He looked over at Mary. "There'll be a mass exodus of people to the West. Anyone who has a score to settle with us has a fine opportunity to make up for lost time."

"We still have the navy," Kittrell replied. He reached over and took the memo from Hedges' lap. "Looking Glass has them up and ready. All you have to do is give the word and we're in business."

"Sure," Hedges quipped. "Half the country's in the dark. Our economy's ruined for the duration of the century. But we still have the power to end civilization." He looked over at Mary. "Only, we don't know where to begin."

The door opened and Scott Marshall entered the room. A five-star army general, Marshall was chairman of the Joint Chiefs of Staff. He moved forward and closed the door. "Mr. President, we're about an hour out of Omaha."

"Offutt?"

"Yes, Mr. President. Offutt Air Force Base. They have a secure command center. We'll be safe there, even from a direct hit. And you'll be in direct communication with our forces."

"Those not on the eastern half of the continent."

"Yes, Mr. President."

Kittrell caught Hedges' eye. "Same place Bush went after the attacks on New York."

"Great." Hedges rolled his eyes. "Now I look like a Republican."

Marshall cleared his throat. "Sir, it's a fully functional facility. It has experienced none of the damage incurred in the East. You'll be able to function more or less normally there."

"Can we reach Washington?"

"CIA has one secure line that works. The Pentagon has two. Both are swamped. We're receiving some updates on conditions, but nothing we can assess yet."

"Any further threats?"

"We're gathering information on that now, sir."

"How long is this going to last?"

"Outages in the East?"

"Yes."

"A while."

"What does that mean?"

"Initial information indicates it will take years to repair the power grid alone, perhaps longer to repair communications systems. Most of them will have to be rebuilt from the ground up."

"How much of the country is affected?"

"The East Coast is in a blackout as far south as Atlanta and west to the Mississippi River. No electricity. No telephones. No radio or television."

"That's a quarter of the country."

"About a third, actually."

"What about Congress and the rest of the government?"

"Congress is waiting on your decision, sir."

"Have we told them where we're going?"

"We'll tell them after we get there."

"Okay. We should get everyone relocated as quickly as possible. We need to be up and running by the time people living in the East realize what's happened. Otherwise, we could have widespread panic."

"We could face that anyway, sir."

"What do you mean?"

"With no electricity, there will be no fresh water. No sewer service. Delivery systems rely on just-in-time replenishment. Food stocks in the East will be at critically low levels by tomorrow."

"What does that mean? Critically low levels."

"They'll be out of food by the end of the week."

90

NEW YORK CITY

HALF AN HOUR LATER Kinlaw glanced up at a green and white street sign. "We're at Fourteenth Street." He gestured toward the street sign. "I didn't realize we had walked this far south." Kinlaw pointed to the right. "There's the Strand."

"The what?"

"Strand Bookstore. Haven't you been to New York before?"

"Yes," Hoag replied. "But right now I'd like to be somewhere else." He placed his hands on his hips. "What are we gonna do, Dennis?"

"We gotta get to somebody."

"Get to somebody? Get to somebody and do what?"

"Tell them what's going on. Tell them about the ships and the missiles and Nasser Hamid."

"It's a really good theory, but we don't even have enough to write a report."

Kinlaw stopped and leaned close to Hoag. "Listen, David. Our country has been attacked. I don't need enough information to write a report." He backed away. "I know what happened, and I know what's going to happen."

Hoag looked stricken. "What are you talking about? What's going to happen?"

"Another strike," Kinlaw answered.

"Where?"

"Here. Los Angeles. Israel probably."

"Israel?"

"Why else would Iran strike us?" Kinlaw stopped and held up his fingers. "Only two reasons to hit us. They feel threatened by us, or they have something else they want to do and know we'd stop them if they tried." He tapped Hoag on the chest, his eyes bright and clear. "We were right. We analyzed this, did some creative research, a little speculation, and we were right. They hit us first because their real target is Israel. And they know we'd never let them do it otherwise."

"I don't know. Sounds pretty thin to me now."

"Yeah, well, thin is all we've ever had. What we need to do now is get out of the blast zone far enough that we can find a phone—one that works—so we can get in touch with someone. NORAD, PAC COM in Hawaii. Someone's always up." Kinlaw looked around and his eyes lit up. "Come on," he grinned.

Across the street a 1969 Ford pickup truck was parked at the curb. Kinlaw hurried toward it. Hoag lingered behind. "I think it's too late for all that." His voice mimicked the downcast look on his face. "They'll strike wherever they're going to strike. Besides, we'd have to walk out of here and, I gotta tell you, I'm feeling pretty tired right now."

Kinlaw pushed in the vent window on the driver's side of the truck. He reached his arm through the vent window and pulled up the door latch. Hoag stepped up behind him to watch. Kinlaw smiled at him. "Somebody is always in control." He handed Hoag his leather satchel and opened the truck door. "We gotta make sure they know who did this." He took a seat in the truck behind the steering wheel and leaned forward, tucking his head and torso beneath the dash.

Hoag clutched the leather satchel and leaned against the truck, just in front of the door. "You should have spoken up when this first began. Back when we were in the room with Winston's bright young minds."

"We'd still be right here doing the same thing."

"You think?"

"I didn't speak up, but I did go to work. We worked your idea. That's how we know who actually did this." Blue sparks flew from wires under the dash. "Besides, I always believed you," Kinlaw chuckled. More sparks flew. "I just didn't want everyone to know it." Kinlaw raised his head. "Look, you know as well as I do, we have thousands of missiles ready to strike anywhere in the world. None of them need a connection to the White House to launch. If they don't know who did this, they'll hit the wrong place. Pakistan or Russia or China. Someplace like that. And then everyone else will launch their missiles." He disappeared beneath the dash again.

"Hey!" A man up the street shouted. "Hey! That's my truck!" He started toward them at a run.

Kinlaw touched the wires together once more. The truck engine groaned then started. He twisted the wires tightly together and slammed the driver's door shut. "Get in," he shouted.

Hoag hurried around the truck and jumped in on the other side. "How come this one works?"

"It doesn't have a computer." Kinlaw pressed the clutch with his foot, put the truck in gear, and steered it away from the curb.

91

PHILADELPHIA

AFTER AN HOUR OF WEAVING around stalled traffic, Kinlaw and Hoag reached the Williamsburg Bridge on the east side of Manhattan. From there they crossed into Brooklyn and slowly worked their way south. By then, people were wandering the streets, peering into abandoned vehicles, taking things they should have left alone.

"This doesn't look like a great neighborhood." Hoag glanced around. "Why are we going this way? New Jersey was the other way. We should have gone that way."

"Can't go that way. Only way to get to New Jersey from downtown is through the tunnel. We don't want to get trapped in there." He pointed through the front windshield. "There's a bridge down here to Staten Island."

"No bridges to New Jersey?"

"Yeah, if you want to spend hours going north to the George Washington Bridge or up to Yonkers."

"Oh."

Two hours later they reached the Verrazano-Narrows Bridge. They wound their way past stalled vehicles and crossed to Staten Island without any trouble. On the west side of the Island, they turned south onto the New Jersey Turnpike and headed toward Philadelphia. Stranded cars and trucks on the highway were spaced far enough apart that Kinlaw was able to steer around them without slowing. For the next hour and a half they drove without incident, but at the outskirts of Philadelphia things changed.

Near Bordentown, the highway was clogged with cars and trucks that were tangled in an accident that stretched for three miles. Confused and angry drivers who had been involved in the crash became embroiled in a fight that quickly grew into a riot. Fueled by fear, rioters roamed from car to car attacking passengers and stealing whatever they could find. As Kinlaw and Hoag came on the scene, the sight of a functioning pickup truck brought the melee to a halt.

Kinlaw eased the truck onto the emergency strip and idled past the wreckage. Startled rioters stared and watched, their bloody faces tracking the truck as it rolled by. Hoag shifted positions on the seat. "Dennis, I don't like the look of this."

"Me, either," Kinlaw replied.

Then a voice in the crowd cried out. "Get that truck." All at once, the mob surged forward. Kinlaw downshifted and pressed the gas pedal. The engine rumbled as the truck picked up speed.

To the left, the crowd ran along the highway, darting between crumpled cars, all the while drawing closer and closer to the pick-up. As they ran, they called out to those farther ahead, waving and pointing in a frantic effort to head off the truck. Kinlaw pressed the gas pedal closer to the floor. The truck bounced and rocked as they sped along the emergency strip.

A little farther down the road, a guardrail approached. Hoag pointed. Kinlaw nodded. "I see it."

"What are we going to do?"

"Hold on."

Hoag stuck his legs out straight and braced himself against the floorboard beneath the dash. He gripped the armrest with his right hand and pushed his left down hard against the seat. "I'm not sure about this," he groaned.

"Me either."

When they were just a few feet from the rail, Kinlaw whipped the truck to the right sending it careening down a grassy embankment. As they neared the bottom, he steered the truck to the left, shifted gears and pressed the gas pedal. Dirt and grass flew in the air as the truck raced along the embankment.

The crowd was now in full pursuit. From the highway, they descended like a wave rolling down from the pavement toward the truck. Brandishing tire irons and jack handles, they rushed down the embankment, shouting and screaming in bloodcurdling yells. The hair on the back of Kinlaw's neck stood up. "This could be close."

"What?" Hoag glanced around. "What could be close?" Kinlaw pointed out the windshield. Hoag's eyes grew wide as he saw a drainage ditch up ahead. Hoag looked over at Kinlaw once more. "What do we do?"

"Hold on."

"You said that before."

"Better hold on tighter this time."

Kinlaw pressed the gas pedal all the way to the floor. The truck responded with more speed. All the while, the crowd closed in from the left, coming closer and closer, sweeping down from the highway. Kinlaw ignored them and kept his eyes focused on the rapidly approaching ditch.

From the left an angry man reached the truck and lunged for the door handle. His hands slapped against the side of the truck as he struggled to hold on then tumbled to the ground. Behind him someone threw a hammer. It banged against the back of the cab and ricocheted into the air. Still, Kinlaw kept the gas pedal pressed to the floor.

When they reached the ditch, the front of the truck sailed through the air as if taking flight. Midway to the opposite side it seemed to hang in midair, then it slammed into the ditch bank on the opposite side, striking the ground just in front of the rear axles. It sat there lodged at a precarious angle, the front wheels off the ground. Kinlaw and Hoag stared up at the sky. Behind them they heard a roar of laughter from the crowd.

Kinlaw pressed the clutch pedal and shoved the truck into a lower gear. The rear wheels spun in the soft dirt, flinging dust and gravel into the air. Then there was a thud from the truck bed behind them. The truck rocked from side to side as two men climbed in back. Waving their hands in the air triumphantly, they laughed and shouted and jumped up and down. Sensing victory at last, the crowd surged forward. Just as it seemed Kinlaw and Hoag had reached the end, the rear wheels caught traction. The truck shot forward sending the men in back tumbling to the ground. Kinlaw shifted gears and shoved the gas pedal to the floor. The truck raced along the embankment once more, leaving the crowd behind.

Ahead of them, an exit ramp led to the right. Kinlaw steered the truck up the embankment, onto the pavement and sped down the ramp away from the craziness. Hoag turned to look out the back window. Kinlaw glanced in the rearview mirror. Behind them, the crowd turned on each other, frantically swinging their tire irons and jack handles. Hoag faced forward. Kinlaw propped his arm on the window ledge.

They rode in silence for a while, then Hoag looked over at Kinlaw. "That was scary."

"I thought we were gone."

"It was like something from a movie."

"Like after the Rapture?"

"Yeah. After the Rapture."

"I wouldn't want to be here then."

"Me either."

"You could do something about that."

"About what?"

"About not being here then."

"Yeah. But when does the Rapture occur?"

"Like Vic said, no one knows for sure. And you don't even have to believe the Rapture will ever occur. That's not what a relationship with God is about."

"What's it about?"

"Loving Him and doing what He says." Kinlaw looked over at Hoag. "And," he shrugged, "if the Rapture comes, you're out of here. If it doesn't, you get to go through whatever happens knowing God is right there with you."

Hoag propped his arm against the door and stared ahead. Kinlaw slowed the truck and turned onto the next exit ramp. Hoag looked at him. "What are you doing?"

"Getting off this highway."

"Why?"

"We're going in the wrong direction."

"How do you know?"

"The sun is in our eyes. We're headed west. We need to be going south."

92

MARYLAND COUNTRYSIDE

LATE THAT AFTERNOON Kinlaw slowed the truck. Hoag, who had been asleep, raised his head from the window ledge and looked around to find they were driving down a two-lane road. Rolling farmland spread out on either side. He rubbed his eyes. "Where are we?"

"I'm not sure." Kinlaw downshifted. The truck slowed further. "Somewhere in Maryland."

"We're stopping?"

Kinlaw pointed up ahead. "Looks like that store is open. We need gas." He pressed the brake and steered the truck from the highway onto a gravel parking lot. Two gas pumps stood on a concrete island between the highway and the store. Kinlaw brought the truck to a stop near the pumps and climbed from the cab. Hoag got out on the opposite side.

Near the front door of the building, an old man sat on an upturned bucket. Dressed in a tan work shirt and faded overalls, he wore a green cap with a John Deere logo on the front.

"Good afternoon," Kinlaw said.

"Afternoon," the man replied.

"Got any gas?"

"Got a little." The old man stood.

Hoag stretched his arms out wide and yawned. "Where are we?"

"Long Corner."

"Long Corner? Long Corner where?"

"Maryland." The old man gave Hoag a puzzled look. "How long you been asleep?"

"Awhile," Hoag chuckled. "Never heard of Long Corner, Maryland."

"We ain't never heard of you, either." The old man lifted his cap, pushed back his hair, and settled the cap back on his head. "And we like it that way." He looked at Kinlaw. "You want to fill up?"

Kinlaw raised an eyebrow. "You have that much gas?"

"Sure."

Kinlaw gestured over his shoulder. "Pumps work?"

"Nah." The old man shook his head. "Power's out. Been out all day. Folks say it may take a while to come back on." His eyes sparkled. "But I got a hand pump and a five gallon bucket."

"Can't we just pump it straight into the tank on the truck?"

The old man smiled. "Got to measure it so I know what to charge you for it." He gestured with a nod of his head and started toward the end of the building. "Come on."

Kinlaw followed him. "What's the price?"

"Same as always." The old man pointed over his shoulder. "Price is on the sign."

Hoag chimed in. "You could get two hundred dollars a gallon for it today."

The old man glanced in Hoag's direction. "And that'd be a sorry way to treat my neighbors."

"Neighbors?"

"Son, I've been open since five this morning." The old man stopped and turned to face them. "You two are the first people I've seen today that I don't know." He pointed in the distance. "I know everybody around here for five miles in every direction, and they know me. Whatever caused the power to go out will pass. Before long, people will forget all about it. But they'll remember me." He tapped Hoag on the chest. "I want them to remember me right."

Using a hand pump and the five gallon bucket on which the old man had been sitting, Kinlaw and Hoag filled the pickup truck with gas. Half an hour later they were back on the road.

As they drove toward the fading afternoon sun, Hoag sat propped against the passenger door. "That old man didn't care whether he sold his gas or not."

"Didn't have a line waiting in the parking lot either."

"No one around there seemed to be panicking."

"Seemed rather peaceful."

"Ignorance is bliss."

"Maybe that old man knows something the people in Philadelphia didn't."

"What could he know that would make him peaceful even when we've been hit by a nuclear bomb and half the country's in the dark?"

Kinlaw raised an eyebrow. "Not what, but who."

"Who?"

"Who could you know that would make you that peaceful?"

"I guess you're talking about God."

Kinlaw grinned. "I guess so."

Hoag folded his arms across his chest. "So, what does it take to be a Christian? I mean, officially a Christian."

Kinlaw was amused by the question. "Actually," he smiled, "you just ask."

"Ask?"

"You pray."

"I've never prayed."

"Follow me," Kinlaw replied. "I'll walk you through it. I'll say a sentence, you repeat it out loud."

"I don't know."

"Yes, you do." Kinlaw reached over and slapped Hoag on the shoulder. "You've been thinking about this since that day we were at Vic Hamilton's house. Here we go. Just say the words out loud as I say them."

As they drove down the highway, Kinlaw led Hoag through a simple but profound prayer. "God, I know I have been living outside of your control, and that has separated me from you. I am sorry. Please forgive me. I want to love you and serve you with all my heart. I know that Jesus is Lord and you raised him from the dead. Rule and reign over my life from this day forward. Amen."

When they were finished, Hoag looked over at Kinlaw. "That's it?"

"That's it." Kinlaw glanced at Hoag. "Are you okay?"

Hoag blinked back tears. "I'm fine," he whispered.

93

CIA HEADQUARTERS
LANGLEY, VIRGINIA

THE SKY WAS DARK WHEN Hoag and Kinlaw reached the outskirts of Washington. They picked their way carefully through stalled traffic and reached the main gate at CIA headquarters a little before seven. Unlike the dark countryside around them, lights on the CIA campus glowed brightly. Hoag brought the truck to a stop at the gate. A guard came from the guardhouse. "May I help you?"

Kinlaw handed the guard his building pass. "I'm Dennis Kinlaw." He pointed across the seat. "This is David Hoag." After a check of their employee identification, the guard waved them forward. To their amazement the gate opened under its own power.

Hoag glanced out the window. "I guess Operations Support did their job."

"Looks like they kept the lights on anyway."

When they reached the building, a security officer stationed at the front entrance recognized them at once. "Winston Smith is waiting for you. He's in a conference room down the hall to the right."

Inside, Kinlaw and Hoag found Winston Smith in the Operations Support conference room, where he was seated at the far end of the table. A grin swept over his face as they entered the room. "Gentlemen." He pushed back his chair and stood. "You finally decided to join us?"

"We know who did it," Kinlaw blurted out. "We've got to get word to the president. We can't let them—"

"I know," Winston interrupted. "A missile launched from a cargo ship. The *Panama Clipper*. Twenty-five miles off New York harbor."

"How did you know?"

"Jenny told us."

"Jenny?"

"Yeah. She told us about it and the other two ships."

Kinlaw was puzzled. "Other ships?"

"The *Amazon Cloud* and the *Santiago*. The director thinks this was the work of Al-Qa'ida."

"Al-Qa'ida?" Kinlaw frowned. "Why would he think Al-Qa'ida did it?"

"Those cargo ships are owned by Pakistan Shipping. Nabhi Osmani controls the company. Bin Laden controls Osmani."

"Maybe so, but the missiles were Iranian and so were the warheads. Do they really think bin Laden built nuclear warheads in his Afghan cave?"

"No." Winston had a sobering look. "They think he got them from Pakistan."

"That's crazy," Kinlaw protested. "We gotta stop them. Where's the director?"

"Omaha."

"Omaha?" Kinlaw felt deflated. "What's he doing in Omaha?"

"Everybody's headed that way. President set up a command center at Offutt Air Force Base. Congress is moving out there. Supreme Court. Entire government will be located there by next month."

"Why?"

"In case you haven't noticed, other than this compound, nothing works anymore."

Kinlaw pulled a chair from the table and flopped down on it. "Then why are you here?"

"Somebody had to stay behind to run things here."

Kinlaw sighed. "Is this a permanent move?"

"East Coast will be inoperable for a long time. Your kids will be grandparents before this gets fixed. If at all."

Hoag spoke up. "Is Jenny with them?"

"No." Winston shook his head. "She's in her office."

"Now?"

"Yeah. Most of us have been living here the past two days. She's got a—" By then, Hoag was already at the door. "Take the stairs," Winston called. "The elevator doesn't work." He looked at Kinlaw and shrugged. "I guess he'll figure it out for himself."

"Has anyone heard how things are in Rockville?"

"I think they're about like everywhere else. No electrical power, but no physical damage either." Winston took a seat. "You want to get home?"

"Yeah. But I guess I better wait and see what David wants to do." Kinlaw leaned back in the chair and closed his eyes. "I'll give him a few minutes."

"You hungry?"

"Starving."

Winston caught someone's attention. A young staff member appeared. "Get us a sandwich and something to drink."

"Yes, sir."

Kinlaw opened his eyes. "The cafeteria's open?"

"Yeah. Operations got us up and running almost immediately. Some of the switches took a hit, but the generators are shielded. Voltage fluctuations knocked out some of the monitors, but we've pieced things together enough to keep going." He leaned back and folded his hands behind his head. "We can debrief later. After you eat, you should go home. Find out about your wife. Which reminds me, how did you guys get down here from New York?"

"Found an old pickup truck. Didn't have a computer. Wasn't affected by the blast."

"You found it?"

"Sort of," Kinlaw shrugged. "I had to tinker with the switch to get it started."

"You hot-wired a truck," Winston laughed. "I knew you guys would show up." He laughed again. "You got here quicker than I thought, but I knew you'd get here." He took a deep breath. "All the same, your wife needs to see you. There isn't much you can do here right now." He stood. "Take a few days and get things straight at home."

94

EGYPT, NEAR THE GAZA BORDER

NASSER HAMID STOOD INSIDE the tent and scanned over the missile once more. After a moment he stepped to the cab of the truck and opened the door. He reached inside and took a green webbed belt from the seat. A smile spread across his face as he read the words, "A. Kirkland, U.S. Army," printed in plain block letters on the inside edge. Taken from one of the dead American soldiers, the belt had been a trophy presented to him by the sniper team guarding the Zagros Mountains near Al-Akbar. Hamid strapped the belt around his waist over the top of his white thawb and cinched it tight. Quietly, he closed the cab door, ducked beneath the tent flap, and stepped outside.

High above the warm desert sand, the night was ablaze with stars. Hamid turned in every direction, scanning the sky for any sign of a plane, an intruder, or a warning. All he saw was a great, dark expanse. First reports from America indicated the missile from the *Panama Clipper* had done its job. In an instant, that single explosion denied the East Coast electricity, phones, television, and radio. Food and drinking water would soon be in short supply. Financially and economically America was ruined. All that remained was to finish the plan.

The plan. Hamid sighed. An angry scowl descended over his face. *Nothing ever goes according to plan*. He kicked the sand in disgust.

As originally conceived, missiles from all three ships were to rain down on America in a single, coordinated attack. The first would take out the electrical grid, then two more on the East and the West Coast would obliterate Los Angeles and Washington, D.C. America would be powerless. It would still have the power to retaliate with its navy, but the entire nation would be living in 19th century conditions. Then they could get on with the real point of the operation—the destruction of Israel.

The plan had worked perfectly until the Chinese killed that FBI agent. If Wu could have held his temper another day, the *Santiago* would have sailed from Guangzhou and Los Angeles would be a wasteland. But no, Wu could not wait. When the FBI discovered the agent's body, it was a simple matter to figure out where he had been, which cost the ship two days in port while they investigated. Now the *Santiago* was not yet in range and the *Amazon Cloud* was floating in the Atlantic awaiting final instructions, an easy target if the American satellites could find it. Surely by now they had figured out where the first missile had been launched.

Hamid glanced at his watch and pressed a button to illuminate the face. It was three in the morning in the desert. He calculated in his head. *Eight at night in Washington, D.C.*, he thought.

With the *Santiago* delayed, the timing of their plan had changed. Priorities were reordered. Tel Aviv now was more important than Los Angeles. Tel Aviv first, and then all of Israel would be laid waste. But he must wait. "Sunrise," he said to himself. "At sunrise we shall rain upon Little Satan the power of the sun." He placed his hands on his hips. "And then the Mahdi will come."

95

CIA HEADQUARTERS
LANGLEY, VIRGINIA

HOAG MADE HIS WAY DOWNSTAIRS and walked quietly to Jenny's office. He stood at the door and watched her sorting through stacks of files that covered her desk. Cardboard boxes were stacked on the floor nearby. "I'll have some boxes for you in a minute," she said, without looking up. Hoag leaned against the doorframe and waited. Still unaware of his presence, Jenny closed the file on her desk and turned to shove it in a box. When she looked up, she gasped.

"Hello, Jenny," he said softly.

For a moment she stared at him as if not able to comprehend what she was seeing. Then slowly she stood. Hoag leaned away from the doorframe and stepped forward. She moved from behind the desk and slipped her arms around his waist.

"I wasn't sure I'd ever see you again, and the next minute I was certain you'd show up. And then I was—" she began to cry.

Hoag leaned over and kissed her, then kissed her again. "I wasn't sure you'd see me either," he whispered. "Are you all right?"

"Yes," she nodded. "And you?"

"I'm fine." She leaned away and wiped her eyes with her fingers. "I went back and looked at the tapes. I found two more ships. This is what you were working on, wasn't it? Missiles launched from cargo ships."

"Yes," Hoag replied. He leaned forward and kissed her again, then pulled her close. "I love you," he whispered.

Jenny buried her face in his chest. "I love you, too."

"You weren't hurt?"

"No." She shook her head. "We didn't even feel the explosion."

"What about radiation? Has anyone checked for radiation levels?"

"They've been monitoring as best they can, but the air samplers don't work."

Hoag sighed. "Nothing works." He guided her back to her seat at the desk then pulled a chair next to hers and sat down. Jenny leaned over and rested her head against him. Hoag slipped his arm around her shoulder. She looked up at him. "What was New York like without electricity?"

"There were cars everywhere. Just stopped in the street. We were the only thing moving. Coming out of the city we passed cars parked all the way across the bridge but not a person in sight. It was like they had all vanished. I began to wonder if what Dennis had said wasn't true."

"What?"

"About the Rapture and all that." Hoag squeezed her shoulder. "I thought maybe it had happened, and you'd be gone."

Jenny draped her arm across his chest. "I'm still here."

"When we got down to Philadelphia, it was like taking a trip through a horror movie. Cars abandoned on the highway. People running around like lunatics. Fighting. Stealing. When they saw the truck was running they turned on us." He sighed and shook his head. "Then I was sure the Rapture had come."

"Oh, David," Jenny chuckled. "Dennis was with you."

"Yeah. I guess so. But that's what I was thinking. And I didn't want to be without you. I realized what a mess I'd made of things, and I didn't want to be like that anymore." His eyes looked deep into hers. "I wanted to be like you and David and actually know that I was known by God."

Jenny squeezed him even closer. "I was praying."

"I know," he whispered.

Using his foot, Hoag scooted a trashcan from beneath the desk and propped his feet on it. "But we're here, and the Rapture hasn't come yet, which means there's still time to do something."

"Yes," Jenny nodded. "There's still hope."

"You found three ships?"

Jenny sat up and wiped her eyes again. "We already knew about the *Panama Clipper*. That's where the missile came from that hit us. But they also loaded the same kind of containers on two other ships. The *Amazon Cloud* and the *Santiago*. *Amazon Cloud* left Yemen for Newport, Virginia. I'm sure it's out there in the Atlantic, just waiting. The *Santiago* is headed for Long Beach."

"Does anyone know about this?"

"I told Winston. He took me to the director, and they sent the information to the president." Her shoulder's sagged. "But they think this was Al-Qa'ida, using missiles from Pakistan."

"That's crazy." Hoag sat up, suddenly alert. "We have to tell them."

"They aren't here."

"Where are they?"

"Everyone's headed to Omaha."

"Offutt Air Force Base."

"Yes."

"You said they sent the information to the president. How? How did they send it to him? I thought everything was down."

"We have one secure line that works, from the situation room on the third floor."

"We could send a message from there."

"I tried. We sent them a memo detailing how this was more likely an attack from Iran and not Pakistan, but I don't think anyone's listening."

"We need to get out there to Omaha."

"But how?" Jenny paused and gave him a questioning look. "By the way, how did you and Dennis get here?"

"A pickup truck," Hoag grinned.

"A pickup truck? You found a truck that actually worked?"

"It's old. Doesn't have a computer. Dennis hot-wired it off the street."

"That's funny." Jenny leaned back in her chair and laughed. "Dennis Kinlaw hot-wiring a pickup truck. I wish I could have seen that." She took a breath and then looked at Hoag. "So, what do we do now?"

"I don't know. If we hit Pakistan… They're the wrong people, but that might be the best option. I mean, it would be bad, but they aren't strategic partners with anyone. China would protest, but they wouldn't retaliate. But if we hit Iran, the world could just come unglued."

"You want to go to Omaha?"

Hoag took her hand. "I want to stay right here with you."

"But you want to be in the middle of this."

"It seems like the beginning of the end. Like all those prophecies are finally coming true. At least, it could be. But maybe history reached this point before, where the end was about to happen, and someone stepped up and did the right thing. They averted the end, at least for a little longer."

"Maybe," Jenny shrugged.

"I know God determines the ultimate end, but maybe the reason no one knows the date when it finally happens is because the date depends on our actions, too."

Jenny smiled at him. "You aren't the same person who left for New York the other day."

"No." Hoag sighed. "I'm not."

"I like this David better than that other one."

He pulled her close. "I do, too."

CIA HEADQUARTERS
LANGLEY, VIRGINIA

THE NEXT MORNING Hoag and Jenny met Winston in the courtyard behind the headquarters building. They sat on a wooden bench near the fishpond watching the sun as it rose over the horizon. "I love to watch the sunrise from here," Winston mused. "Nothing like working all night, then coming out here with a cup of coffee to see a new day arrive." He turned sideways and looked down the bench at them. "The air force is sending in a couple of C-17s. They'll be landing at Dulles in an hour. Bringing in generators, trucks, and fuel."

"Good," Hoag replied. "Want me to help?"

Winston glanced at Jenny then back to Hoag. "I want the two of you to get down there to Dulles and fly out to Omaha when those planes return."

"What about Dennis?"

"I sent him home last night. He's with his wife. I'll find a place for him if he wants to go, but right now he needs to look after his family."

Hoag felt sad at the thought of leaving his friend behind, but he was excited about going to Omaha, especially with Jenny.

"So, what will we do in Omaha?"

"The director is assembling a team of analysts. I told him I'd send the two of you out there to help."

"What about you? Aren't you coming?"

"No," Winston shook his head. "For right now, I'll be here."

Hoag didn't like the idea of operating without Winston as his cover. Winston had been more than a supervisor. He had been mentor, friend, and shield against the rough and tumble politics that often marred the agency. The thought of having to work without his protection was troubling. Winston gave Hoag a knowing look. "I'll be around. You won't get rid of me that easily."

"Maybe I could work from here. We have one line that functions. Operations is already working on another."

Winston shook his head. "They'll get the lights on in a few places, fire up the Capitol and the White House for morale, but life on this end of the country will be primitive for a long time to come. If you and Jenny are going to have a future, it'll be somewhere west of the Mississippi." He stood and patted Hoag on the shoulder. "Get moving. I need you two on that plane. They won't wait."

As Winston started across the courtyard, someone called from the building entrance. "Come quick. The EU is making a statement."

Hoag and Jenny hurried after Winston. They rushed inside and down the hall to the conference room, where a crowd had already gathered around a shortwave radio that sat on the table. Winston glanced at a man to his left. "What have they said?"

"Mueller, the German chancellor, is speaking. European Council met. He's been talking about the extent of damage we've incurred."

The voice on the radio continued. "We regret that our friends in America face such a difficult hour, but the consequences of that difficulty fall not only on them but on us as well. We in Europe, as well as citizens of the world in every country, face an uncertain future. In the past we looked to America to address situations like this. It was they who brought stability to our lives and gave us relief for our fears. Now America can no longer respond. No one knows for certain if that great nation shall ever return to its former glory. Meanwhile, life goes on and we must, too.

"Today, the European Union, in concert with the great nations of China and Russia, has taken the unprecedented step of assuring the world's financial markets that our economic life will proceed in an orderly and efficient manner. We in the European community remain economically strong and financially sound. Germany, in particular, had little exposure to American debt. Consequently, Germany and its fellow EU member countries have agreed to inject sufficient amounts of capital in both the Russian and Chinese financial systems to insure that losses on U.S. debt obligations will not cripple their economies.

"In addition, we have agreed to purchase sufficient quantities of oil on the open market to maintain stable supplies throughout Europe. We regret that events have brought us to this point, and we extend our best wishes and deepest sympathies to the people of America, but we cannot sit idly by while the world and our future crumble at our feet." There was a rustling sound, and then an EU spokesman took the microphone for questions.

Those listening in the conference room began to murmur. Someone spoke up. "Josef Mueller is a traitor."

"He had no choice."

"We saved Germany when they were devastated."

"That was a long time ago. They've repaid us many times over."

Jenny leaned close to Hoag. "What does this mean?"

"Josef Mueller is making his play."

"His play?"

"We're out. Germany sees a chance to step up."

"Step up for what?"

"World leadership."

She looked troubled. "A crisis is a great opportunity. He can control the world."

"I didn't think about it like that." Hoag raised an eyebrow. "We talked about this with Vic Hamilton."

"We?"

"Dennis and I."

"You talked about Germany?"

"No. About the Four Horsemen of the Apocalypse."

Winston gave Hoag a nudge. "You two better get moving. There's a truck waiting out front."

"We have trucks?"

"Old ones. Like the one you and Kinlaw drove from New York." Winston nodded toward the door. "Get moving. I want you both on that plane." Hoag felt a lump in his throat. Winston's eyes were misty. "I'll be in touch."

Hoag took Jenny's hand. "Come on. We better go."

Jenny tossed Winston a wave and turned to leave. As she and Hoag walked out the door she looked up at him. "So, what do they mean?"

"What does what mean?"

"The Four Horsemen. What does that mean?"

At the front entrance Hoag pushed open the door and held it for her as they stepped outside. "They aren't creatures, literally. They represent—"

A guard met them at the steps. "Winston Smith said you needed a ride to Dulles."

"Yes."

"Right this way."

Jenny tugged on Hoag's arm. "But, what does it mean?"

"Let's get in the truck. I'll tell you on the way."

ACKNOWLEDGEMENTS

My deepest gratitude goes to the men and women who have agreed to present and past interviews which have laid the foundation for this novel. These include: Israeli Prime Ministers Benjamin Netanyahu, Menachem Begin, Yitzhak Shamir, Ehud Olmert; Yitzhak Rabin, and Shimon Peres; Deputy Prime Minister, Lt. General Moshe Ya'alon, former Chief of Staff, IDF; President Mahmoud Ahmadinejad and more than a dozen Iranian diplomats; Her Majesty Farah Pahlavi, wife of the former Shah of Iran; a special thanks to Iran's last and most powerful ambassador to the U.S., Ambassador Ardeshir Zehedi; former President of the French Republic Valerie Giscard d'Estaing; President of Iraqi Kurdistan Massoud Barzani; editorial journalist Samuel Segev; journalist and terrorism expert Charles Villeneuve; Dr. Parviz Mina, Director, National Iranian Oil Company under the Shah; Dr. Abol-Majid Majidi, Minister of Planning and Budget under the Shah; Hubert Vedrine, adviser to President Francois Mitterrand and Secretary-General from 1991-1995; General Dani Yatom, Former head of Mossad, Israeli Intelligence Service; former Israeli Ambassador to Iran Uri Lubrani; former Israeli Ambassador to the U.S. Dore Gold; Marvin Kalb, award-winning reporter for CBS and NBC; Dr. Alan Dershowitz, professor, Harvard School of Law; Mr. James Woolsey, former director, CIA; Israeli Mossad agent Eliezer Zafrir; General David Ivri, Commander Israeli Air Force and Ambassador to U.S.; General Yitzhak Segev; Dr. Ahmed Tehrani; and Lt. General Shapur Azarbarzin. I especially want to thank Israeli, French, and U.S. intelligence operatives (whose names must remain anonymous.)

My sincere thanks to Joe Hilley without whom this book could not have been possible. I also wish to thank my executive assistant, Lanelle Shaw-Young for her amazing assistance, Arlen Young for his proof-reading skills, and editor Elizabeth Sherman whose insight and suggestions were invaluable. A book project of this magnitude demands a grueling schedule. For her patience, compassion, encouragement, and sacrifice, I am indebted to my beloved wife, Carolyn. This book is dedicated to my newborn grandson, Michael David Evans III, born just as this book was completed.